CONTENTS

PREFACE

In view of the necessity of re-evaluating the technology transfer, the actual work of the Japanese Experience Project has been carried out through two methods -- the formation of a consortium and the research work of the subject matter.

The tasks assigned to the consortium formation are as follows:

(a) review and reappraisal of existing studies;

(b) collection of information concerning on-going researches, researchers involved, and hypotheses and theories developed therein; and

(c) collection of information on experiences of other countries.

This bibliography is a result of the activities in the first field of the consortium formation. This is expected to articulate the subject area that the Japanese Experience Project is dealing with and also to serve the purpose of opening the avenues towards further resarch collaboration with the scholars of the various countries.

July 1980

Takeshi Hayashi
Project Co-ordinator
UN University Project on
Technology Transfer, Transformation,
and Development; the Japanese
Experience

EDITOR'S NOTE

This bibliography lists books, articles in collective volumes, doctoral dissertations and articles in selected journals appeared in English during the period from 1945 to 1979 on the problems of socio-economic development of Japan from circa 1600 to 1940.

The actual work of complilation has been done in association with Mrs. Akiko Ishii.

As regards the books contained, the compilers depend mostly on:

Fukuda, Naomi, ed. Union catalogue of books on Japan in western languages. Tokyo, International House of Japan Library, 1968.

Japan; International House of Japan Library acquisition list, 1955-1979. Tokyo, 1979.

National Diet Library. Catalog of materials on Japan in western languages in the National Diet Library, 1948-1975. Tokyo, Kinokuniya, 1977.

In selection doctoral dissertations, the following pamphlets are used:

Shulman, Frank Joseph, comp. and ed. Doctoral dissertations on Japan and Korea, 1969-1974; a classified bibliographical listing of international research. Ann Arbor, Univ. Microfilms International, 1976.

Japan and the Japanese; a dissertation bibliography. Ann Arbor, Univ. Microfilms International, n.d.

Journals cited are listed on pages iv-viii.

This bibliography is divided into several subject sections and subsections. Both sections and subsections are further divided into four parts: I. books, II. articles in collective volumes, III. doctoral dissertations, and IV. articles in selected journals.

In each part citations are listed alphabetically by author, giving the following information.

I. author, title, place of publication, publisher, year of publication, number of pages

II. contributor, title of article (editor, book's title, place of publication, publisher, year of publication, number of pages of article)

III. author, title, degree earned, date of degree, school name, number of text pages

IV. contributor, title of article, periodical's name (underlined), volume, number, date of publication, number of pages of article

The compilers are mainly concerned with the problems of socio-economic development. Therefore, the coverage is insufficient for politics and also the method of selection is rather discretional. Suggestions and information would be welcome from all sources about important books and articles left out of this bibliography and new works which ought to be included in a planned revised edition.

Anyone who compiles a bibliography enters into many debts to friends and colleagues. The present compilers are especially grateful to the following libraries for permitting access to their facilities and collections:

The Library, Institute of Develoing Economies, Tokyo.

The Library, The Institute of Economic Research, Hitotsubashi University, Tokyo.

The International House of Japan Library, Tokyo.

Finally we thank Mrs. Hatsuko Nakaba and Mrs. Kazuko Shinohara for their painstaking work of typing the manuscript in several forms.

Hirokazu Tada

LIST OF JOURNALS CITED

AMERICAN ECONOMIC REVIEW, Menasha, Wis., American Economic Association. v.35, n.1, Feb. 1945 - v.69, n.4, Sept. 1979.

AMERICAN HISTORICAL REVIEW, New York. v.51, 1945/46 - v.82, n.5, Dec. 1977.

AMERICAN JOURNAL OF AGRICULTURAL ECONOMICS, Menasha, Wis., American Agricultural Economics Association. v.5o, n.1, Feb. 1968 - v.61, n.3, Aug. 1979.
Formerly: JOURNAL OF FARM ECONOMICS. v.27, n.1, Feb. 1945 - v.49, n.5, Dec. 1967.

ANNALS OF THE INSTITUTE OF SOCIAL SCIENCE, Tokyo, Tokyo Univ. n.7, 1966 - n.19, 1978.
Formerly: SOCIAL SCIENCE ABSTRACTS. n.1, 1953 - n.6, 1965.

ANNALS OF THE SCHOOL OF BUSINESS ADMINISTRATION, KOBE UNIVERSITY, Kobe. n.1, 1957 - n.23, 1979.

ASIA BUNKA KENKYU (KOKUSAI KIRISUTOKYO DAIGAKU GAKUHO 3-A), Tokyo. n.1, Oct. 1958 - n.11, May 1979.

ASIA QUARTERLY, Bruxelles, Universite Libre. 1971, n.1 - 1979, n.2.
Formerly: JOURNAL OF SOUTHEAST ASIA AND THE FAR EAST. 1963, n.1 - 1967, n.2.

ASIAN AFFAIRS, Tokyo, Asia Kyokai. v.1, n.1, Mar. 1956 - v.6, n.2, Mar. 1962 (* v.3)
No more published.

ASIAN AFFAIRS, London, Royal Society for Asian Affairs. v.1, pt.1, Feb. 1970 - v.9, pt.2, June 1978.
Formerly: ROYAL CENTRAL ASIAN JOURNAL. v.33, pt.3/4, July/Oct. 1946 - v.56, pt.3, Oct. 1969 (* v.34, pt.1; v.39, pts.2,3 & 4; v.40; v.44, pt.1; v.43, pt.3/4)

ASIAN STUDIES, Quezon City, Univ. of Philippines. v.1, Special Issue 1963 - v.14, n.3, Dec. 1976 (* v.7, n.1; v.14, n.2)

ASIAN SURVEY, Berkeley, Calif., Univ. California. v.1, n.1, Mar. 1961 - v.18, n.12, Dec. 1978.
Formerly: FAR EASTERN SURVEY. v.14, n.1, Jan. 1945 - v.30, Jan./Feb. 1961 (* v.12, n.1-6)

BULLETIN OF CONCERNED ASIAN SCHOLARS QUARTERLY, San Fransisco, Calif. v.3, n.1, Winter/Spring 1971 - v.11, n.2, Apr./June 1979 (* v.3, n.2; v.9, n.3)

BULLETIN OF THE ASSOCIATION FOR JAPANESE STUDIES IN INDIA, New Delhi. v.1, n.1, 1973

BULLETIN OF THE UNIVERSITY OF OSAKA PREFECTURE, Osaka, Series D, v.1, 1957 - v.23, 1979 (*v.13-v.15)

BUSINESS HISTORY REVIEW, Boston, Harvard Univ. 1945 - 1979.

COMPARATIVE STUDIES IN SOCIETY AND HISTORY, The Hague. v.1, n.1, Oct. 1958 - v.21, n.3, July 1979.

CONTEMPORARY JAPAN, Tokyo, Foreign Affairs Association of Japan. v.16, n.1/3, Jan./Mar. 1947 - v.29, n.2, Mar. 1970 (*v.21, n.1-3; v.22, n.1-3)

DAEDALUS, Boston, American Academy of Arts and Sciences.v.89, n.1, Winter 1958 - v.108, n.3, Summer 1979.

THE DEVELOPING ECONOMIES, Tokyo, Institute of Developing Economies. v.1, n.1, Mar. 1962 - v.17, n.2, June 1979.

DOSHISHA SHOGAKU, Kyoto. v.14, n.5, Feb. 1963 - v.31, n.3, Dec. 1979.

ECONOMETRICA, Amsterdam, Econometric Society. v.13, n.1, Jan. 1945 - v.47, n.4, July 1979.

ECONOMIC DEVELOPMENT AND CULTURAL CHANGE, Chicago, Univ. of Chicago. v.1, 1952/53 - v.27, n.4, July 1979.

ECONOMIC HISTORY REVIEW, Utrecht, Economic History Society. First Series. v.14, 1944/1945 - v.18, 1948; Second Series. v.1, n.1, July 1948 - v.32, n.2, May 1979.

EXPLORATIONS IN ECONOMIC HISTORY, Richmond, Ind., Earlham College. v.7, n.1, 1970 - v.15, n.4, 1978.
Formerly: EXPLORATIONS IN ENTREPRENEURIAL HISTORY. 1963 - 1969.

FOOD RESEARCH INSTITUTE STUDIES, Stanford, Calif., Stanford Univ. v.1, n.1, Feb. 1960 - v.16, n.3, 1977/78 (*v.15, n.3-4)

HARVARD JOURNAL OF ASIATIC STUDIES, Boston. v.8, n.3/4, Mar. 1945 - v.39, n.2, Dec. 1979.

HITOTSUBASHI JOURNAL OF ARTS AND SICENCE, Tokyo. v.1, 1960 - v.19, 1979.
Formerly: ANNALS OF THE HITOTSUBASHI ACADEMY. v.1, 1950 - v.10, 1959.

HITOTSUBASHI JOURNAL OF COMMERCE AND MANAGEMENT, Tokyo. v.1, 1961 - v.13, 1978.
Formerly: ANNALS OF THE HITOTSUBASHI ACADEMY. v.1, 1950 - v.10, 1959.

HITOTSUBASHI JOURNAL OF ECONOMICS, Tokyo. v.1, n.1, Oct. 1960 - v.18, n.2, Feb. 1978.
Formerly: ANNALS OF THE HITOTSUBASHI ACADEMY. v.1, 1950 - v.10, 1959.

HITOTSUBASHI JOURNAL OF LAW AND POLITICS, Tokyo. v.1, 1960 - v.8, 1979.
Formerly: ANNALS OF THE HITOTSUBASHI ACADEMY. v.1, 1950 - v.10, 1959.

HITOTSUBASHI JOURNAL OF SOCIAL STUDIES, Tokyo. v.1, 1960 - v.11, 1979.
Formerly: ANNALS OF THE HITOTSUBASHI ACADEMY. v.1, 1950 - v.10, 1959.

HOKUDAI ECONOMIC PAPERS, Sapporo. v.1, 1968/9 - v.4, 1974/5.

INDIAN ECONOMIC JOURNAL, Bombay, Indian Economic Association. v.1, n.1, July 1953 - v.26, n.4/5, Apr./June 1978.

INTERNATIONAL ECONOMIC REVIEW, Osaka, Kansai Economic Federation. v.1, n.1, Jan. 1960 - v.19, n.3, Oct. 1978.

JAPAN QUARTERLY, Tokyo. v.1, n.1, Oct./Dec. 1954 - v.26, n.4, Oct./Dec. 1979 (*v.1, n.2-4)

JAPAN SCIENCE REVIEW, ECONOMIC SCIENCES, Tokyo, Union of Associations of Economic Sciences. n.1, 1953 - n.10, 1965.
No more published.

JAPANESE ECONOMIC STUDIES, White Plains, N.Y. v.1, n.1, Fall 1972 - v.7, n.1, Fall 1978.

JAPANESE STUDIES IN THE HISTORY OF SCIENCE, Tokyo, History of Science Society of Japan. n.1, 1962 - n.17, 1978.

THE JOURNAL OF ASIAN STUDIES, Ann Arbor, Mich., Association for Asian Studies. v.16, n.1, Nov. 1956 - v.38, n.4, Aug. 1979.
Formerly: FAR EASTERN QUARTERLY. v.4, n.2, Feb. 1945 - v.15, n.4, Aug. 1956.

THE JOURNAL OF DEVELOPMENT STUDIES, London. v.1, n.1, Oct. 1964 - v.15, n.4, July 1979.

THE JOURNAL OF ECONOMIC HISTORY, N.Y., Economic History Association. v.5, n.1, 1945 - v.39, n.2, June 1979.

JOURNAL OF INTERDISCIPLINARY HISTORY, Cambridge, Mass. v.4, n.1, Summer 1973 - v.9, n.4, Spring 1979.

JOURNAL OF JAPANESE STUDIES, Seattle, Society for Japanese Studies. v.1, n.1, Autumn 1974 - v.5, n.1, Winter 1979.

THE JOURNAL OF ORIENTAL SOCIETY OF AUSTRALIA, Sydney, Sydney Univ. v.2, n.1, June 1963 - v.10, n.1/2, 1975.

JOURNAL OF POLITICAL ECONOMY, Chicago, Univ. of Chicago. v.55, 1947 - v.87, n.5, pt.2, Oct. 1979.

KEIO BUSINESS REVIEW, Tokyo. n.1, 1962 - n.15, 1978.

KEIO ECONOMIC STUDIES, Tokyo. v.1, 1963 - v.15, 1978.

KEIZAI KENKYU (Hitotsubashi University), Tokyo. v.1, n.1, Oct. 1950 - v.31, n.1, Jan. 1980.

KOBE ECONOMIC AND BUSINESS REVIEW, Kobe. v.1, 1954 - v.25, 1979.

KOBE UNIVERSITY ECONOMIC REVIEW, Kobe. n.1, 1955 - n.24, 1978.

KYOTO UNIVERSITY ECONOMIC REVIEW, Kyoto. v.20, n.1, Apr. 1950 - v.48, n.2, Oct. 1978.
Not published in 1945-49.

MANAGEMENT AND LABOR STUDIES, Tokyo, Keio Univ. n.1, 1962 - n.21, 1972 (*n.18)
No more published.

MODERN ASIAN STUDIES, London, Cambridge Univ. v.1, 1967 - v.12, 1978.

MONUMENTA NIPPONICA, Tokyo, Sophia Univ. v.7, n.1, Apr. 1951 - v.34, n.2, July 1979.

NATIONAL RESEARCH INSTITUTE OF AGRICULTURE BULLETIN, Tokyo. n.1, 1949 - n.6, 1961.
No more published.

OSAKA CITY UNIVERSITY ECONOMIC REVIEW, Osaka. n.1, 1965 - n.14, 1978.

OSAKA ECONOMIC PAPERS, Osaka, Osaka Univ. v.1, 1951 - v.22, n.1/2, Mar. 1974.

OTEMON ECONOMIC STUDIES, Osaka. v.1, 1968 - v.5, 1972.

PACIFIC AFFAIRS, Vancouver, Univ. of British Columbia. v.18, n.1, Mar. 1945 - v.51, n.3, Fall 1978.

PAST AND PRESENT, Oxford, Past and Present Society. n.1, Feb. 1952 - n.82, Feb. 1979.

POPULATION STUDIES, London, London School of Economics. v.1, pt.1, June 1947 - v.33, n.1, Mar. 1979.

QUARTERLY JOURNAL OF ECONOMICS, Cambridge, Mass., Harvard Univ. v.60, n.1, Nov. 1945 - v.93, n.3, Aug. 1979.

RESEARCH IN ECONOMIC HISTORY, Greenwich, Conn. v.1, 1967 - v.4, 1979.

REVIEW OF ECONOMIC STUDIES, Cambridge, Mass., Harvard Univ. v.13, 1945/1946 - v.46, n.4, Oct. 1979.

REVIEW OF ECONOMICS AND STATISTICS, Cambridge, Mass., Harvard Univ. v.27, n.1, Feb. 1945 - v.61, n.3, Aug. 1979.

RIRON KEIZAIGAKU (Toyo Keizai Shimposha), Tokyo. v.1, n.1, Jan. 1950 - v.30, n.2, Dec. 1979.

RURAL ECONOMIC PROBLEMS, Tokyo, International Association for Agricultural Economics in Japan. v.1, n.1, May 1964 - v.4, n.2, Nov. 1967.
No more published.

SOCIAL RESEARCH, N.Y., New School for Social Research. v.12, n.1, Feb. 1945 - v.46, n.2, Summer 1979.

TRANSACTIONS OF THE ASIATIC SOCIETY OF JAPAN, Tokyo, Third Series. v.1, 1948 - v.3, 1954.

UNIVERSITY OF MICHIGAN, CENTER FOR JAPANESE STUDIES OCCASIONAL PAPERS, Ann Arbor, Mich. n.1, 1951 - n.12, 1979.

WASEDA BUSINESS AND ECONOMIC STUDIES, Tokyo. n.1, 1965 - n.13, 1977.

WASEDA ECONOMIC PAPERS, Tokyo. n.1, 1955 - n.17, 1978.

YALE ECONOMIC ESSAYS, New Haven, Conn. v.1, n.1, Spring 1961 - v.11, n.1/2, Spring/Fall 1971.
No more published.

Note: Volumes and numbers marked with * could not be conferred.

BIBLIOGRAPHY

I.

Ajia Keizai Kenkyujo
(Institute of Developing Economies. Economic Growth Division)
A selected bibliography on the economic development of Japan written in English. Tokyo, 1970.
191p.

An annotated catalogue of the exhibition of materials on the study of Japan by foreigners. Tokyo, National Diet Library, 1954.
58p.

Bibliography of the humanistic studies and social relations. Tokyo, Ministry of Education, 1955-1963.
8v.

Borton, Hugh, comp.
A selected list of books and articles on Japan in English, French and German. Cambridge, Harvard Yenching Institute, 1954.
272p.

Ceadel, Eric B.
Classified catalogue of modern Japanese books in Cambridge University Library. Cambridge, W. Heffer and Sons, 1961.
558p.

East-West Center. Institute of Advanced Projects.
Annotated bibliography series, No.6: A guide to social and behavioral science journals in Japan, comp. by Yasumasa Kuroda.

Eells, Walter Crosby
The literature of Japanese education, 1945-1954. Connecticut, Shoe String Press, 1955.
210p.

Fukuda, Naomi, ed.
Union catalog of books on Japan in western languages. Tokyo, International House of Japan Library, 1967.
534 p.

Gusinde, Martin and Chiye Sano
An annotated bibliography, Ainu studies by Japanese scholars. Tokyo, Heibonsha, 1962.
109p. (Collectanea Universitati Catholicae Nanzan)

Haring, Douglas G.
A list of books and articles on Ryukyu. Rev. ed. Syracuse, N.Y., Syracuse Univ., 1963.
102p.

Haring, Douglas, G., comp.
The Ryukyu research collection; holdings and desiderata as of May 1964, Syracuse Univ. Library and Maxwell Graduate School of Citizenship and Public Affairs. Syracuse, N.Y., 1964.
79p.

Higa, Shuncho, ed.
Bibliography of the Ryukyus. Naha, Univ. of the Ryukyus, 1962.
118p.

Ichimura, Shinichi and Toru Yano
Books on Japan; an assorted bibliography. Kyoto, Center for Southeast Asian Studies, 1974.
105p.

Japan. Ministry of Education
Introductions to scientific works in humanities and social sciences published in Japan. Tokyo, 1951.
223p.

Japan. Ministry of Foreign Affairs
Checklist of archives, in the Japanese Ministry of Foreign Affairs, Tokyo, Japan, 1868-1945, microfilmed for the Library of Congress 1949-51, compiled by Cecil H. Uyehara. Washington, Library of Congress, 1954.
262p.

Japan. Nihon Gakujutsu Kaigi
(Science Council of Japan)
Japanese annual bibliography of economics. Tokyo, 1971-1976.
7v.

Japan; International House of Japan
Library acquisition list, 1955-1975. Tokyo, International House of Japan Library, 1975.
242p.

Japan; International House of Japan
Library acquisition list, 1955-1979. Tokyo, International House of Japan Library, 1979.
316p.

Japanese National Committee of Historical Science
Bibliography of Japanese historiography (1969-1973) Tokyo, Univ. of Tokyo Press, 1976.
248p.

Japanese National Committtee of Historical Science
Recent trends in Japanese historiography; bibliographical essays. Tokyo, Japan Society for the Promotion of Science, 1972.
541p.

Kokuritsu Kokkai Toshokan
(National Diet Library)
Catalog of materials on Japan in western languages in the National Diet Library, April 1948-December 1963. Tokyo, 1963.
306p.

Kokuritsu Kokkai Toshkan
(National Diet Library)
Catalog of materials on Japan in western languages in the National Diet Library, fomerly in the collection of the Ueno Library, 1872-1960. Tokyo, 1966.
166p.

Kokuritsu Kokkai Toshokan
(National Diet Library)
Catalog of materials on Japan in western languages in the National Diet Library, 1948-1975. Tokyo, Kinokuniya, 1977.
388p.

Kokuritsu Kyoiku Kenkyujo. Fuzoku Kyoiku Toshokan (National Institute of Education. Education Library)
A list of documents in English on education in Japan. Tokyo, 1974.
27p.

Kokusai Kirisutokyo Daigaku
(International Christian Library)
Books on Japan in western languages. Tokyo, 1971.
139p.

Kokusai Koryu Kikin
(Japan Foundation)
Books on Japanese history and foreign relations; acquisition catalogue of the Japan Foundation Library, no.1. Tokyo, 1974.
97p.

Kokusai Koryu Kikin
(Japan Foundation)
An introductory bibliography for Japanese studies. Tokyo, Univ. of Tokyo Press, 1974-
(5v.)

Komiya, Ryutaro
A bibliography of studies in English on the Japanese economy. Tokyo, Univ. of Tokyo Press, 1966.
52p. (Research materials series)

McGovern, Melvin P
A list of Nagasaki maps printed during the Tokugawa era. The Hague, Mouton, 195-
20p. maps.

Passin, Herbert
Japanese education; a bibliography of materials in the English language. N.Y., Teachers College Press, 1970.
135p.

Rosovsky, Henry, comp.
Quantitative Japanese economic history; an annotated bibliography and a survey of U. S. holdings. Berkeley, Univ. of California, 1961.
173p.

Saito, Masaei, comp.
A select list of books on Tokyo, 1868-1971. Ann Arbor, Mich., Univ. of Michigan, Asia Library, 1975.
126p.

Sakamaki, Shunzo
Ryukyu; a bibliographical guide to Okinawan studies, surveying important primary sources and wrintings in Ryukyuan, Japanese, Chinese and Korean. Honolulu, Univ. of Hawaii Press, 1963.
353p.

Sakamaki, Shunzo
Ryukyuan research resources at the University of Hawaii. Honolulu, Univ. of Hawaii, Social Science Research Institute, 1965.
454p. (Ryukyuan Research Center research series)

Sasaki, Shigeshi, ed.
Publishing in Japan; present and past. Tokyo, Japan Book Publishers Association, 1969.
99p.

Silberman, Bernard S.
Japan and Korea; a critical bibliography. Tucson, Ariz., Univ. of Arizona Press, 1962.
120p.

Spaulding, Robert M., Jr. and John W. Hall
Japanese history; bibliography of sources in European languages.
1962.
73p.

Taguchi, Kirsten Yumiko
An annotated catalogue of Ainu material in the East Asian Institute of Aarhus University. Copenhagen, Scandinavian Institute of Asian Studies, 1974.
136p.

Teichler, Ulrich and Friedrich Voss
Bibliography on Japanese education; postwar publications in western languages. Munchen, Verlag Dokumentation, 1974.
294p.

Teng, Ssu-Yu, ed.
Japanese studies on Japan and the Far East; a short biographical and bibliographical introduction.
Hong Kong, Hong Kong Univ. Press, 1961.
485p.

Tokyo Joshi Daigaku. Hikaku Bunka Kenkyusho (Tokyo Women's Christian Univ. Institute for Comparative Studies of Culture)
Books on Japan and Asia. Tokyo, 1970-
3v.

U. S. Dept. of the Army
Ryukyu Islands; a bibliography.
Washington, 1967.
105p.

University of Michigan. Center for Japanese Studies
Bibliographical series. Ann Arbor, Univ. of Michigan Press, 1950-
(10v.)

No.1: A guide to Japanese reference and research materials in the field of political science, ed. by Robert E. Ward. 1950. Rev. ed. 1961.
No.2: A bibliography of Japanese dialects, ed. by Robert H. Brower. 1950.
No.3: Bibliographical materials in the Japanese language on Far Eastern archaology and ethnology, ed. by Richard K. Beardsley. 1950.
No.4: Japanese history; a guide to Japanese reference and research material, ed. by John W. Hall. 1954.
No.5: Japanese economics; a guide to Japanese reference and research materials, ed. by Charles F. Remer and Saburo Kawai. 1956.
No.6: Japanese geography; a guide to Japanese reference and research materials, ed. by Robert B. Hall and Toshio Noh. 1956. Rev. ed. 1970.
No.7: Japanese religion and philosophy; a guide to Japanese reference and research materials, ed. by Donald Holzman.
No.8: Japanese literature of the Showa period; a guide to Japanese reference and research materials, ed. by Joseph K. Yamagiwa. 1959.
No.9: Japanese language studies in the Showa period, ed. by Joseph K. Yamagiwa. 1961.
No.10: Japanese sociology and social anthropology, comp. by Richard K. Beardsley and Takashi Nakano. 1970.

Yamaguchi, Kosaku, ed.
A bibliography on Japanese history. Odaka, Institute of International Relations, St. Andrew's Univ., 1969. 112p.

Young, John, comp.
Checklist of microfilm reproduction of selected archives of the Japanese army, navy, and other government agencies 1868-1945. Washington, Georgetown Univ. Press, 1959. 144p.

IV.

Aima, Seiho
General bibliography on the impact of western culture in Japan. Monumenta Nipponica, v. 19, no.3/4. 1964. pp. 168-185.

Bibliography on economics published in Japan in western languages 1956-1958. Annals of the Hitotsubashi academy, v. 10, no.1. Aug. 1959. pp. 108-139.

Kuroda, Andrew Y.
Periodicals in occupied Japan. Pacific affairs, v. 22, no.1. Mar. 1949. pp. 43-52.

Saito, Osamu
List of references in Japanese on Japan. Keio economic studies, v. 10, no.2. 1973. pp. 95-96.

DICTIONARY

I.

Goedertier, Joseph M.
A dictionary of Japanese history. N.Y., Weatherhill, 1968. 415p.

Iwai, Seiichi, ed.
Biographical dictionary of Japanese history, tr. by Burton Watson. Tokyo, Kodansha International Ltd., 1978. 655p.

Papinot, E.
Historical and geographical dictionaby of Japan. N.Y., Frederick Ungar, 1964. 2v. illus.

Toyo Keizai Shimposha
Japanese-English dictionary of economic terms. Tokyo, 1950. 671p.

CHRONOLOGY

I.

Kai, Miwa and Philip B. Yampolsky, ed.
Political chronology of Japan, 1885-1957. N.Y., Columbia Univ., 1957.
63p. (East Asian Institute studies)

Tsuchihashi, Yachita
Japanese chronological table from 601 to 1972 A.D. Tokyo, Sophia Univ., 1972.
128p. (Monumenta Nipponica monographs)

RESEARCH TRENDS

I.

Hall, John Whitney
Japanese history; new dimensions of approach and understanding. 2d ed. Washington, Service Center for Teachers of History, 1966.
69p.

International Congress of Historical Sciences, 11th, Stockholm, 1960.
Le Japon au XIe Congres International des Sciences Historiques a Stockholm - l'etat actuel et les tendances des etudes historiques au Japon. Tokyo, Nippon Gakujutsu Shimkokai, 1960.
482p.
Contents are written in English

International Congress of Historical Sciences, 12th, Vienna, 1965.
Japan at the XIIth International Congress of Historical Sciences in Vienna. Tokyo, Nippon Gakujutsu Shinkokai, 1965.
431p.

Kokusai Kirisutokyo Daigaku (International Christian Univ.)
Approaches to the "History of thought" - transformation of modern Japan. Tokyo, 1966.
145p. (Asian cultural studies)

Sumiya, Mikio and Koji Taira, ed.
An outline of Japanese economic history, 1603-1940; majo works and research findings. Tokyo, Univ. of Tokyo Press, 1979.
372p.

UNESCO, Japanese National Commission
Research in Japan in history of Eastern and Western cultural contacts; its development and present situation. Tokyo, 1957.
154p.

II.

Borton, Hugh
Modern Japanese economic historians. (W. G. Beasley and E. G. Pulleyblank, ed. Historians of China and Japan. London, Oxford Univ. Press, 1961. pp. 288-306)

Boxer, C. R.
Some aspects of western historical writing on the Far East, 1500-1800. (W. G. Beasley and E. G. Pulleyblank, ed. Historians of China and Japan. London, Oxford Univ. Press, 1961. pp. 307-321)

Hanley, Susan B. and Kozo Yamamura
Quantitative data for use in historical research on Japan. (W. R. Lorwin and J. M. Price, ed. The dimensions of the past; materials, problems and opportunities for quantitative work in history. New Haven, Yale Univ. Press, 1971. pp. 503-530)

Hata, Ikuhiko
Japanese historical writing on the origins of the Pacific War. Australian National Univ., Papers on modern Japan, v. 2. Canberra, 1968. pp. 79-90)

Hudson, G. F.
British historical writing on Japan. (W. G. Beasley and E. G. Pulleyblank, ed. Historians of China and Japan. London, Oxford Univ. Press, 1961. pp. 322-327)

Shinohara, Miyohei
A survey of the Japanese literature on small industry. (Bert F. Hoselitz, ed. The role of small industry in the process of economic growth. The Hague Mouton, 1968. pp. 3-113. Bibl. pp. 91-113. and also cf. Committee for Translation of Japanese Economic Studies. Translations of Japanese economic studies, no. 43, Tokyo, International House of Japan, 1959-64. 133p. Bibl. pp. 103-133)

Takagaki, Torajiro
Researches in the economic history of Japan in the early Meiji era and the Okuma documents. (Naosaku Uchida, ed. Social and economic aspects of Japan. Seijo Gakuen Jubilee year 1917-1967. Tokyo, Economic Institute of Seijo Univ., 1967. pp. 1-16)

Yamamura, Kozo
Recent research in Japanese economic history. (R. E. Gallman, ed. Recent developments in the study of economic and business history. Connecticut, JAI Press, 1977. pp. 221-246)

IV.

Akita, George
An examination of E. H. Norman's scholarship. Journal of Japanese studies, v. 3, no.2, Summer 1977. pp. 375-419.

Bell, J. F.
Origins of Japanese academic economics. Monumenta Nipponica, v. 16, nos. 3/4. Oct. 1960/Jan. 1961. pp. 43-68.

Broadbridge, Seymour
The economic development of Japan 1870 to 1920; a review article. Journal of development studies, v. 4, no.2. Jan. 1968. pp. 268-287.

Hanley, Susan B. and K. Yamamura
A quiet transformation in Tokugawa economic history. Journal of Asian studies, v. 30, no.2. Feb. 1971, pp. 373-384.

Honjō, Eijirō
The development of the economics in Japan. Bulletin of University of Osaka Prefecture, series D, v. 1. 1957. pp. 1-14.

Honjō, Eijirō
Introduction of Western economics into Japan. Bulletin of University of Osaka Prefecture, series D, v. 6. 1962. pp. 1-19.

Ishigaki, Hiromi
Influence of American economics on economic thinkings in Japan. Hokudai economic papers, v. 2. 1970/1971. pp. 77-87.

Kawashima, Yoko
Research on Japanese economy; contributions by western economists. Keio economic studies, v. 1. 1963. pp. 168-181.

Kawata, Tadashi and Saburo Ninomiya
The development of the study of international relations in Japan. Developing economies, v. 2, no.2. June, 1964. pp. 190-204.

Kita, Kuichi
Public utility economics and its problems in Japan. Japan science review, economic sciences, v. 2. 1955. pp. 1-20.

Komatsu, Yoshitaka
The birth, development and recent trends of economic history in Japan; an outline with special reference to Waseda University. Waseda economic papers, no. 2. 1958. pp. 15-27.

Komatsu, Yoshitaka
The study of economic history of Japan. Economic history review, 2nd series, v. 14, no.1. Aug. 1961. pp. 115-120.

Kubota, Akiteru
Three economists of Waseda University, 1886-1920. Waseda economic papers, no. 2. 1958. pp. 1-14.

Ohashi, Ryuken
The study of statistics in Japan; its development, present state and future task. Keio University economic review, v. 29, no.2. Oct. 1959. pp. 40-77.

Okuma, Ichiro
Research on Japanese economy; part I, contributions by Japanese economists. Keio economic studies, v. 1. 1963. pp. 157-167.

Shimazaki, Takao
Introduction to the economic thought of Japan. Keio economic studies, v. 5. 1968. pp. 11-34.

Teranishi, Juro
A survey of economic studies of prewar Japan. Japanese economic studies, v. 1, no.2. Winter, 1972/73. pp. 47-98, Bibl. pp. 89-98.

Yamamura, Kozo
A note on Japan business history; review and recent books. Business history review, v. 44, no.1. Spring 1970. pp. 126-130.

Yamamura, Kozo
Recent research in Japanese economic history, 1600-1945. Research in economic history, supplement 1. 1977. pp. 221-245. Bibl. pp. 237-245.

Yamamura, Kozo
Towards a reexamination of the economic history of Tokugawa Japan, 1600-1867. Journal of economic history, v. 33, no.3. Sept. 1973. pp. 509-546.

HISTORY

EARLY MODERN AND MODERN PERIOD

I.

Allen, Louis
Japan, the years of triumph; from feudal isolation to Pacific empire. N.Y., American Heritage Press, 1971. 127p.

Australian National University. Research School of Pacific Studies.
Papers on modern Japan, ed. by D. C. S. Sissons. Canberra, 1965-1968. 2 v.
Contents:
- Vol. I.: the development of interest groups and the pattern of modernization in Japan, by Takeshi Ishida. pp. 1-17.
- The associational basis of decision-making in the Liberal-Democratic Party, by Haruhiro Fukui. pp. 18-33.
- Faction and ideology in postwar Japanese socialism by J. A. A. Stockwin, pp. 34-49.
- Human rights under the Japanese constitution, by D. C. S. Sissons. pp. 50-69. - Japanese economic experience and Southeast Asia, by E. S. Crawcour. pp. 70-82.
- Japanese-Australian trade by P. Drysdale. pp. 83-98. - Japan's trade policy, by Kiyoshi Kojima, pp. 99-127. - Japan's foreign aid policy, by Kiyoshi Kojima. pp. 128-137.
- Vol. II.: Japan's post-war foreign policy, by Masataka Koosaka. pp. 1-25.
- The liberal-Democratic Party and constitutional revision, by Haruhiro Fukui. pp. 26-45. - Government Departments and the making of foreign policy towards Okinawa, by Akio Watanabe. pp. 46-61. - Post-war

Japanese security and rearmament; with special reference to Japanese-American relations, by Shunsaku Katoo. pp. 62-78.
- Japanese historical writing on the origins of the Pacific War, by Ikuhiko Hata. pp. 79-90. - Dissolution of the Japanese Lower House, by D. C. S. Sissons. pp. 91-135.

Beasley, W. G. and E. G. Pulleyblank, ed.
Historians of China and Japan. London, Oxford Univ. Press, 1961. 351p. (Historical writing on the peoples of Asia)
Contents:
Introduction: (a) Chinese historical writing, (b) Japanese historical writing, (c) Western historical writing on China and Japan, by E. G. Pulleyblank and W. G. Beasley. pp.1-23.
- The ancient Chinese chronicles and the growth of historical ideals, by P. van der Loon. pp. 24-30 - Notes on the historiography of the Han period, by A. F. P. Hulsewe. pp. 31-43.
- The organization of Chinese official historiography; principles and methods of the standard histories from the T'ang through the Ming Dynasty, by Lien-sheng Yang. pp. 44-59.
- The veritable records of the Ming Dynasty, 1368-1644, by Wolfgang Franke, pp. 60-77. L'histoire comme guide de la pratique bureaucratique (les monographies, les encyclopedies, les recueils de statuts), by E. Balazs. pp. 78-94. - Chinese biographical writing, by D. C. Twitchett. pp. 95-114. - Some aspects of Chinese private historiography in the thirteenth and fourteenth centuries, by Herbert Franke. pp. 115-134. - Chinese historical criticism; liu chihchi and ssu-ma kuang, by E.G. Pulleyblank. pp. 135-166.
- Chang Hsueh-ch'eng and his historiography, by P. Demieville. pp. 167-185.
- Historical writing in twentieth-century China; notes on its background and development, by J. Gray, pp. 186-212.
- Early Japanese chronicles; the six national histories, by G. W. Robinson. pp. 213-228 - Japanese historical writing in the eleventh to fourteenth centuries, by G. W. Robinson and W. G. Beasley. pp. 229-243.
- Japanese historical writing in the Tokugawa period (1603-1868) by W. G. Beasley and Carmen Blacker. pp. 245-263. - Shigeno Yasutsugu and the modern Tokyo tradition of historical writing by Jiro Numata. pp. 264-287
- Modern Japanese economic historians, by Hugh Borton. pp. 288-306.
- Some aspects of western historical writing on the Far East, 1500-1800, by C. R. Boxer. pp. 307-321.
- British historical writing on Japan by G. F. Hudson. pp. 322-327.
- The social history of Mongol nomadism by Owen Lattimore. pp. 328-344
- Index, p. 345.

Beasley, William G.
The modern history of Japan. London, Weidenfeld and Nicolson, 1963. 352p. illus. maps. (The Weidenfeld and Nicolson Asia-Africa series)

Borton, Hugh, ed.
Japan. Ithaca, N.Y., Cornell Univ. Press, 1950. 320p.
Contents:
- The land, by Robert Burnett Hall, pp. 1-9.
- Political divisions and population by Robert Burnett Hall. pp. 10-15.
- The people, by John F. Embree. pp. 16-30.
- The natural resources, by Norton S. Ginsburg. pp. 31-45.
- Agriculture, by W. I. Ladejinsky. pp. 46-63.
- Industrial development, by William W. Lockwood. pp. 64-80.
- Trade, by William W. Lockwood. pp. 81-93.
- Labor relations, by Miriam S. Farley. pp. 94-109.
- Transportation and communications, by Stanley Nehmer. pp. 110-126.
- Financial development, by Jerome B. Cohen. pp. 127-143.
- Government, by Chitoshi Yanaga. pp. 144-159.
- Way of life, by Douglas G. Haring. pp. 160-173.

- Religion, by A. K. Reischauer. pp. 174-191.
- Cultural life, by Daniel Crump Buchanan. pp. 192-206.
- Scientific research, by Seishi Kikuchi. pp. 207-218.
- The fine arts, by Harold G. Henderson. pp. 219-231.
- Architecture, by Alexander C. Soper pp. 232-239.
- Language, by Joseph K. Yamagiwa. pp. 240-242.
- Literature, by Joseph K. Yamagiwa. pp. 243-257.
- History; from earliest times to 1853, by G. B. Sansom. pp. 258-270.
- Development of the modern state, 1850-1945, by Hugh Borton. pp. 271-284.
- Foreign relations, 1931-1945, by Joseph W. Ballantine. pp. 285-297.
- Occupation, by Jane M. Alden. pp. 298-312.
- Index of persons and places, p.313

Borton, Hugh
Japan's modern century. N.Y., Ronald Press, 1955.
524p. illus. maps.

Chatterji, Bijan Raj
Modern Japan; Perry to Sato. 3d rev. and enl. ed., Meerut, Meenakshi Prakashan, 1966.
128p.

Craig, Albert M and Donald H. Shively, ed.
Personality in Japanese history. Berkeley, Univ. of California Press, 1970.
481p.
Contents:
- Perspectives on personality in Japanese history, by Albert M. Craig. pp. 1-28.
- Human nature in the Japanese myths, by John C. Pelzel. pp. 29-56.
- Ikeda Mitsumasa and the Bizen flood of 1654, by John W. Hall. pp. 57-84.
- Tokugawa Tsunayoshi, the Genroku Shogun, by Donald H. Shively. pp. 85-126.
- Okura Nagatsune and the technologists, by Thomas C. Smith. pp. 127-154.
- Oshio Heihachiro (1793-1837), by Tetsuo Najita. pp. 155-179.
- Political reconsilitation in the Tokugawa Bakufu; Abe Masahiro and Tokugawa Nariaki, 1849-1852, by Conrad Totman. pp. 180-208.
- Shimazu Nariakira and the emergence of national leadership in Satsuma, by Robert K. Sakai. pp. 209-233.
- The Bakumatsu intellectual in action; Hashimoto Sanai in the political crisis of 1858, by George M. Wilson. pp. 234-263.
- Kido Koin and Okubo Toshimichi; a psycho-historical analysis, by Albert M. Craig. pp. 264-308.
- Mutsu Munemitsu, by Maricos B. Jansen. pp. 309-334.
- The other Ito; a political failure, by George Akita. pp. 335-372.
- Kayahara Kazan and Japanese cosmopolitanism, by Akira Iriye. pp. 373-398.
- Nagai Ryutaro; the tactical dilemmas of reform, by Peter Duns. pp. 399-424.
- Akutagawa Ryunosuke and the negative ideal, by Howard S. Hibbett. pp. 425-451.

Dilts, Marion May
The pageant of Japanese history. 3d. ed. N.Y., Longmans, Green, 1961.
368p. illus. maps.

Dunn, Charles J.
Everyday life in traditional Japan. London, Batsford, 1969.
197p. illus. map. (Everyday life series)

Duus, Peter
The rise of modern Japan. Boston, Houghton Mifflin, 1976.
298p.

Fairbank, John K., Edwin O. Reischauer, and Albert M. Craig
East Asia; the modern transformation. Boston, H. Mifflin 1965.
955p. (A history of East Asian civilization, v. 2)

Fairbank, John K., Edwin O. Reischauer, and Albert M. Craig.
East Asia; transformation and tradition. Boston, H. Mifflin, 1973.
955p.

Fairbank, John K. and Edwin O. Ruischauer
East Asia; the great tradition. Boston, H. Mifflin, 1960.
738p. (A history of Eastern civilization, v. 1)

Gibson, Michael
The rise of Japan. N.Y., Wayland Publishers, 1972.
128p.

Gubbins, John H.
The making of modern Japan. Reprint ed. Freeport, N.Y., Books for Libraries Press, 1971.
316p.

Hall, John Whitney
Japan, from prehistory to modern times. N.Y., Delacorte Press, 1970.
395p. illus. maps. (Delacorte world history)

Halliday, Jon
A political history of Japanese capitalism. N.Y., Pantheon, 1975.
466p.

Hane, Mikiso
Japan; a historical survey. New York, Scribner, 1972.
650p.

Honjo, Eijiro
The social and economic history of Japan. Kyoto, Institute for Research in Economic History of Japan, 1935.
Reprint ed. by Russell and Russel, 1965.
405p.

Ienaga, Saburo
History of Japan. 7th ed. Tokyo, Japan Travel Bureau, 1963.
262p. illus. maps. (Tourist library)

Kajima, Morinosuke
The emergence of Japan as a world power 1895-1925. Tokyo, Tuttle, 1968.
403p. maps.

Kennedy, Malcolm D.
A history of Japan. London, Weidenfeld and Nicolson, 1963.
365p. maps.

Kumar, S. and S. Jain
History of modern Japan, 1850-1975. 2d ed. New Delhi, S. Chand, 1978.
188p.

Latourette, Kenneth Scott
The history of Japan. Rev. ed. N.Y., Macmillan, 1956.
299p. illus. maps.

Lehmann, Jean-Pierre
The image of Japan; from feudal isolation to world power, 1850-1905. London, George Allen & Unwin, 1978.
208p.

Livingston, Jon, ed.
Imperial Japan, 1800-1945. New York, Pantheon Books, 1973.
600p. (The Japan reader, 2)
Incl. bibliography.

Contents:
- Part I: Japan's feudal origins; 1800-1868, pp. 3-6.
- 1. Impressions of feudal Japan; Memoirs of a captivity in Japan, by Captain Vasilii, pp. 7-12.
- 2. Feudalism and its decline, p. 13.

- 2. Agriculture, p. 240.
- Landlords and village society, by Fukutake Tadashi. pp. 240-244.
- The power structure of the hamlet, by Fukutake Tadashi. pp. 245-250.
- The tenant movement, by Wakukawa Seiyei. pp. 251-256.
- 3. Education and the position of women, p. 256.
- The emperor's birthday, by Sydney Greenbie. p. 256.
- The Japanese educational system, by Herbert Passin. pp. 257-270.
- After a fruitless argument, by Ishikawa Takuboku. p. 271.
- Student enthusiasts, by Peter Duus. pp. 272-273.
- Rather than cry, by Ishikawa Takuboku. p. 274.
- A Japanese husband, by Ishimoto Shidzué. pp. 275-286.
- 4. Labor and industry, p. 285.
- The great combines, by William Lockwood. pp. 285-290.
- Labor, repression, and the public police act, by Ayusawa Iwao. pp. 291-297.
- The early socialist movement, by George O. Totten. III. pp. 298-304.
- Japan's economic position; the progress of industrialization, by John Orchard. pp. 305-310.
Japanese laborers, by Matsukata Kōjirō. pp. 311-312.
- Are miners human beings?, by Ishimoto Shidzué. pp. 313-317.
- The effects of the world war on industrialization, by John Orchard. pp. 318-321.
- The rice riots of 1918, by Arthur Young. pp. 322-326.
The new labor and the Japanese communists, by George O. Totten, III. pp. 327-331.
- Government suppression of the labor movement, by John Orchard. pp. 332-335.
- 5. The twenties and beyond, p. 336.
- Japan's economy in transition, by William Lockwood. pp. 336-341.
- Japan as a political organism, by T. A. Bisson. pp. 342-348.

Part IV: Depression, militarism, and war: 1929-1945. pp. 349-354.
- 1. Political economy, 1929-1936. pp. 353-354.
- The Genyōsha; a study in the origins of Japanese imperialism, by E. H. Norman. pp. 355-367.
- Japan's quest for autonomy, by James Crowley. pp. 368-370.
- Trade, armament, industrial expansion, 1930-1938, by William Lockwood. pp. 371-377.
- The concentration of economic control, by G. C. Allen. pp. 378-383.
- 2. Labor, peasants, women, conscription, repression. p. 384.
- Social democratic reactions to war and totalitarianism, by George O. Totten, III. pp. 385-396.
- The Japanese communist party, by John K. Emmerson. pp. 397-404.
- The Japanese situation and the duty of the Japanese communist party, by Communist International, 1932. pp. 405-409.
- Labor's lot in the war period, by Ayusawa Iwao. pp. 410-412.
- The way of the gods, by Helen Mears, pp. 413-423.
- The Japanese family system as seen by a Japanese woman, by Hani Setsuko. pp. 424-430.
- Tenancy and aggression, by R. P. Dore. pp. 431-438.
- Suye mura - the life history of the individual, by John Embree. pp. 439-444.
- Wartime local government, by Kurt Steiner. pp. 445-448.
- Japan - land and men, by Lawrence Hewes. p. 449.
- War and the rural areas, by R. P. Dore. pp. 450-451.
- 3. Political economy, 1936-1945, p. 452.
- The Zaibatsu and the war, by Eleanor Hadley, pp. 452-455.
- Increase in Zaibatsu predominance in wartime Japan, by T. A. Bisson, pp. 456-457.
- The Zaibatsu's wartime role, by T. A. Bisson. pp. 458-464.
- 4. The Japanese people and the war, p. 465.
- Hunger in the mountains, by Gwen Terasaki. pp. 465-474.
- Tokyo burns, by Robert Guillain. pp. 475-484.

- Zone of emptiness, by Noma Hiroshi.
pp. 485-488.
- Fires and the plain, Ōoka Shōhei,
pp. 489-494.

Maraini, F.
Japan; patterns of continuity.
Tokyo, Kōdansha International, 1971.
246p.

Mason, R. H. P. and J. G. Caiger
A history of Japan.
Tokyo, C. E. Tuttle, 1973.
334p.

Mayo, Marlene J., ed.
The emergence of imperial Japan; self-defense or calculated aggression? Lexington, Mass., Heath, 1970.
105p. (Problems in Asian civilizations)
Contents:
- Traditional expanionism, by Robert T. Pollard. pp. 13-18.
- Response to western aggression, by Hyman Kublin. pp. 19-24.
- A question of timing and not of goals, by W. G. Beasley. pp. 25-30.
- Lingering militarism, by John M. Maki, pp. 31-34.
- The confucian world order, by M. Frederick Nelson. pp. 35-38.
- Requirements of national security, by James Crowley. pp. 39-46.
- Ultranationalist societies, by E. Herbert Norman. pp. 47-54.
- Pan-Asianism, by Marius Jansen. pp. 55-58.
- National mission, by Sannosuke Matsumoto. pp. 59-68.
- Capitalism and imperialism, by O. Tanin and E. Yohan. pp. 69-74.
- Capitalism, international politics, and the emperor system, by Shōichi Fujii. pp. 75-82.
- A rebuttal to economic determinism, by Hilary Conroy. pp. 83-88.
- Blueprint for conquest, by George Kerr. pp. 89-94.
- Unexpected happenings, by Hilary Conroy, pp. 95-100.
- Suggestions for additional reading. p. 101.

Meyer, Milton Walter
Japan; a concise history. Boston, Allyn and Bacon, 1966.
226p. illus. maps.

Moulder, Frances V.
Japan, China and the modern world economy; toward a reinterpretation of East Asian development, ca. 1600 to ca. 1918. London, Cambridge Univ. Press, 1977.
x, 255p.

Murdoch, James
A history of Japan. London, Routledge & K. Paul, 1949.
3 v. maps.

Najita, Tetsuo
Japan. Englewood Cliffs, N.J., Prentice-Hall, 1974.
152p.

Nakamura, Kichisaburo
The formation of modern Japan, as viewed from legal history. Tokyo, Centre for East Asian Cultural Studies, 1962.
127p. (East Asian cultural studies series)

Nish, Ian
The story of Japan. London, Faber and Faber, 1968.
238p. illus, maps.

Norbeck, Edward
Changing Japan. New York, Holt Rinehart and Winston, 1965.
82p. illus. map. (Case studies in cultural anthropology)

Norman, E. H.
Japan's emergence as a modern state. N.Y., Institute of Pacific Relations, 1940.
254p. (I. P. R. inquiry series)

Norman, E. H.
Origins of the modern Japanese state; selected writings of E. H. Norman, ed. by J. W. Dower. New York, Pantheon Books, 1975.
497p.

Reischauer, Edwin O.
Japan; past and present. 3d. rev. ed. Tokyo, Tuttle, 1964.
323p. maps.

Reischauer, Edwin O.
Japan; the story of nation. Tokyo, Tuttle, 1970.
345p.

Reischauer, Edwin O.
The Japanese. Cambridge mass., and London, Belknap Press of Harvard Univ. Press, 1977.
443p.
published enl. ed. in 1978. 464p.

Reischauer, Edwin O. and Albert M. Craig
Japan; tradition and transformation. New York, G. Allen & Unwin, 1979.
347p.

Sadler, A. L.
A short history of Japan. 2d ed. London, Angus and Robertson, 1963.
359p. illus. maps.

Sansom, Sir George Bailey
A history of Japan. London, Cresset Press, 1958-64.
3 v. illus. maps.

Sansom, Sir George Bailey
Japan; a short cultural history. Rev. ed. N. Y., Appleton-Century-Crofts, 1943.
554p. illus. maps.
Illustrated ed. 1962. 558p.

Sansom, Sir George Bailey
Japan in world history. Tokyo, Kenkyusha, 1965.
121p.

Scheiner, Irwin, ed.
Modern Japan; an interpretive anthology. New York, MacMillan, 1974.
270p.
Contents:
- Japan's cultural identity; some reflections on the work of Watsuji Tetsuro, by Robert N. Bellah. pp. 3-8.
- Japan's world order, by Seizaburo Sato. pp. 9-17.
- From Suye mura; a Japanese village, by John F. Embree. pp. 18-38.
- From the Chrysanthemum and the sword, by Ruth Benedict. pp. 39-50.
- The social perception of skin color in Japan, by Hiroshi Wagatsuma. pp. 51-78.
- From Tokugawa religion, by Robert N. Bellah. pp. 79-94.
- Old values and new techniques in the modernization of Japan, by Thomas C. Smith. pp. 95-103.
- The castle town and Japan's modern urbanization, by John Whitney Hall. pp. 104-121.
- Some recent approaches to Japanese nationalism, by Kenneth B. Pyle pp. 122-134.
- The significance of nationalism in modern Japanese thought, by Sannosuke Matsumoto. pp. 135-139.
- From Christian converts and social protest in Meiji Japan, by Irwin Scheiner. pp. 140-150.
- Achievement orientation, social self-identity, and Japanese economic growth, by George A. deVos. pp. 151-164.
- From the autobiography of Yukichi Fukuzawa, by Yukichi Fukuzawa. pp. 165-175.
- Inoue Kowashi (1843-1895) and the Meiji educational system, by Joseph Pittau. pp. 176-189.
- Freedom and the concept of people's rights, by Daikichi Irokawa. pp. 190-201.

- Characteristics of Japanese intellectuals, by Chie Nakane, pp. 202-207.
- Japanese thought, by Masao Maruyama. pp. 208-215.
- Tradition and trauma in the contemporary Japanese novel, by Howard Hibbett. pp. 216-232.
- Fukuzawa, Uchimura, and Okakura; Meiji intellectuals and westernization, by Masao Maruyama. pp. 233-247.
- Japan and the ethics of fatalism, by David W. Plath. pp. 248-254.
- Tate no Kai and selected writings, by Yukio Mishima. pp. 255-259.
- 'Economic animal' reconsidered, by Yoshiyuki Hagiwara. pp. 260-270.

Seth, Ronald
Milestones in Japanese history. Philadelphia, Chilt Book Co., 1969.
167p. illus, map.

Skrzypczak, Edmund, ed.
Japan's modern century. A special issue of Monumenta Nipponica prepared in celebration of the Centennial of the Meiji Restoration. Tokyo, Sophia Univ., 1968.
207p.
Contents:
- Fukuzawa Yukichi's 'Departure from Asia'; a prelude to the Sino-Japanese War, by Miwa Kimitada. pp. 1-26 .
- Ōkuma Shigenobu; modernization and the west, by Joyce C. Lebra. pp. 27-40.
- Ancestor worship in Yatsuka Hozumi's state and constitutional theory, by Atsuko Hirai. pp. 41-50.
- The aims and content of school courses in Japanese history, 1872-1945, by John Caiger. pp. 51-82.
- Suehiro Tetchō; a Meiji political novelist, by Iwamoto Toshio. pp. 83-114.
- Saikaku and the modern Japanese novel, by Richard Lane. pp. 115-132.
- Meiji period translators and translations, by Hide Ikebara Inada. pp. 133-160.
- Artistic trends in the Meiji period, by Fernando Gutiérrez. pp. 161-190.
- Japan as a model for developing nations, by Douglas H. Mendel. pp. 191-207.

Storry, Richard
A history of modern Japan. Harmondsworth, Middlesex, Penguin Books, 1960.
287p. map.

Takekoshi, Yosaburo
The economic aspects of the history of the civilization of Japan. London, Dawsons of Pall Mall, 1978.
3 v.

Tiedemann, Arthur E., ed.
An introduction to Japanese civilization. New York, Columbia, Univ. Press, 1974.
622p.
Contents:
- Part one: the history of Japan
I. Early Japan, by H. Paul Varley. pp. 3-32.
- II. The age of the Court Nobles, by H. Paul Varley. pp. 33-60.
- III. The age of the military houses, by H. Paul Varley, pp. 61-97.
- IV. Tokugawa Japan, by Conrad Totman. pp. 98-130.
- V. Late Tokugawa and early Meiji Japan, by Marlene J. Mayo. pp. 131-180.
- VI. The era of fulfillment; 1877-1911, by Roger F. Hackett. pp. 181-216.
- VII. Taisho and early Shōwa Japan, by Arthur E. Tiedemann. pp. 217-246.
- VIII. The road to war: 1931-1945, by Richard Storry. pp. 247-276.
- IX. Japan since 1945, by Lawrence Olson, pp. 277-308.
- Part two: Aspects of Japanese civilization.
- X. Japanese religion, by W. M. Theodore de Bary. pp. 309-328.
- XI. The art of Japan, by Hugo Munsterbery. pp. 329-376.
- XII. Literature, by Donald Keene. pp. 375-422.
- XIII. Economic and cultural geography, by Norton Ginsburg. pp. 423-460.

- XIV. The premodern economy, by E. S. Crawcour. pp. 461-486.
- XV. The modern economy, by E. S. Crawcour. pp. 487-514.
- XVI. Japanese society, a sociological view, by Koya Azumi, pp. 515-536.
- XVII. Modern political institute, by Ardath Burks. pp. 537-568.
- XVIII. Japanese law, a profile, by Dan F. Henderson. pp. 569-591.

Tiedemann, Arthur E.
Modern Japan; a brief history. rev. ed. Princeton, N.J., Van Nostrand, 1962.
193p. (Anvil original)

Tsunoda, Ryusaku, Wm. Theodore de Bary and Donald Keene
Sources of the Japanese tradition. N.Y., Columbia Univ. Press, 1958.
928p. maps. (Records of civilization; sources and studies)

Uchida, Naosaku and Kotaro Ikeda
Social and economic aspects of Japan. Seijo Gakuen Jubilee year 1917-1967. Tokyo, Economic Institute of Seijo Univ., 1967.
263p.
Contents:
- Researches in the economic history of Japan in the early Meiji era and the Okuma documents, by Torajiro Takagaki. pp. 1-16.
- Shigenobu Okuma; his view on Japan's international balance of payments, by Shumpei Okada. pp. 17-42.
- Finanzielle und fiskalische mabnahmen der regierung zue pflege des kapitals in der fruhen Meiji zeit (1868-1890), by Kotaro Ikeda. pp. 43-64.
- The demerits of high economic growth; creeping inflation and forced savings, by Osamu Arii. pp. 65-90.
- Japan's economic growth and social welfare, by Tadashi Saito. pp. 91-110.
- Industrialization ahd the change of wage structure in Japan, by Hyosaburo Matsuzaka. pp. 111-140.
- Marketing in Japan - retrospection and perspective, by Giichi Fukami. pp. 141-166.
- Public transport investment in Japan, by Kiyoshi Okada. pp. 167-182.
- The impact of joint councils on collective bargaining in Japan, by Tadashi Mitsufuji. pp. 183-220.
- The role of the emperor in postwar Japan, by Ryusuke Suda. pp. 221-238.
- Social and economic problems of the overseas Chinese in Southeast Asia, by Naosaku Uchida. pp. 239-263.

Varley, H. Paul
A syllabus of Japanese civilization. N.Y., Columbia Univ. Press, 1968.
98p. maps. (Companions to Asian studies)

Wakefield, Harold
New paths for Japan. N.Y., Oxford Univ. Press, 1948.
222p.

Williams, Barry
Emerging Japan. N.Y., McGraw-Hill, 1969.
143p. illus. maps. (Modern times)

Williams, Harold S.
Shades of the past, or indiscreet tales of Japan. Tokyo, Tuttle, 1959.
357p. illus.

Yanaga, Chitoshi
Japan since Perry. N.Y., McGraw-Hill, 1949.
723p.

Yanaga, Chitoshi
Japanese people and politics. N.Y., Wiley, 1956.
408p.

Yoshida, Shigeru
Japan's decisive century 1867-1967. N.Y., Praeger, 1967. 110p. illus.

II.

Sansom, Sir George Bailey
History; from earliest times to 1853. (Hugh Borton, ed. Japan. Ithaca, N.Y., Cornell University Press, 1950. pp. 258-270)

Sato, Seizaburo
Japan's world order. (Irwin Scheiner, ed. Modern Japan; an interpretive anthology. New York, MacMillan, 1974. pp. 9-17)

Storry, Richard
The road to war; 1931-1945. (Arthur E. Tiedemann, ed. An introduction to Japanese civilization, New York, Columbia Univ. Press, 1974. pp. 247-276)

Tiedemann, Arthur E.
Taishō and early Showa Japan. (Arthur E. Tiedemann, ed. An introduction to Japanese civilization. New York, Columbia Univ. Press, 1974. pp. 217-246)

Yanaihara, Tadao
A short history of modern Japan. (Seiichi Tobata, ed. The modernization of Japan - I. Tokyo, Institute of Asian Economic Affairs, 1966. pp. 3-48)

HISTORY OF SCIENCE AND TECHNOLOGY

I.

Nakayama, Shigeru
A history of Japanese astronomy; Chinese background and Western impact. Cambridge, Mass., Harvard Univ. Press., 1969. 329p. illus. (Harvard-Yenching Institute monograph series)

Nakayama, Shigeru, ed.
Science and society in modern Japan; selected historical sources. Tokyo, Univ. of Tokyo Press, 1974. 337p.
Contents:
- History of science; a subject for the frustrated, by Nakayama Shigeru. pp. 3-18.
- Arithmetic in a class society; notes on arithmetic in the Europen Renaissance, by Ogura Kinnosuke. pp. 19-23.
- Methodological approaches in the development of the meson theory of Yukawa in Japan, by Taketani Mitsuo. pp. 24-38.
- On concepts of technology by Hoshino Yoshiro. pp. 39-50.
- Toward a truly free labor force; a review of Nakaoka Tetsuro's the future of man and labor, by Shizume Yasuo. pp. 51-56.
- Reflections on the history of science in Japan, by Oya Shin'ichi. pp. 57-71.
- A history of universities; an overview - from the viewpoint of science history, by Nakayama Shigeru. pp. 72-80.
- The shifting center of scientific activity in the West; from the 16th to the 20th century, by Yuasa Mitsutomo. pp. 81-103.
- Statistical approaches to the history of science, by Yagi Eri. pp. 104-150.
- Society for the study of materialism; Yuiken, by Oka Kunio. pp. 151-157.
- The Japanese research system and the establishment of the Institute of Physical and Chemical Research, by Itakura Kiyonobu and Yagi Eri. pp. 158-201.
- Social conditions for prewar Japanese research in nuclear physics, by Hiroshige Tetu. pp. 202-220.
- The elementary particle theory group, by Kaneseki Yoshinori. pp. 221-252.
- Marxism and biology in Japan, by Nakamura Teiri. pp. 253-269.
- Grass-roots geology; Ijiri Shoji and the Chidanken, by Nakayama Shigeru. pp. 270-289.
- A basic theory of Kogai, by Ui Jun. pp. 290-311.
- An annotated bibliography of English language works on the social history of modern Japanese science, by James Bartholomew. pp. 312-328.
- Index, p. 329.

Sugimoto, Masayoshi and David L. Swain
Science and culture in traditional Japan; A. D. 600-1854. Cambridge, Mass., MIT Press, 1978.
498p.

Sugita, Genpaku
Dawn of Western science in Japan; Rangaku kotohajime, tr. by Ryozo Matsumoto and Eiichi Kiyooka. Tokyo, Hokuseido, 1969.
74p. illus.

Tezuka, Tatsumaro
The introduction of Western culture into Japan in the age of her modernization. Tokyo, Tokyo Metropolitan Government, 1967.
31p. illus. (Tokyo municipal news supplement)

Tsuge, Hideomi, ed.
Historical development of science and technology in Japan. Tokyo, Kokusai Bunka Shinkokai, 1961.
200p. illus. maps. (Series on Japanese life and culture v. 5)

II.

Craig, Albert
Science and confucianism in Tokugawa Japan. (Marius B. Jansen, ed. Changing Japanese attitudes toward modernization. Princeton, Princeton University Press, 1965. pp. 133-166)

Hirosige, Tetu
Social conditions for prewar Japanese research in nuclear physics. (Shigeru Nakayama, ed. Science and society in modern Japan; selected historical sources. Tokyo, University of Tokyo Press, 1974. pp. 202-220)

Itakura, Kiyonobu and Eri Yagi
The Japanese research system and the establishment of the Institute of Physical and Chemical Research. (Shigeru Nakayama, ed. Science and society in modern Japan; selected historical sources. Tokyo, University of Tokyo Press, 1974. pp. 158-201)

Nakayama, Shigeru
History of science; a subject for the frustrated. (Shigeru Nakayama, ed. Science and society in modern Japan; selected historical sources. Tokyo, University of Tokyo Press, 1974. pp. 3-18)

Oka, Kunio
Society for the study of materialism; Yuiken. (Shigeru Nakayama, ed. Science and society in modern Japan; selected historical sources. Tokyo, University of Tokyo Press, 1974. pp. 151-157)

Oya, Shin'ichi.
Reflections on the history of science in Japan. (Shigeru Nakayama, ed. Science and society in modern Japan; selected historical sources. Tokyo, University of Tokyo Press, 1974. pp. 57-71)

Smith, Thomas C.
Okura Nagatsune and the technologists. (Albert M. Craig, ed. Personality in Japanese history. Berkeley, University of California Press, 1970. pp. 127-154)

Smith, Thomas C.
Old values and new techniques in the modernization of Japan. (Irwin Scheiner, ed. Modern Japan; an interpretive anthology. New York, MacMillan, 1974. pp. 95-103)

Yagi, Eri
Statistical approaches to the history of science. (Shigeru Nakayama, ed. Science and society in modern Japan; selected historical sources. Tokyo, University of Tokyo Press, 1974. pp. 104-150)

IV.

Aoki, Kunio and Tohru Nakagawa
A review of the history of the development of science museums in Japan. Japanese studies in the history of science, no. 17. 1978. pp. 1-12.

Asaoka, Hiroshi
The process of formation of commodity-science in Japan. Hitotsubshi journal of arts and sciences, v. 19 no.1. Nov. 1978. pp. 30-39.

Bartholomew, James R.
Why was there no scientific revolution in Tokugawa Japan? Japanese studies in the history of science, no. 15. 1976. pp. 111-126.

Hashimoto, Michio
Development of social consciousness in the history of public health of Japan. Japanese studies in the history of science, no. 3. 1964. pp. 127-183. Bibl. 183-184.

Hirose, Hideo
The European influence on Japanese astronomy. Monumenta Nipponica, v. 19, nos. 3/4. 1964. pp. 61-80

Hiroshige, Tetu
Social conditions for the researches of nuclear physics in pre-war Japan. Japanese studies in the history of science, no. 2. 1963. pp. 80-93.

Hiroshige, Tetu
Studies of history of physics in Japan. Japanese studies in the history of science, no.1. 1962. pp. 26-34.

Honda, Kin-ya
A survey of Japanese mathematics during the last centenary. Japanese studies in the history of science, no. 16. 1977. pp. 1-16.

Imazu, Kenji
The beginning of electric engineers in Japan. Japanese studies in the history of science, no. 17. 1978. pp. 13-36.

Kamatani, Chikayoshi
The history of research organization in Japan. Japanese studies in the history of science, no. 2. 1963. pp. 1-79.

MacLean, J.
The significance of Jan Karel van den Broek (1814-1865) for the introduction of western technology into Japan. Japanese studies in the history of science, no. 16. 1977. pp. 69-90.

MacLean, J.
Von Siebold and the importation of Japanese plants into Europe via the Netherlands. Japanese studies in the history of science, no. 17. 1978. pp. 43-80.

Nakayama, Shigeru
Japanese studies in the history of astronomy. Japanese studies in the history of science, no. 1. 1962. pp. 14-22.

Otsuka, Yasuo
A short history of bioethics in Japan. Japanese studies in the history of science, no. 16. 1977. pp. 17-22.

Oya, Shin-ichi
A short note on the history of Japanese mathematics. Japanese studies in the history of science, no. 1. 1962. pp. 23-25.

Saito, Torao
The Japanese element in modern architecture. Japan quarterly, v. 9, no.4. Oct./Dec. 1962. pp. 419-428.

Sippel, Patricia
Aoki Konyo (1618-1769) and the beginnings of Rangaku. Japanese studies in the history of science, no. 11. 1971. pp. 127-162.

Tanaka, Minoru
A note on the development of chemistry in Japan. Japanese studies in the history of science, no. 7. 1968. pp. 61-70.

Tsuzuki, Yojiro and Akiko Yamashita
History of the chemistry of taste in Japan. Japanese studies in the history of science, no. 7. 1968. pp. 1-28.

Tsuzuki, Yojiro and Akiko Yamashita
On the studies of history of chemistry in Japan. Japanese studies in the history of science, no. 4. 1965. pp. 41-57.

Ueno, Masuzo
The western influence on natural history in Japan. Monumenta Nipponica, v. 19, nos.3/4. 1964. pp. 81-105.

Watanabe, Masao and Yūko Ose
General academic trend and the evolution theory in late nineteenth century Japan; a statistical analysis of the contemporary periodicals. Japanese studies in the history of science, no. 7. 1968. pp. 129-142.

Yajima, Suketoshi
The European influence on physical science in Japan. Monumenta Nipponica, v. 19, nos.3/4. 1964. pp. 106-117.

Yamazaki, Toshio
Japan's contributions to the modern history of technology. Japanese studies in the history of science, no. 1, 1962. pp. 45-50.

Yuasa, Mitsutomo
The growth of scientific communities in Japan. Japanese studies in the history of science, no. 9. 1969. pp. 137-158.

Yuasa, Mitsutomo
History of science and technology in Japan. Japanese studies in the history of science, no. 10. 1970 pp. 1-16.

Yuasa, Mitsutomo
Scientific revolution in nineteenth century Japan. Japanese studies in the history of sceience, no. 2. 1963. pp. 119-126.

TOKUGAWA PERIOD

POLITICS AND SOCIETY

I.

Bolitho, Harold
Treasures among men; the Fudai Daimyo in Tokugawa Japan. New Haven, Yale Univ. Press, 1974. 278p.

Dore, Ronald Philip
Education in Tokugawa Japan. London, Routledge and Kegan Paul, 1965. 346p. illus. map. (International library of sociology and social reconstruction)

Duus, Peter.
Feudalism in Japan. New York, A. Knopf, 1969. 116p. maps. (Studies in world civilization)

Hall, John Whitney
Tanuma Okitsugu 1719-1788; forerunner of modern Japan. Cambridge, Mass., Harvard Univ. Press, 1955. 208p. (Harvard-Yenching Institute monograph series)

Hall, John W. and Marius B. Jansen, ed.
Studies in the institutional history of early modern Japan. Princeton, Princeton University Press, 1968. 396p.
Contents:
- The Tokugawa period and Japanese feudalism, by Joseph R. Strayer. pp. 1-14.
- Feudalism in Japan; a reassessment, by John Whitney Hall. pp. 15-51. (Reprinted from *Comparative studies in society and history*, v. 5, no.1. Oct. 1962)
- The new look of Tokugawa history, by J. W. Hall. pp. 55-64.
- Foundations of the modern Japanese Daimyo, by J. W. Hall. pp. 65-77 (Reprinted from *Journal of Asian studies*, v. 20, no.3. May 1961).
- The Ikeda House and its retainers in Bizen, by J. W. Hall. pp. 79-88.
- Tosa in the sixteenth century; the 100 article code of Chōsokabe Motochika, by Marius B. Jansen. pp. 89-114. (Reprinted from *extremus*, v. 10, no.1. Apr. 1963)
- Tosa in the seventeenth century; the establishment of Yamauchi Rule, by Marius B. Jansen. pp. 115-129.
- The consolidation of power in Satsuma-han, by Robert Sakai. pp. 131-139.
- Materials for the study of local history in Japan; pre-Meiji Daimyo records, by J. W. Hall. pp. 143-168. (Reprinted from *Harvard journal of Asiatic studies*, v. 20, nos. 1/2. June 1957)
- The castle town and Japan's modern urbanization, by J. W. Hall. pp. 169-188. (Reprinted from *Far Eastern quarterly*, v. 15, no. 1. Nov. 1955).
- Changes in Japanese commerce in the Tokugawa period, by E. S. Crawcour. pp. 189-202. (Reprinted from *Journal of Asian studies*, v. 22, no.4. Aug. 1963).
- The evolution of Tokugawa law, by Dan Fenno Henderson. pp. 203-229.
- Bakufu versus Kabuki, by Donald H. Shively. pp. 231-261. (Reprinted from *Harvard journal of Asiatic studies*, v.18, nos.3/4. Dec. 1955)
- The Japanese village in the seventeenth century, by Thomas C. Smith. pp. 263-282. (Reprinted from *Journal of economic history*, v. 12, no.1. Winter 1952).
- The land tax in the Tokugawa period, by Thomas C. Smith. pp. 283-299. (Reprinted from *Journal of Asian studies*, v. 18, no.1. Nov. 1958)
- Village autonomy and articulation with the state, by Harumi Befu. pp. 301-314. (Reprinted from *Journal of Asian studies*, v. 25, no.1. Nov. 1965).
- Tokugawa and modern Japan, by Marius B. Jansen. pp. 317-330. (Reprinted from *Japan quarterly*, v. 12, no.1. 1965).
- Tosa during the last century of Tokugawa rule, by Marius B. Jansen. pp. 331-347.
- Talent and the social order in Tokugawa Japan, by R. P. Dore. pp. 349-361. (Reprinted from *Past and present*, no. 21. Apr. 1962)
- The restoration movement in Chōshu, by Albert Craig. pp. 363-373. (Reprinted from *Journal of Asian studies*, v. 18, no.2. Feb. 1959).
- From Tokugawa to Meiji in Japanese local administration, by J. W. Hall. pp. 375-386.

Haraguchi, Torao
The status system and social organization of Satsuma; a translation of the Shumon tefuda aratame jomoku.
Tokyo, Univ. of Tokyo Press, 1975. 257p.

Inoue, Mitsusada
Introduction to Japanese history - before the Meiji Restoration. Tokyo, Kokusai Bunka Shinkokai, 1962. 124p. illus. maps. (Series on Japanese life and culture).

Lewis, Archibald
Knights and samurai; feudalism in Northern France and Japan. London, T. Smith, 1974. 101p.

Perrin, Noel
Giving up the gun; Japan's reversion to the sword, 1543-1879. Boston, D. R. Godine, 1979.
122p.

Totman, Conrad
The collaspe of the Tokugawa Bakufu, 1862-1868. Honolulu, Univ. of Hawaii Press, 1980.
448p.

Totman, Conrad D.
Politics in the Tokugawa Bakufu 1600-1843. Cambridge, Mass., Harvard Univ. Press, 1967.
346p. (Harvard East Asian series)

Tsukahira, Toshio G.
Feudal control in Tokugawa Japan; the Sankin Kotai system. Cambridge, Mass., Harvard Univ. Press, 1966.
228p. (Harvard East Asian series)

Webb, Herschel
The Japanese imperial institution in the Tokugawa period. N.Y., Columbia Univ. Press, 1968.
296p. (Studies of the East Asian Institute)

Wigmore, John Henry, ed.
Law and justice in Tokugawa Japan. Tokyo, Kokusai Bunka Shinkokai, 1967-70.
3v. illus, maps.

II.

Beasley, W. G.
Feudalism and its decline; the samurai tradition. (Jon Livingston, ed. Imperial Japan, 1800-1945, New York, Pantheon Books, 1973. pp. 15-18)

Beasley, W. G. and Carmen Blacker
Japanese historical wrinting in the Tokugawa period (1603-1868) (W. G. Beasley and E. G. Pulleybland, ed. Historians of China and Japan. London, Oxford Univ. Press, 1961. pp. 245-263)

Hall, John Whitney
Feudalism in Japan; a reassessment. (John W. Hall, and Marius B. Jansen, ed. Studies in the institutional history of early modern Japan. Princeton, Princeton Univ. Press, 1968. pp. 15-51. Reprinted from Comparative studies in studies in society and history, v. 5, no.1. Oct. 1962)

Hall, John Whitney
The nature of traditional society; Japan. (Robert E. Ward and D. A. Rustow, ed. Political modernization in Japan and Turkey. Princeton, Princeton Univ. Press, 1964. pp. 14-41)

Hall, John Whitney
The new look of Tokugawa history. (John W. Hall, and Marius B. Jansen, ed. Studies in the institutional history of early modern Japan. Princeton, Princeton Univ. Press, 1968. pp. 55-64)

Henderson, Dan Fenno
The evolution of the Tokugawa law. (John W. Hall and Marius B. Jansen, ed. Studies in the institutional history of early modern Japan, Peinceton, Princeton Univ. Press, 1968. pp. 203-229)

Jansen, Marius B.
Tokugawa and modern Japan. (John W. Hall and Marius B. Jansen, ed. Studies in the institutional history of early modern Japan. Princeton, Princeton Univ. Press, 1968. pp. 317-330. Reprinted from Japan quarterly, v. 12, no.1. 1965)

Mayo, Marlene J.
Late Tokugawa and early Meiji Japan. (Arthur E. Teidemann, ed. An introduction to Japanese civilization. New York, Columbia Univ. Press, 1974. pp. 131-180)

Reischauer, Edwin O.
Japanese feudalism. (Rushton Coulborn, ed. Feudalism in history. Hamden, Conn., Archon Books, 1965. pp. 26-48)

Sansom, G. B.
Feudalism and its decline; economic trends. (Jon Livingston, ed. Imperial Japan, 1800-1945. New York, Pantheon Books, 1973. pp. 21-25)

Storry, Richard
Feudalism and its decline; change in Tokugawa society. (Jon Livingston, ed. Imperial Japan, 1800-1945. New York, Pantheon Books, 1973. pp. 19-20)

Strayer, Joseph R.
The Tokugawa period and Japanese feudalism. (John W. Hall and Marius B. Jansen, ed. Studies in the institutional history of early modern Japan. Princeton, Princeton Univ. Press, 1968. pp. 1-14)

Yasuba, Yasukichi
Another look at the Tokugawa heritage with special reference to social conditions. (International Development Center of Japan. Papers and proceedings of the conference on Japan's historical development experience and contemporary developing countries; issues for comparative analysis. Feb. 11-16, 1978. Tokyo, 1978. pp. 1-24)

III.

Brooks, William Lyman
Outcaste society in early modern Japan. Ph.D. 1976. Columbia University.
360p.

Dicenzo, Ronald John
Daimyo, domain and retainer band in the seventeenth century; a study of institutional development in Echizen, Tottori and Matsue. Ph.D. 1978. Princeton University.
228p.

Miller, John Holmes
Social disorder in late Tokugawa Japan. Ph.D. 1975. Princeton University.
278p.

Mitsui, Masato
Shimazu Shigehide 1745-1833; a case study of Daimyo leadership. Ph.D. University of Hawaii.
311p.

Odo, Franklin Shoichiro
Saga Han; the feudal domain in Tokugawa Japan. Ph.D. 1975. Princeton University.
322p.

IV.

Beasley, W. G.
Politics and the Samurai class structure in Satsuma 1858-1868. Modern Asian studies, v. 1, pt.1, Jan. 1967. pp. 47-58.

Hall, John Whitney
E. H. Norman on Tokugawa Japan. Journal of Japanese studies, v. 3, no.2. Summer 1977. pp. 365-374.

Hall, John Whitney
Feudalism in Japan; a reassessment. Comparative studies in society and history, v. 5, no.1. Oct. 1962. pp. 15-51.

Hall, John Whitney
Materials for the study of local history in Japan; pre-Meiji Daimyo records. Harvard Journal of Asiatic studies, v. 20, no.1/2. June 1957. pp. 187-212.

Hall, John Whitney
Materials for the study of local history in Japan; pre-Meiji village records. Univ. of Michigan, Center for Japanese studies occasional paper, no. 3. 1952. pp. 1-14.

Hall, John Whitney
Rule by status in Tokugawa Japan. Journal of Japanese studies, v. 1, no.1. Autumn 1974. pp. 39-49.

Henderson, Dan Fenno
"Contracts" in Tokugawa Japan. Journal of Japanese studies, v. 1, no.1. Autumn 1974. pp. 51-90.

Irimajiri, Yoshinaga
Feudal crisis in Tokugawa Japan; the historical preconditions of Meiji restoration. Waseda business and economic studies, no. 6. 1970. pp. 1-16.

Irimajiri, Yoshinaga
The socio economic causes and consequences of the Meiji restoration; social movements in the late Tokugawa and early Meiji periods. Waseda business and economic studies, no. 3. 1967. pp. 23-38.

Jansen, Marius B.
Tokugawa and modern Japan. Japan quarterly, v. 12, no.1. Jan./Mar. 1965. pp. 27-38.

Kee Il Choi
Tokugawa feudalism and the emergence of the new leaders of early modern Japan. Explorations in entrepreneurial history, v. 9, no.2. 1956.

Moore, Ray A.
Adoption and samurai mobility in Tokugawa Japan. Journal of Asian studies, v. 29, no.3. May 1970. pp. 617-632.

Moore, Ray A.
Samurai discontent and social mobility in the late Tokugawa period. Monumenta Nipponica, v. 24, nos.1/2. 1969. pp. 79-91.

Nagahara, Keiji
The historical premises for the modernization of Japan; on the structure of the Tokugawa Shogunate. Hitotsubashi journal of economics, v. 3, no.1. Oct. 1962. pp. 61-72.

Shively, Donald H.
Sumptuary regulation and status in early Tokugawa Japan. Harvard journal of Asiatic studies, vol. 25. 1964/1965. pp. 123-164.

Soranaka, Isao
The Kansei reforms - success or failure? Monumenta Nipponica, v. 33, no.2. Summer 1978. pp. 151-164.

Toby, Ronald P.
Reopening the question of Sakoku; diplomacy in the legitimation of the Tokugawa Bakufu. Journal of Japanese studies, v. 3, no.2. Summer 1977. pp. 323-363.

Totman, Conrad
Fudai Daimyo and the collapse of the Tokugawa Bakufu. Journal of Asian studies, v. 34, no.3. May 1975. pp. 581-592.

Totman, Conrad
Political succession in Tokugawa Bakufu; Abe Masahiro's rise to power, 1843-1845. Harvard journal of Asian studies, v. 26. 1966. pp. 102-124.

Totman, Conrad
Tokugawa Yoshinobu and Kōbugattai; a study of political inadequacy. Monumenta Nipponica, v. 30, no.4. Winter 1975. pp. 393-403.

Toyoda, Takeshi
The character of the feudal society in Japan. Annals of the Hitotsubashi academy, v. 8, no.1. Oct. 1957. pp. 29-35.

ECONOMY GENERAL

I.

Frost, Peter
The bakumatsu currency crisis. Cambridge, Mass., East Asian Research Center, 1970.
79p. (Harvard East Asian monographs)

Hauser, William B.
Economic institutional change in Tokugawa Japan; Osaka and Kinai cotton trade. New York and London, Cambridge University Press, 1974.
239p.

Honjo, Eijiro
Economic theory and history of Japan in the Tokugawa period. Reprint ed. N.Y., Russell and Russell, 1965.
350p.

Sheldon, Charles David
The rise of the merchant class in Tokugawa Japan, 1600-1868; an introductory survey. New York, Russell and Russell, 1958.
205p. (Monographs of the Association for Asian Studies 5)

Takizawa, Matsuyo
The penetration of money economy in Japan and its effects upon social and political institutions. Reprint ed. N.Y., AMS Press, 1968.
159p.

Toyoda, Takeshi
A history of pre-Meiji commerce in Japan. Tokyo, Kokusai Bunka Shinkokai, 1969.
107p. maps. (Japanese life and culture series)

Volker, T.
The Japanese porcelain trade of the Dutch East India Company after 1683. Leiden, E. J. Brill, 1959.
92p. illus. (Mededelingen van het Rijksmuseum voor Volkenkunde)

Yamamura, Kozo
A study of samurai income and entrepreneurship; quantitative analyses of economic and social aspects of the samurai in Tokugawa and Meiji Japan. Cambridge, Mass., Harvard Univ. Press, 1974.
243p.

II.

Bendix, Richard
Preconditions of development, a comparison of Japan and Germany. (Ronald P. Dore, ed. Aspects of social change in modern Japan. Princeton, Princeton University Press, 1967. pp. 27-68)

Crawcour, E. S.
Changes in Japanese commerce in the Tokugawa period. (J. W. Hall and M. B. Jansen, ed. Studies in the institutional history of early modern Japan. Princeton, Princeton University Press, 1968. pp. 189-202. Reprinted from Journal of Asian studies, v. 22, no.4. Aug. 1963).

Crawcour, E. S.
The premodern economy.
(Arthur E. Tiedemann, ed. An introduction to Japanese civilization. New York, Columbia Univ. Press, 1974. pp. 487-514)

Crawcour, E. Sydney
The Tokugawa heritage. (W. W. Lockwood, ed. The state and economic enterprise in Japan. Princeton, Princeton Univ. Press, 1965. pp. 17-44)

Ihara, Saikaku
Samurai, merchants, and townsmen; the Japanese family storehouse or the millionaires' gospel modernized. (Jon Livingston, ed. Imperial Japan, 1800-1945. New York, Pantheon Books, 1973. pp. 72-79)

Smith, T. C.
Economic changes; the decision to industrialize; motivation to industrialize.
(Jon Livingston, ed. Imperial Japan, 1800-1945. New York, Pantheon Books, 1973. pp. 108-115)

III.

Mitchnick, Les.
Traditional and transitional tax systems during the early modern period; a case study of Chōshū Han, 1600-1873. Ph.D. 1972. University of California at Los Angeles.
354p.

Neville, Edward L.
The Development of Transportation in Japan; a case study of Okayama han, 1600-1868. Ph.D. 1958.
University of Michigan.

Sakihara, Mitsugu
The significance of Ryukyu in Satsuma finances during the Tokugawa period. Ph.D. 1971. University of Hawaii. 327p.

IV.

Broadbridge, Seymour
Economic and social trends in Tokugawa Japan. Modern Asian studies, v. 8, pt. 3. July 1974. pp. 347-372.

Cooper, Michael
The mechanics of the Macao-Nagasaki silk trade. Monumenta Nipponica, v. 27, no. 4. Winter 1972. pp. 423-433.

Crawcour, E. Sydney
Changes in Japanese commerce in the Tokugawa period. Journal of Asian studies, v. 22, no.4. Aug. 1963. pp. 387-400.

Crawcour, E. Sydney
The development of a credit system in seventeenth century Japan.
Journal of economic history, v. 21, Sept. 1961. pp. 342-360.

Crawcour, E. Sydney
Documentary sources of Tokugawa economic and social history.
Journal of Asian studies, v. 20, no. 3 May 1961. pp. 343-351.

Crawcour, E. Sydney
The Japanese economy on the eve of modernization. Journal of Oriental Society of Australia, v. 2, no.1. June 1963. pp. 34-41.

Crawcour, E. Sydney
Kawamura Zuiken; a seventeenth-century entreprenuer. Transactions of the Asiatic Society of Japan, Third series, v. 9. May 1966. pp. 28-50.

Crawcour, E. Sydney
Some observations on merchants, a translation of Mitsui Takafusa's Chonin Koken Roku, with an introduction and notes. Transactions of the Asiatic Society of Japan, Third series, 8. Dec. 1961. pp. 1-139.

Crawcour, E. Sydney
The Tokugawa period and Japan's preparation for modern economic growth. Journal of Japanese studies, v. 1, no.1. Autumn 1974. pp. 113-125.

Crawcour, E. S. and Kozo Yamamura
The Tokugawa monetary system; 1787-1868. Economic development and cultural change, v. 18, no.4. pt. 1. July 1970. pp. 489-518.

Duffy, William J. and Kozo Yamamura
Integration of Tokugawa monetary markets, 1787-1867; a spectral analysis. Explorations in economic history. 8. June 1971.

Duffy, William J. and Kozo Yamamura
Monetization and integration of markets in Tokugawa Japan; a spectral analysis. Explorations in entrepreneurial history, v. 8, no.4. Summer 1971. pp. 395-423.

Flershem, Robert G.
Some aspects of Japan sea trade in the Tokugawa period. Journal of Asian studies, v. 23, no.3. May 1964. pp. 405-416.

Flershem, Robert G. and N. Yoshiko
Nakano family documents; Satsuma-Chōshu trade, 1855-1866. Monumenta Nipponica, v. 26, nos.1/2. 1971. pp. 1-16.

Hall, John Whitney
The Tokugawa Bakufu and the merchant class. Univ. of Michigan, Center for Japanese studies occasional papers, no. 1, 1951. pp. 26-34.

Hauser, William B.
The diffusion of cotton processing and trade in Kinai region in Tokugawa Japan. Journal of Asian studies, v. 33, no.4. Aug. 1947. pp. 633-649.

Horie, Yasuzo
The feudal states and the commercial society in the Tokugawa period. Kyoto University economic review, v. 28, no.2. Oct. 1958. pp. 1-16.

Kuroha, Hyōjirō
Commerce of Osaka in the Tokugawa era. Bulletin of University of Osaka Prefecture, series D, v. 9. 1965. pp. 1-15.

Miyamoto, Mataji
The merchants of Osaka. 1-2. Osaka economic papers, pt. 1, v. 7, no.1. Sept. 1958, pp. 1-13.
pt. 2, v. 15, no.1, Nov. 1966. pp. 11-32.

Miyashita, Koichi
"Money economy" in the Tokugawa era. Kobe University economic review, no. 8. 1962. pp. 1-20.

Mori, Yasuhiro
Loans to Daimyōs by the Ōsaka money changers. Osaka economic papers, v. 15, no.2. Mar. 1967. pp. 19-28.

Nakamura, Satoru
The historical preconditions of the formation of capitalism in Japan. Kyoto University economic review, v. 43, nos.1/2. Apr./Oct. 1973. pp. 30-44.

Nishikawa, Shunsaku
Productivity, subsistence, and by-employment in the mid-nineteenth century Chōshū. Explorations in entrepreneurial history, v. 15, no. 1. 1978. pp. 69-83.

Nishimura, Takao
The English factory at Hirado. Bulletin of University of Osaka Prefecture. series D. v. 1. 1957. pp. 47-52.

Ohkura, Takehiko and Hiroshi Shimbo
The Tokugawa monetary policy in the eighteenth and nineteenth centuries. Explorations in entrepreneurial history, v. 15, no.1. 1978. pp. 101-124.

Ramseyer, J. Mark
Thrift and diligence; house codes of Tokugawa merchant families. Monumenta Nipponica, v. 34, no.2. Summer 1979. pp. 209-230.

Sakai, Robert K.
The Satsuma-Ryukyu trade and the Tokugawa seclusion policy. Journal of Asian studies, v. 23, no.3. May 1964. pp. 391-403.

Sakihara, M.
Ryūkyū's tribute-tax to Satsuma during the Tokugawa period. Modern Asian studies, v. 6, pt. 3. July 1972. pp. 329-336.

Sakudō, Yōtarō
Currency in Japanese feudal society. Osaka economic papers, v. 4, no.1. June 1955. pp. 17-30.

Sakudō, Yōtarō
Growth of securities market in feudal Japan. Osaka economic papers, v. 8, no.2. Mar. 1960. pp. 25-40.

Sakudō, Yōtarō
Monetary system in feudal Japan. Osaka economic papers, v. 5, no.1. Aug. 1956, pp. 33-57.

Sasaki, Seiji
A chronological table of modern Japanese shipping. no. 1; 1600-1799. no. 2; 1800-1912. Kobe economic and business review, v. 11-12. 1964-1965. pp. 113-124, 15-38.

Smith, Thomas C.
Pre-modern economic growth; Japan and the West. Past and present. no. 60. Aug. 1973. pp. 127-160.

Toyoda, Takeshi
Japanese guilds. Annals of the Hitotsubashi academy, v. 5, no.1. Oct. 1954. pp. 72-85.

Wakita, Osamu
The Kokudaka system; a device for unification. Journal of Japanese studies, v. 1, no.2. Spring 1975. pp. 297-320.

Yamamura, Kozo
The increasing poverty of the samurai in Tokugawa Japan, 1600-1868. Journal of economic history, v. 31, no.2. June 1971. pp. 378-406.

POPULATION AND LABOUR

I.

Hanley, Susan B. and Kozo Yamamura
Economic and demographic change in preindustrial Japan, 1600-1800. Princeton, Princeton Univ. Press, 1978. xiii, 409p.

II.

Hanley, Susan B.
Population trends, Bizen Province in Okayama. (D. V. Glass and R. Revelle, ed. Population and social change. London, E. Arnold, 1972. pp. 437-449)

Hanley, Susan B. and K. Yamamura
Population trends and economic grwoth in preindustrial Japan. (D. V. Glass and R. Revelle, ed. Population and social change, London, E. Arnold, 1972. pp. 451-499)

III.

Hanley, Susan
Population trends and economic development in Tokugawa Japan. Ph.D. 1971. Yale University.

IV.

Hanley, Susan B.
Fertility, mortality and life expectancy in pre-modern Japan. Population studies, v. 28, Mar. 1974. pp. 127-142.

Hanley, Susan B.
Migration and economic change in Okayama during the Tokugawa period. Keio economic studies, v. 10, no.2. 1973. pp. 19-35.

Hanley, Susan B.
Population trends and economic development in Tokugawa Japan; the case of Bizen province in Okayama. Daedalus, v. 97, no.2. 1968. pp. 622-635.

Hanley, Susan B.
Toward an analysis of demographic and economic change in Tokugawa Japan; a village study. Journal of Asian studies, v. 31, no.3. May 1972. pp. 515-538.

Hayami, Akira
The demographic analysis of a village in Tokugawa Japan; Kando-shinden of Owari province, 1771-1871. Keio economic studies, v. 5. 1968. pp. 50-88.

Hayami, Akira
Labour migration in a pre-industrial society; a study tracing the life histories of the inhabitnats of a village. Keio economic studies, v. 10, no.2. 1973. pp. 1-17.

Hayami, Akira
The population at the beginning of the Tokugawa period; an introduction to the historical demography of pre-industrial Japan. Keio economic studies, v. 4. 1966/67. pp. 1-28.

Saito, Osamu
The labor market in Tokugawa Japan; wage differentials and the real wage level, 1727-1830. Explorations in entrepreneurial history, v. 15, no.1. Jan. 1978. pp. 84-100.

AGRICULTURE AND VILLAGE STRUCTURE

I.

Borton, Hugh
Peasant uprisings in Japan of the Tokugawa period. 2d ed. with a new introduction. N.Y., Paragon Book Reprint Corp., 1968. 219p.

Chambliss, William Jones
Chiaraijima village; land tenure, taxation, and local trade 1818-1884. Tucson, Univ. of Arizona Press, 1965. 159p. (Association of Asian Studies, monographs and papers)

Henderson, Dan Fenno
Village "contract" in Tokugawa Japan; fifty speciments with English translation and comments. Seattle, Univ. of Washington Press, 1975.
234p.

Smith, Thomas C.
The agrarian origins of modern Japan. Stanford, Stanford Univ. Press, 1959. 250p. illus. maps. (Stanford studies in the civilizations of Eastern Asia)

Smith, Thomas C.
Nakahara; family farming and population in a Japanese village, 1717-1830. Stanford, Calif., Stanford Univ. Press, 1977.
183p.

II.

Befu, Harumi
Duty, reward, sanction, and power; four-cournered office of the Tokugawa village headman. (Bernard S. Silberman, etc. ed. Modern Japanese leadership; transition and change. Tucson, Univ. of Arizona Press, 1966. pp. 25-50)

Befu, Harumi
Village autonomy and articulation with the state. (John W. Hall and Marius Jansen, ed. Studies in the institutional history of early modern Japan. Princeton, Princeton Univ. Press, 1968. pp. 301-314. Reprinted from Journal of Asian studies, v. 25, no.1. Nov. 1965)

Borton, Hugh
The peasants; peasant uprisings in Japan of the Tokugawa period. (Jon Livingston, ed. Imperial Japan, 1800-1945. N.Y., Pantheon Books, 1973. pp. 49-55)

Kikuchi, Toshio
Geographical function of the reclamation settlements during the period of the Shogunate, 1603-1867. (International Geographical Union. Regional conference in Japan, 1957. Proceedings of IGU regional conference in Japan. Tokyo, 1959. pp. 349-354)

Norman, E. H.
The countryside and the cities, peasant protest and the land tax. (Jon Livingston, ed. Imperial Japan, 1800-1945. New York, Pantheon Books, 1973. pp. 124-128)

Scheiner, Irwin
Benevolent lords and honorable peasants; rebellion and peasant consciousness in Tokugawa Japan. (Tetsuo Najita and Irwin Scheiner, ed. Japanese thought in the Tokugawa period, 1600-1868; methods and metaphors. Chicago, University of Chicago Press, 1978. pp. 39-62)

Smith, Thomas C.
The countryside and the cities; agrarian distress and taxation. (Jon Livingston, ed. Imperial Japan, 1800-1945, New York, Pantheon Books, 1973. pp. 129-131)

Smith, Thomas C.
The Japanese village in the seventeenth century. (John W. Hall and Marius B. Jansen, ed. Studies in the institutional history of early modern Japan. Princeton, Princeton University Press, 1968. pp. 263-282. Reprinted from Journal of economic history, 12, 1952)

Smith, Thomas C.
The land tax in the Tokugawa period. (John W. Hall and Marius B. Jansen, ed., Studies in the institutional history of early modern Japan. Princeton, Princeton University Press, 1968. pp. 283-299. Reprinted from Journal of Asian studies, v. 18, no.1. Nov. 1958)

Umemura, Mataji
Note on economic development in agriculture in the Tokugawa period. (Kazushi Ohkawa and Yujiro Hayami, ed. Economic growth; the Japanese experience since the Meiji era; proceedings of the second conference held by the Japan Economic Research Center, June 26 - July 1, 1972 in Japan. Tokyo, Japan Economic Research Center, 1973. v. 1. pp. 175-183)

Yamamura, Kozo
Pre-industrial landholding patterns in Japan and England. (Albert M. Craig, ed. Japan; a comparative view. Princeton, N.J., Princeton Univ. Press, 1979. pp. 276-323)

III.

Soranaka, Isao
Agrarian growth and social change in Tokugawa Japan. Ph. D. 1974. The University of Wisconsin at Madison, 1974. 335p.

Vlastos, Stephen Gregory
Tokugawa peasant movements in Fukushima; conflict and peasant mobilization. Ph.D. 1977. University of California, Berkeley. 206p.

IV.

Araki, Moriaki
Development of the agricultural production and its productivity in the Tokugawa Shogunate. Annals of the Institute of Social Science, no. 7. 1966. pp. 34-40.

Choi, Kee IL
Technological diffusion in agriculture under the Bakuhan system. Journal of Asian studies, v. 30, no.4. Aug. 1971. pp. 749-759.

Eng, Robert Y. and Thomas C. Smith
Peasant families and population control in eighteenth century Japan. Journal of interdisciplinary history, v. 6, no. 3. Winter 1976. pp. 417-445.

Fruin, W. Mark
Farm family migration; the case of Echizen in the nineteenth century. Keio economic studies, v. 10, no.2. 1973. pp. 37-46.

Ōishi, Kaichiro
The differentiation of the peasantry and peasants' movement in the process of disintegration of feudal and seigneurial land property in Japan. Annals of the Institute of Social Science, no. 12. 1971. pp. 43-50.

Shimbo, Hiroshi
A study of the growth of cotton production for the market in the Tokugawa era. Kobe University economic review, no. 1. 1955. pp. 55-70.

Smith, Thomas C.
Farm family by-employments in pre-industrial Japan. Journal of economic history, v. 29, no.4. Dec. 1969. pp. 687-715.

Smith, Thomas C.
The land tax in the Tokugawa period. Journal of Asian studies, v. 18, no.1. Nov. 1958. pp. 3-20.

Takeyasu, Shigeji
The farm rent in Kawachi district in the late Tokugawa period. Bulletin of University of Osaka Prefecture, series D, v. 2. 1958. pp. 108-112.

Varner, Richard E.
The organized peasant; the Wakamonogumi in the Edo period. Monumenta Nipponica, v. 32, no.3. Autumn 1977. pp. 459-483.

URBAN PROBLEMS

I.

Alcock, Sir Rutherford
The capital of the Tycoon; a narrative of a three years' residence in Japan. N.Y., Greenwood Press, 1969. 2 v. illus. maps.

Mogi, Hitoshi
A historical study of the development of Edo 1600-1860. Tokyo, City and Town Planners, 1966.
198p. illus. maps.

Ponsonby-Fane, Richard A. B.
Kyoto; the old capital of Japan 794-1869. Kyoto, Ponsonby-Memorial Society, 1956.
454p. illus.

Rozman, Gilbert
Urban networks in Ch'ing China and Tokugawa Japan. Princeton, N.J. Princeton Univ. Press, 1973.
355p.

II.

Beasley, W. G.
Samurai, merchants, and townsmen; town life and Tokugawa culture. (Jon Livingston, ed. Imperial Japan, 1800-1945. New York, Pantheon Books, 1973. p. 63)

Hall, John W.
The castle town and Japan's modern urbanization. (John W. Hall and Marius B. Jansen, ed. Studies in the institutional history of early modern Japan. Princeton, Princeton University Press, 1968. pp. 169-188. Reprinted from Far Eastern quarterly, v. 15, no.1. Nov. 1955)
also published (Irwin Scheiner, ed. Modern Japan; an interpretive anthology. New York, MacMillan, 1974. pp. 104-121)

Smith, Robert J.
Pre-industrial urbanism in Japan; a consideration of multiple traditions in a feudal society. (Thomas C. Smith ed. City and village in Japan. Chicago, University of Chicago Press, 1960. pp. 241-257)

IV.

Rozman, Gilbert
Edo's importance in the changing Tokugawa society. Journal of Japanese studies, v. 1, no.1. Autumn 1974. pp. 91-112.

Smith, Robert J.
Aspects of mobility in pre-industrial Japanese cities. Comparative studies in society and history, v. 5, no.4. July 1963. pp. 416-423.

Smith, Robert J.
Pre-industrial urbanism in Japan; a consideration of multiple traditions in a feudal society. Economic development and cultural change, v. 9, no.1, pt.2. Oct. 1960. pp. 241-257. Bibl. p. 255-257.

RELIGION AND THOUGHT

I.

Bellah, Robert N.
Tokugawa religion; the values of pre-industrial Japan. Boston, Free Press,1957. 249p.
also published by Boston, Beacon Press, 1970.

Earl, David Magarey
Emperor and nation in Japan; political thinkers of the Tokugawa period. Seattle, Univ. of Washington Press, 1964.
270p.

Harootunian, H. D.
Toward restoration; the growth of political consciousness in Tokugawa Japan. Berkeley, Univ. of California Press, 1970.
421p.

Henderson, Dan Fenno.
Conciliation and Japanese law; Tokugawa and modern. Seattle, Univ. of Washington Press, 1964.
2 v. (Association for Asian Studies monographs)
also published Tokyo Univ. Press, 1964.

Ishiguro, Tadaatsu, ed.
Ninomiya Sontoku; his life and 'Evening talks'. Tokyo, Kenkyusha, 1955.
246p. illus.

Maruyama, Masao
Studies in the intellectual history of Tokugawa Japan, tr. by Mikiso Hane. Tokyo, Univ. of Tokyo Press, 1974.
383p.

Najita, Tetsuo and Irwin Scheiner, ed.
Japanese thought in the Tokugawa period, 1600-1868; methods and metaphors. Chicago, Univ. of Chicago Press, 1978.
209p.
Contents:
- Method and analysis in the conceptual portrayal of Tokugawa intellectual history,by Tetsuo Najita, pp. 3-38.
- Benevolent lords and honorable peasants; rebellion and peasant consciousness in Tokugawa Japan, by Irwin Scheiner. pp. 39-62.
- The consciousness of archaic form in the new realism of Kokugaku, by H. D. Harootunian. pp. 63-104.
- Saussure's linguistic theories and the study of Japanese intelectual history, by Shigeki Niiyama, pp. 105-136.
- Baigan and Sorai; continuities and discontinuities in eighteenth-century Japanese thought, by Robert N. Bellah, pp. 137-152.
- Ogyu Sorai and the distinguishing features of Japanese confucianism, by Bito Masahide, pp. 153-160.
- The constitutionalism of Inoue Kowashi, by Yukichi Sakai. pp. 161-180.
- The idea of heaven; a Tokugawa foundation for natural rights, by Sannosuke Matsumoto. pp. 181-200.
- Contributors. p. 201. Index. p. 203.

Ogyu, Sorai
Distinguishing the way; Bendo, tr. with an introduction and notes by Olof G. Lidin. Tokyo, Sophia Univ., 1970.
130p. (Monumenta Nipponica monographs).

Ogyu, Sorai
The political writings of Ogyu Sorai, tr. and ed. by J. R. McEwan. London, Cambridge Univ. Press, 1962.
153p. (Univ. of Cambridge Oriental publications)

Spae, Joseph John.
Ito Jinsai; a philosopher, educator and sinologist of the Tokugawa period. Peiping, Catholic Univ. of Peking, 1948.
278p. illus. (Monumenta Serica, monograph)

Van Straelen, Henry
Yoshida Shoin; forerunner of the Meiji Restoration; a biographical study. Leiden, Brill, 1952.
149p. (Monographies du T'oung pao)

II.

Bellah, Robert N.
Baigan and Sorai; continuities and discontinuities in eighteenth century Japanese thought. (Tetsuo Najita and Irwin Scheiner ed. Japanese thought in the Tokugawa period, 1600-1868; methods and metaphors. Chicago, University of Chicago Press, 1978. pp. 137-152)

Bellah, Robert N.
From Tokugawa religion.
(Irwin Scheiner, ed. Modern Japan; and interpretive anthology. New York, MacMillan, 1974. pp. 79-94)

Bito, Masahide
Ogyu Sorai and the distinguishing features of Japanese confusianism.
(Tetsuo Najita and Irwin Scheiner, ed. Japanese thought in the Tokugawa period, 1600-1868; methods and metaphors. Chicago, University of Chicato Press, 1978. pp. 153-160)

Dore, Ronald
The thought of men; the thought of society, the educational system and ideologies by the Tokugawa period.
(Kokusai Kirisutokyo Daigaku. Studies on modernization of Japan by Western scholars. Tokyo, 1962. pp. 73-86)

Harootunian, H. D.
The consciousness of archaic form in the new realism of Kokugaku.
(Tetsuo Najita and Irwin Scheiner ed. Japanese thought in the Tokugawa period, 1600-1868; methods and metaphors. Chicago, University of Chicago Press, 1978. pp. 63-104)

Jansen Marius B.
Conciliar thought in late Tokugawa time in the case of Sakamoto Ryōma.
(Kokusai Kirisutokyo Daigaku. Studies on modernization of Japan by Western scholars. Tokyo, 1962. pp. 57-72)

Lane, Richard
Saikaku and the modern Japanese novel. (Edmund Skrzypczak, ed. Japan's modern century. A special issue of Monumenta Nipponica prepared in celebration of the centennial of the Meiji restoration. Tokyo, Siphia University, 1968. pp. 115-132)

Matsumoto, Sannosuke
The idea of heaven; a Tokugawa foundation for natural rights theory.
(Tetsuo Najita and Irwin Scheiner, ed. Japanese thought in the Tokugawa period, 1600-1868; methods and metaphors. Chicago, University of Chicago Press, 1978. pp. 181-200)

Najita, Tetsuo
Method and analysis in the conceptual portrayal of Tokugawa intellectual history. (Tetsuo Najita and Irwin Scheiner, ed. Japanese thought in the Tokugawa period, 1600-1868; methods and metaphors. Chicago, University of Chicago Press, 1978. pp. 3-38)

Niiyama, Shigeki
Saussure's linguistic theories and the study of Japanese intellectual history. (Tetsuo Najita and Irwin Scheiner, ed. Japanese thought in the Tokugawa period, 1600-1868; methods and metaphors. Chicago, University of Chicago Press, 1978. pp. 105-136.

Sakai, Robert K.
Simazu Nariakira and the emergence of national leadership in Satusma.
(Albert M. Craig, ed. Personality in Japanese history. Berkeley, University of California Press, 1970. pp. 209-233)

Sakai, Yukichi
The constitutionalism of Inoue Kowashi. (Tetsuo Najita and Irwin Scheiner, ed. Japanese thought in the Tokugawa period, 1600-1868; methods and metaphors. Chicago, University of Chicago Press, 1978. pp. 161-180)

Yazaki, Takeo
Samurai, merchants, and townsmen; The samurai family and feudal ideology.
(Jon Livingston, ed., Imperial Japan, 1800-1945. New York, Pantheon Books, 1973. pp. 57-62)

IV.

Dore, R. P.
Talent and the social order in Tokugawa Japan. Past and present, no.21. Apr. 1962. pp. 60-72.

Honjō, Eijirō
The anti-feudalistic thought in Tokugawa period. Bullentin of University of Osaka Prefecture, series D, v. 7. 1963. pp. 1-14.

Horie, Yasuzo
Confucian concept of state in Tokugawa Japan. Kyoto University economic review, v. 32, no.2. Oct. 1962. pp. 26-38.

Jansen, Marius B.
New materials for the intellectual history of nineteenth-century Japan. Harvard journal of Asiatic studies, v. 20, no.3/4. Dec. 1957. pp. 567-597.

Kimoto, Kōzō and Koji Takata
A proem to the socio-economic thought of Seiryo Kaiho (1755-1817); prefatorial remarks to an inquiry into the modernity and obsolescence of the ideas of Seiryo Kaiho, a prominent thinker on Japanese mercantilism in the latter Edo period. Osaka City University economic review, no. 11. 1975. pp. 31-34.

Morris, I. I.
Economic realism in the later works of Ihara Saikaku, with special reference to Seken munesanyō. Transactions of the Asiatic Society of Japan, 3rd ser. v. 7. Nov. 1959. pp. 1-30.

Nakamura, Hajime
Suzuki Shozan, 1579-1655 and the spirit of capitalism in Japanese Buddhism. Monumenta Nipponica, v. 22, nos.1/2. 1967. pp. 1-14.

Norman, E. Herbert
Andō Shōeki and the anatomy of Japanese feudalism. Transactions of Asiatic Society of Japan, 3rd series, v. 2. Dec. 1949. 340p.

Steele, M. W.
Katsu Kaishu and the limits of Bakumatsu nationalism. Asia bunka kenkyu, no.10. Nov. 1978. pp. 65-76.

Ueda, Tatsunosuke
Saikaku's 'Economic man'. Annals of the Hitotsubashi academy, v. 7, no.1. Oct. 1956. pp. 10-32.

ENCOUNTER WITH THE WEST

I.

Barr, Pat
The coming of the barbarians; the opening of Japan to the West 1853-1870. N.Y., Dutton, 1967. 236p. illus. map.

Beasley, William Gerald
Great Britain and the opening of Japan, 1834-1858. Londong, Luzac, 1951. 227p.

Beasley, William Gerald
Japan and the West in the mid nineteenth century; nationalism and the origins of the modern state. London, Oxford Univ. Press, 1969. 23p.

Beasley, William Gerald, ed.
Select documents on Japanese foreign policy 1853-1868. London, Oxford Univ. Press, 1955. 359p.

Boxer, Charles Ralph
Jan Compagnie in Japan 1600-1850; an essay on the cultural, artistic and scientific influence exercised by the Hollanders in Japan from the seventeenth to the nineteenth centuries. 2d rev. ed. The Hague, M. Nijhoff, 1950.
198p. illus.

Brooks, Charles Wolcott
Japanese wrecks, stranded and picked up adrift in the North Pacific Ocean. Fairfield, Wash., Ye Galleon Press, 1964.
23p. map.

Bush, Lewis
77 Samurai; Japan's first embassy to America; based on the book by Itsuro Hattori. Tokyo, Kodansha International, 1968.
248p. illus. maps.

Chang, Richard T.
From prejudice to tolerance; a study of the Japanese image of the West 1826-1864. Tokyo, Sophia Univ., 1970.
237p. (Monumenta Nipponica Monographs)

Cocks, Richard
Diary of Richard Cocks; cape merchant in English factory in Japan, 1615-1622. Edward M. Thompson, ed. New York, B. Franklin, 1965.
2 v. (Hakluyt Society 1st. series, no.66-67)

Dulles, Foster Rhea
Yankees and Samurai; America's role in the emergence of modern Japan, 1791-1900. N.Y., Harper and Row, 1965.
275p. illus. map.

Fox, Grace
Britain and Japan 1858-1883. London, Oxford Univ. Press, 1969.
627p. illus. maps.

Goodman, Grant K.
The Dutch impact on Japan, 1640-1853. Leiden, Brill, 1967.
242p. maps. (Monographies du T'oung pao)

Graff, Henry F., ed.
Bluejackets with Perry in Japan; a day-by-day account kept by master's mate John R. C. Lewis and cabin boy William B. Allen. N. Y., New York Public Library, 1952.
181p. illus.

Harris, Townsend
The complete journal of Townsend Harris, first American Consul and Minister to Japan, introduction and notes by Mario Emilio Cosenza. Rev. ed. Tokyo, Tuttle, 1959.
616p. illus.

Heusken, Henry
Japan journal 1855-1861, tr. and ed. by Jeannette C. van der Corput and Robert A. Wilson. New Brunswick, N. J., Rutgers Univ. Press, 1964.
247p. illus.

Higashi Ajia Bunka Kenkyu Senta (Centre for East Asian Cultural Studies)
Acceptance of Western culture in Japan, from the sixteenth to the mid-nineteenth century. Tokyo, 1964.
185p. illus.

Kanai, Madoka
A diary of William Cleveland, Captain's clerk on board the Massachusetts. Quezon City, Univ. of the Philippines, Institute of Asian Studies, 1965.
43p. (Asian studies monograph series)

Keene, Donald
The Japanese discovery of Europe 1720-1830. Rev. ed. Stanford, Stanford Univ. Press, 1969.
255p. illus.

Kojima, Matajiro
Commodore Perry's expedition to Hakodate, May 1854; a private account with illustrations. Hakodate, Hakodate Kyodo Bunkakai, 1953.
2 v. illus. map.

Medzini, Meron
French policy in Japan during the closing years of the Tokugawa regime. Cambridge, Mass., East Asian Research Center, Harvard University, 1971.
245p. (Harvard East Asian monographs, 41)

Miyoshi, Masao
As we saw them; the first Japanese embassy to the United States, 1860, Berkeley, Univ. of California Press, 1979.
300p.

Morison, Samuel Eliot
Old Bruin; Commodore Matthew C. Perry 1794-1858. Boston, Little, Brown, 1967.
482p. illus. maps.

Muragaki, Tanso
Kōkai Nikki; the diary of the first Japanese embassy to the United States of America, by Muragaki Awaji-no-kami. Tokyo, Foreign Affairs Association of Japan, 1958.
209p. illus. map.

Paske-Smith, M.
Western barbarians in Japan and Formosa in Tokugawa days, 1603-1868. 2d ed. N.Y., Paragon Book Reprint Corp., 1968.
431p. illus. maps.

Perry, Matthew Calbraith
The Japan expedition 1852-1854; the personal journal of Commodore Matthew C. Perry, ed. by Roger Pineau.
Washington, Smithsonian Institution Press, 1968.
241p. illus. maps.

Perry, Matthew Calbraith
Narrative of the expedition of an American squadron to the China Seas and Japan under the command of Commodore M. C. Perry, United States Navy, comp. at his request and under his supervision by Francis L. Sidney Wallach. N.Y., Coward-McCann, 1952.
305p. illus.

Pompe van Meerdervort, J. L. C.
Doctor on Desima; selected chapters from Jhr J. L. C. Pompe van Meerdervort's Vijf jaren in Japan (five years in Japan) 1857-1863, tr. and annotated by Elizabeth P. Wittermans and John Z. Bowers.
Tokyo, Sophia Univ., 1970.
144p. (Monumenta Nipponica monographs)

Preble, George Henry
The opening of Japan; a diary of discovery in the Far East 1853-1856. From the original manuscript in the Massachusetts Historical Society, ed. by Boleslaw Szczesniak. Norman, Univ. of Oklahoma Press, 1962.
453p. illus.

Raffles, Sir Stanford
Report on Japan to the secret committee of the English East India Company. London, Curzon Press, 1971.
252p. (Records of Asian history)

Roberts, John G.
Black ships and rising sun; the opening of Japan to the West. N.Y., Julian Messner, 1971.
191p.

Rogers, Philip Graham
The first Englishman in Japan; the story of Will Adams. London, Harvill Press, 1956.
144p. map.

Sansom, Sir George Bailey
The Western world and Japan; a study in the interaction of European and Asiatic cultures. N.Y., Knopf, 1951.
504p. illus. map.

Satow, Sir Ernest
A diplomat in Japan, with an introduction by Gordon Daniels. Tokyo, Oxford Univ. Press, 1968.
427p. illus. maps. (Oxford in Asia historical reprints)

Statler, Oliver
The black ship scroll; an account of the Perry expedition at Shimoda in 1854 and the lively beginnings of people-to-people relations between Japan and America . . .
With translations by Richard Lane, and scroll paintings in full color by an anonymous Japanese eyewitness.
Tokyo, Tuttle, 1963.
80p. illus. maps.

Statler, Oliver
Shimoda story. N.Y., Random House, 1969.
627p. illus. maps.

Tamarin, Alfred
Japan and the United States; early encounters 1791-1860. N.Y., Macmillan, 1970.
260p. illus.

Treat, Payson J.
Diplomatic relations between the United States and Japan, 1853-1895. Gloucester, Mass, P. Smith, 1963.
2 v.

Treat, Payson J.
Japan and the United States, 1853-1921. Boston, H. Mifflin, 1921.
283p.

Warinner, Emily V.
Voyager to destiny; the amazing adventures of Manjiro, the man who changed world twice . . .
Indianapolis, Bobbs-Merrill, 1956.
267p. illus. maps.

Williams, Harold S.
Foreigners in Mikadoland. Tokyo, Tuttle, 1963.
310p. illus.
also published in 1972.

II.

Howes, John F.
Japanese christians and American missionaries. (Marius B. Jansen, ed. Changing Japanese attitutdes toward modernization. Princeton, Princeton Univ. Press, 1965.
pp. 337-368)

Soviak, Eugene
On the nature of western progress; the journal of the Iwakura embassy. (Donald H. Shively, ed. Tradition and modernization in Japanese culture. Princeton, Princeton Univ. Press, 1971. pp. 7-34)

IV.

Ayusawa, Shintaro
Geography and Japanese knowledge of world geography. Monumenta Nipponica, v. 19, nos.3/4. 1964. pp. 41-60.

Farley, Miriam S.
Japan and the West. Pacific affairs, v. 23, no.1. Mar. 1950. pp. 77-82.

Goncharov, I. A.
A Goncharov's account of Russia's attempt to open Japan in 1853, tr. by Kathleen Price. Univ. of Michigan, Center for Japanese Studies occasional papers, no.2. 1952. pp. 1-29.

Goodmand, Grant K.
A translation of Otsuki Gentaku's Ransetsu Benwaku. Univ. of Michigan, Center for Japanese Studies occasional papers, no.3. 1952. pp. 71-99.

Hawks, Francis L., comp.
Commodore Perry's expedition to Japan, excerpt. Contemporary Japan, v. 17, no.1/6-7/12. Apr./June-July/Dec. 1947.
v. 18, no.1/3. Jan./Mar. 1949.
pp. 150-181, 295-360, 50-97.

Higuchi, Kiyoyuki
The opening of Japan and western culture. Contemporary Japan, v. 22, no.4/6. 1953. pp. 233-248.

Iwao, Seiichi
A Dutch doctor in old Japan. Japan quarterly, v. 8, no.2. Apr./June 1961. pp. 170-178.

Jones, Hazel J.
Bakumatsu foreign employees. Monumenta Nipponica, v. 29, no.3. Autumn 1974. pp. 305-327.

Kamikawa, Hikomatsu
Commodore Perry's expedition and the growth of a modern Japan. Contemporary Japan, v. 22, no.4/6. 1953. pp. 163-177.

Macfarlane, Duncan
Some early English contacts with Japan. Asian affairs (J. of the Royal Society for Asian Affairs), v. 60 (new series, v. 4) pt.1. Feb. 1973. pp. 81-85.

McMaster, John
Alcock and Harris; foreign diplomacy in Bakumatsu Japan. Monumenta Nipponica, v. 22, nos.3/4. 1967. pp. 305-367.

Miyauchi, D. Y.
Yokoi Shonan's response to the foreign intervention in late Tokugawa Japan, 1853-1862. Modern Asian studies, v. 4, no.3. July 1970. pp. 269-290.

Mounicou, Pierre
Father Mounicou's Bakumatsu diary, 1856-64, tr. with an introduction by Paul C. Blum. Transactions of the Asiatic Society of Japan, 3rd ser. v. 13. Dec. 1976. pp. 5-103.

Numata, Jiro
The acceptance of western culture in Japan; general observation. Monumenta Nipponica, v. 19, nos.3/4. 1964. pp. 1-8.

Numata, Jiro
The introduction of Dutch language. Monumenta Nipponica, v. 19, nos.3/4. 1964. pp. 9-19.

Onorato, Michael P.
The opening of Japan, 1849-1854; America "finds the key." Asian studies, v. 6, no.3. Dec. 1968. pp. 286-296.

Paul, Huibert
De Coningh on Deshima; Mijn Verblijf in Japan, 1856. Monumenta Nipponica, v. 32, no.3. Autumn 1977. pp. 347-364.

Szczesniak, Boleslaw
Letters of Homer Crane Blake - concerning his naval expedition to China, Japan and Korea, 1869-1872. Monumenta Nipponica, v. 13, nos.1/2. Apr./July 1957. pp. 1-38.

MEIJI PERIOD HISTORY

I.

Beasley, William Gerald
The Meiji restoration. Stanford, Stanford Univ. Press, 1972. 513p.

Bolitho, Harold
Meiji Japan. N.Y., Cambridge Univ. Press, 1977. 48p. (History of mankind series)

Craig, Albert M.
Choshu in the Meiji Restoration. Cambridge, Mass., Harvard Univ. Press, 1961.
385p. (Harvard historical monographs)

Fujii, Jintaro, ed.
Outline of Japanese history in the Meiji era, tr. and adapted by Hattie K. Colton. Tokyo, Obunsha, 1958.
544p. illus. (Centenary Cultural Council series)

Higashi Ajia Bunka Kenkyu Senta (Center for East Asian Cultural Studies)
The Meiji Japan through contemporary sources. Tokyo, 1969-1972.
3 v.

Jansen, Marius B.
Sakamoto Ryoma and the Meiji Restoration. Princeton, Princeton Univ. Press, 1961.
423p. illus.

McLaren, Walter Wallace
A political history of Japan during the Meiji era 1867-1912. N.Y., Russell and Russell, 1965.
380p.

Shibusawa, Keizo
Japanese life and culture in the Meiji era, tr. and adapted by Charles S. Terry. Tokyo, Obunsha, 1958.
397p. illus. (Centenary Culture Council series)

Shibusawa, Keizo, ed.
Japanese society in the Meiji era, tr. and adapted by Aora H. Culbertson and Kimura Michiko. Tokyo, Obunsha, 1958.
527p. illus. (Centenary Cultural Council series

Silberman, Bernard S.
Ministers of modernization; elite mobility in the Meiji Restoration 1868-1873. Tucson, Univ. of Arizona Press, 1964.
135p. map.

Wilson, Robert A.
Genesis of the Meiji government in Japan, 1868-1871. Berkeley, Univ. of California Press, 1957.
149p. (Univ. of Calif. publications in history)

Yanagita, Kunio, ed.
Japanese manners and customs in the Meiji era, tr. and adapted by Charles S. Terry. Tokyo, Obunsha, 1957.
335p. illus. (Centenary Cultural Council series)

II.

Brown, Sidney de Vere
Okubo Toshimichi and the first Home Ministry bureaucracy; 1873-1878. (Bernard S. Silberman, etc. ed. Modern Japanese leadership; transition and change. Tucson, Univ. of Arizona Press, 1966. pp. 195-232)

Craig, Albert M.
Fukuzawa Yukichi; the philosophical foundations of Meiji nationalism. (Robert E. Ward, ed. Political development in modern Japan. Princeton, Princeton Univ. Press, 1968. pp. 99-148)

Craig, Albert M.
Kido Koin and Okubo Toshimichi; a psycho-historical analysis. (Albert M. Craig, ed. Personality in Japanese history. Berkeley, Univ. of California Press, 1970. pp. 264-308)

Fukuzawa, Yukichi
From the autobiography of Yukichi Fukuzawa. (Irwin Scheiner, ed. Modern Japan; an interpretive anthology. N.Y., MacMillan, 1974. pp. 165-175)

Hackett, Roger F.
The era of fulfillement; 1877-1911. (Arthur E. Tiedemann, ed. An introduction to Japanese civilization. N.Y., Columbia Univ. Press, 1974. pp. 181-217)

Hackett, Roger F.
The Meiji leaders and modernization; the case of Yamagata Aritomo. (Marius B. Jansen, ed. Changing Japanese attitudes toward modernization. Princeton, Princeton Univ. Press, 1965. pp. 243-282)

Hackett, Roger F.
Political modernization and Meiji Genro. (Robert E. Ward, ed. Political development in modern Japan. Princeton, Princeton Univ. Press, 1968. pp. 65-98)

Lebra, Joyce C.
Okuma Shigenobu; modernization and the west. (Edmund Skrzypczak, ed. Japan's modern century. A special issue of Monumenta Nipponica prepared in celebration of the centennial of the Meiji Restoration. Tokyo, Sophia University, 1968. pp. 27-40)

McEwan, John R.
The confucian ideology and modernization of Japan; as illustrated in the Meiji edition of the Denshun Nenju Gyoji. (Seiichi, Tobata, ed. The modernization of Japan - I. Tokyo, Institute of Asian Economic Affairs, 1966. pp. 229-242. Reprinted from Developing Economies, vo. 3, no.4. Dec. 1965. pp. 560-572)

Norman, E. H.
Economic changes; the decision to industrialize; early industrialization. (Jon Livingston, ed. Imperial Japan, 1800-1945. N.Y., Pantheon Books, 1973. pp. 116-122)

Shively, Donald H.
The Japanization of the middle Meiji. (Donald H. Shively, ed. Tradition and modernization in Japanese culture. Princeton, Princeton Univ. Press, 1971. pp. 77-120)

III.

Chung, Hee Chae
Politics, strains, and structural changes; the Meiji Restoration case. Ph.D. 1969. University of Pennsylvania. 207p.

Conte, James Thomas
Overseas study in the Meiji period; Japanese students in America, 1867-1902. Ph.D. 1977. Princeton University. 214p.

Evans, David Christian
The Satsuma faction and professionalism in the Japanese naval officer corps of the Meiji period, 1868-1912. Ph.D. 1978. Stanford University. 364p.

Griesy, Paul Val
The Dōshisha, 1875-1919; the indigenization of an institution. Ed.D. 1973. Columbia University (Teachers College) 580p.

Hoare, James Edward
The Japanese treaty ports, 1868-1899; a study of the foreign settlements. Ph.D. 1971. University of London. 392p.

Hoover, Willaim Davis
Godai Tomoatsu (1836-1885); an economic statesman of early Meiji Japan. Ph.D. 1973. The University of Michigan.
417p.

Humphreys, Leonard Alfred
The imperial Japanese army, 1918-1929; the disintegration of the Meiji military system. Ph.D. 1975 Stanford University.
406p

Leavell, James Berry, III.
The development of the modern Japanese police system; transition from Tokugawa to Meiji. Ph.D. 1975. Duke University.
183p.

IV.

Brown, Sidney Qevere
Ōkubo Toshimich; his political and economic policies in early Meiji Japan. Journal of Asian studies, v. 21, no.2. Feb. 1962. pp. 183-198.

Daniels, Gordon
The Japanese civil war (1868) a British view. Modern Asian studies, v. 1, pt.3. July 1967. pp.241-264.

Hane, Mikiso
Early Meiji liberalism; an assessment. Monumenta Nipponica, v. 24, no.4. 1969. pp. 353-371.

Horie, Hideichi
Revolution and reform in Meiji restoration. Kyoto University economic review, v. 22, no.1, Apr. 1952. pp. 23-34.

Ishida, Takeshi
Cultural contacts and the new style of thinking; the case of Fukuzawa Yukichi. Annals of the Institute of Social Science, no. 19. 1978. pp. 92-101.

Kelley, A. C. and J. G. Williamson
Writing history backwards; Meiji Japan revisited. Journal of economic history, v. 31, no.4. Dec. 1971. pp. 729-776.

McEwan, J. R.
The confucian ideology and modernization of Japan; as illustrated in the Meiji edition of the Denshun Nenchu Gyoji. Developing economies, v. 3, no.4. Dec. 1965. pp. 560-572.
cf. Seiichi, Tobata, ed. The modernization of Japan.

Maruyama, Masao
Fukuzawa, Uchimura, and Okakura; Meiji intellectuals and westernization. Developing economies, v. 4, no.4. Dec. 1966. pp. 594-611.

Perry, John Curtis
Great Britain and the emergence of Japan as a naval power. Monumenta Nipponica, v. 21, nos.3/4. 1966. pp. 305-321.

Pittau, Joseph
Inoue Kowashi, 1834-1895 and the formation of modern Japan. Monumenta Nipponica, v. 20, nos.3/4. 1965. pp. 253-282.

Pyle, Kenneth B.
Advantages of followership: German economics and Japanese bureaucrats, 1890-1925. Journal of Japanese studies, v. 1, no.1. Autumn 1974. pp. 127-164.

Silberman, Bernard S.
Bureaucratic development and the structure of decision-making in Japan, 1868-1925. Journal of Asian studies, v. 29, no.2. Feb. 1970. pp. 347-362.

Silberman, Bernard S.
Bureaucratic development and the structure of decision-making in the Meiji period. Journal of Asian studies, v. 27, no.1. Nov. 1967. pp. 81-94.

Silberman, Bernard S.
Bureaucratization of the Meiji state; the problem of succession in the Meiji restoration, 1868-1900. Journal of Asian studies, v. 35, no.3. May 1976. pp. 421-430.

Silberman, Bernard S.
Criteria recruitment and success in the Japanese bureaucracy, 1868-1900; "traditional" and "modern" criteria in bureaucratic development. Economic development and cultural change, v. 14, no.2. Jan. 1966 pp. 158-173.

Sippel, Patricia
Popular protest in early modern Japan; the Bushu outburst. Harvard journal of Asiatic studies, v. 37, no.2. Dec. 1977. pp. 273-322.

Soviak, Eugene
The case of Baba Tatsui; western enlightenment, social change and the early Meiji intellectual. Monumenta Nipponica, v. 18, nos.1/4. 1963. pp. 191-235.

Sugiyama, Chuhei
The development of economic thought in Meiji Japan. Modern Asian studies, v. 2, pt.4. Oct. 1968. pp. 325-342.

Teters, B.
Press freedom and the 26th Century affair in Meiji Japan. Modern Asian studies, v. 6, pt.3. July 1972. pp. 337-351.

Tōyama, Shigeki
Politics, economics, and the international environment in the Meiji and Taisho periods. Developing economies, v. 4, no.4. Dec. 1966. pp. 419-446.

FOREIGN EXPERTS

I.

Barr, Pat.
The Deer Cry Pavilion; a story of westerners in Japan 1868-1905. London, Macmillan, 1968. 282p. illus.

Beauchamp, Edward R.
An American teacher in early Meiji Japan. Honolulu, Univ. Press of Hawaii, 1976. 154p.

D'Anethan, Baron Albert
The D'Anethan dispatches from Japan, 1894-1910; the observations of Baron Albert d'Anethan, Belgian minister plenipotentiary and ean of the diplomatic corps, selected and ed. with a historical introduction by George Alexander Lensen. Tokyo, Sophia Univ., 1967. 272p. illus.

Gowen, Herbert Henry
Five foreigners in Japan. Freeport, N.Y., Books for Libraries Press, 1963. 283p. (Essay index reprint series)

Siemes, Johannes
Hermann Roesler and the making of the Meiji state; an examination of his background and his influence on the founders of modern Japan. Tokyo, Sphia Univ., 1968. 252p.

Umetani, Noboru
The role of foreign employees in the Meiji era in Japan. Tokyo, 1971. 109p. (Institute of Developing Economies, occasional papers series. no.9)

Williams, Harold S.
Tales of the foreign settlements in Japan. Tokyo, Tuttle, 1958. 351p. illus.

III.

Beauchamp, Edward Robert
William Elliot Griffs and Japan; Yatoi, historian, and educational educator. Ph.D. 1973. University of Washington. 216p.

IV.

Arima, Seiho
The western influence on Japanese military science, shipbuildings and navigation. Monumenta Nipponica v. 19, nos.3/4. 1964. pp. 118-145.

Beasley, W. G.
Sir Harry Parkes and the Meiji restoration. Transactions of the Asiatic Society of Japan, 3rd ser. v. 12. Dec. 1975. pp. 21-38.

Beauchamp, Edward R.
Griffis in Japan; the Fukui interlude, 1871. Monumenta Nipponica, v. 30, no.4. Winter 1975. pp. 423-452.

Chatam House
Factors in the settlement with Japan. Pacific affairs, v. 18, no.1. Mar. 1945. pp. 40-54.

Daniels, Gordon
The British role in the Meiji restoration; a re-interpretive note. Modern Asian studies, v. 2, pt.4. Oct. 1968. pp. 291-314.

Hara, Yoshio
From westernization to Japanization; the replacement of foreign teachers by Japanese who studied abroad. Developing economies, v. 15, no.4. 1977. pp. 440-461.

Hirose, Shizuko
British attitudes towards the Meiji restoration. Contemporary Japan, v. 29, no.2. Mar. 1970. pp. 293-303.

Honjo, Eijiro
Foreigners employed by Meiji Government and their contribution to development of our economy and eonomics. Bulletin of University of Osaka Prefecture, series D, v. 5. 1961. pp. 1-15.

Ion, A. Hamish
Edward Warren Clark and early Meiji Japan; a case study of cultural contact. Modern Asian studies, v. 11, pt.4. Oct. 1977. pp. 557-572.

Jones, Hazel J.
The formulation of Meiji policy toward the employment of foreigners. Monumenta Nipponica, v. 23, nos.1/2, 1968. pp. 9-30.

Nish, I. H.
Dr. G. E. Morison and Japan. Journal of Oriental Society of Australia, v. 2, no.1. June 1963. pp. 42-47.

Rohan, Kieran M.
Lighthouses and the Yatoi experience of R. H. Brunton. Monumenta Nipponica, v. 20, nos.1/2. 1965. pp. 64-80.

Watanabe, Masao
American science teachers in the early Meiji period. Japanese studies in the history of science, no.15. 1976. pp. 127-144.

Watanabe, Masao
John Thomas Gulick; American evolutionist and missionary in Japan. Japanese studies in the history of science, no.5. 1966. pp. 140-149.

Williams, Harold S.
Two remarkable Australians of old Yokohama. Transactions of the Asiatic Society of Japan, 3rd ser. v. 12. Dec. 1975. pp. 51-69.

MODERN ECONOMY

STATISTICS

I.

Ajia Keizai Kenkyujo (Institute of Developing Economies)
One hundred years of agricultural statistics in Japan. Tokyo, 1969. 270p.

Japan, Economic Counsel Board
Nihon keizai to kokumin shotoku; the English version in national income and national economic accounts of Japan, 1930-50. Tokyo, Gakuyo Shobo, 1954.

Kayo, Nobufumi
Statistical surveys on agriculture in Japan. Tokyo, Agriculture, Forestry and Fisheries Productivity Conference, 1960. 48p. map.

Nihon Ginko (Bank of Japan)
Hundred year statistics of the Japanese economy; English tr. of explanatory notes, footnotes. Tokyo, 1966. 2v.

Nihon Ginko, Tokeikyoku (Bank of Japan, Statistics Dept.)
Supplement to hundred-year statistics of the Japanese economy. Tokyo, 1966. 2v.

Nihon Kaihatsu Ginko (Japanese Development Bank)
Facts and figures on the Japanese economy. Tokyo, 1964. 171p. illus.

POPULATION

I.

Glass, David Victor and Roger Revelle, ed.
Population and social change. London, E. Arnold, 1972. 520p.
Contents:
- The treatment of population in history textbooks, by David Landes. pp. 23-42.
- Historical demography, by Luvis Henry. pp. 43-54.
- Historical sociology and the study of population, by J. A. Banks. pp. 55-70.
- The importance of the quality of the data in historical demography, by T. H. Hollingsworth. pp. 71-86.
- Demographic factor and early modern economic development, by Joseph J. Spenglerl. pp. 87-98.
- Economic development and the fertility transition, by David M. Heer. pp. 99-114.
- Intellectual and demographic history, by John T. Noonan, Jr. pp. 115-135.
- Marriage and marital fertility, by Etienne van de Walle. pp. 137-151.
- Early fertility decline in Austria-Hungary; a lesson in demographic transition, by Paul Demeny. pp. 153-172.
- Fertility and population growth in Spain in the eighteenth and nineteenth centuries, by Massimo Livi-Bacci. pp. 173-184.
- Fertility controls in pre-industrial Norway, by Michael Drake. pp. 185-198.
- Replacement for generations of Danish females, 1840/1844-1920/1924, by P. C. Matthiessen. pp. 199-212.
- The demographic transition of the province of Quebec, by Jacques Hanripin and Yves Peron. pp. 213-232.

- Certain demographic characteristics of the plague epidemic in France, 1720-1772, by Jean-Noel Biraben. pp. 233-241.
- Mortality in pre-industrial England; the example of Colyton, Devon, over three centuries, by E. A. Wrigley. pp. 243-273.
- Notes on the demography of London at the end of the seventeenth century, by D. V. Glass. pp. 275-285.
- When was the great plague? Mortality in London, 1563 to 1663, by Lan Sutherland. pp. 287-320.
- Legitimate fertility and infant mortality in France during the eighteenth century; a comparison, by Pierre Goubert. pp. 321-330.
-Historical demography and the social and economic development of Netherlands, by Bernard H. Slicker van Bath. pp. 331-346.
- Who were the English and Scots immigrants to the United States in the late nineteenth century?, by C. J. Erickson. pp. 347-381.
- Biological problems and opportunities, of isolation among the islanders of Triotan da Cunha, by H. E. Lewis, V. F. Roberts, and A. W. F. Edwards. pp. 383-417.
- Study of the historical demography of India, by Ajit Das Gupta. pp. 419-435.
- Population trends Bizen Province in Okayama, by Susan B. Hanley. pp. 437-449.
- Population trends and economic growth in pre-industrial Japan, by Susan B. Hanley and Kozo Yamamura. pp. 451-499.

Nomura, Kanetaro
On cultural conditons affecting population trends in Jpan. Tokyo. 1953.
35p. (Science Council of Japan, Division of Economics and Commerce, economic series, no.2)

Taeuber, Irene Barnes
The population of Japan. Princeton, Princeton Univ. Press, 1958.
461p. maps.

Ueda, Masao
Population problems in Japan. Tokyo, International Society for Educational Information, 1975.
112p. (Changing Japan series)

UNESCO, Japanese National Commission.
Manual of demographic statistics in Japan. Tokyo, 1958.
250p.

Uyeda, Teijiro
The growth of population and occupational changes in Japan, 1920-1935. New York, AMS Press, 1978.
16, 3p.
Under the auspices of Institute of Pacific Relations reprinting of the 1936 ed.

II.

Kawashima, Takeyoshi and Kurt Steiner
Modernization and divorce rate trends in Japan. (Thomas C. Smith, ed. City and village in Japan. Chicago, University of Chicago Press, 1960. pp. 213-240)

Morita, Yuzo
An estimation on the actual birth - and death - rates in the early Meiji period of Japan. (Committee for Translation of Japanese Economic Studies. Translation of Japanese economic studies. no.30. Tokyo, International House of Japan, 1959-64. 44p.)

Ohbuchi, Hiroshi
Demographic transition in the process of Japanese industrialization.
(Hugh Patrick, ed. Japanese industrialization and social consequences. Berkeley, University of California Press, 1976. pp. 329-362)

Spengler, Joseph J.
Demographic factors and early modern economic development. (D. V. Glass and R. Revelle, ed. Population and social change. London, E. Arnold, 1972. pp. 87-98)

Tachi, Minoru and Yoichi Okazaki
Economic development and population growth - with special reference to South-East Asia. (Seiichi, Tobata, ed. The modernization of Japan - I. Tokyo, Institute of Asian Economic Affairs. pp. 165-184)

Taeuber, Irene B.
Population and labor force in the industrialization of Japan, 1850-1950. (Simon Kuznets, W. E. Moore and J. J. Spengler, ed. Economic growth; Brazil, India, Japan. Durham, N.C., Duke University Press, 1955. pp. 316-362)

Taeuber, Irene B.
Urbanization and population change in the development of modern Japan. (Thomas C. Smith, ed. City and village in Japan. Chicago, University of Chicago Press, 1960. pp. 1-28)

IV.

Dore, R. P.
Japanese rural fertility; some social and economic factors. Population studies, v. 7, pt. 1. July 1953. pp. 62-88.

Horie, Yasuzo
The life structure of the Japanese people in its historical aspects. Kyoto University economic review, v. 21, no.1. Apr. 1951. pp. 1-22.

Kawashima, Takeyoshi and Kurt Steiner
Modernization and divorce rate trends in Japan. Economic development and cultural change, v. 9, no.1. pt.2. Oct. 1960. pp. 213-240.

Minami, Ryoshin
Population migration away from agriculture in Japan. Economic development and cultural change, v. 15, no.2. pt. 1. Jan. 1967. pp. 183-201.

Minoguchi, Tokijiro
Increasing populations and industrial structures. Annals of the Hitotsubashi academy, v. 10, no.1. Aug. 1959. pp. 81-90.

Morita, Yuzo
Estimated birth and death rates in the early Meiji period of Japan. Population studies, v. 17, no.1. July 1963. pp. 33-56.

Mosk, Carl
The decline of marital fertility in Japan. Population studies, v. 33, no.1. Mar. 1979. pp. 19-38.

Mosk, Carl
Fecundity, infanticide, and food consumption in Japan. Explorations in entrepreneurial history, v. 15, no.3. July 1978. pp. 269-289.

Silver, Morris
Births, marriages, and income fluctuations in the United Kingdom and Japan. Economic development and cultural change, v. 14, no.3. Apr. 1966. pp. 302-315.

Tachi, Minoru
The population problem. Japan quarterly, v. 5, no.1. Jan./Mar. 1958. Changing Japan 4. pp. 103-172.

Tachi, Minoru and Yoichi Okazaki
Economic development and population growth. Developing economies, v. 3, no.4. Dec. 1965. pp. 497-515.

Taeuber, Irene B.
Japan's demographic transition re-examined. Population studies, v. 14, no.1. July 1960. pp. 28-39.

Taeuber, Irene B.
Urbanization and population change in the development of modern Japan. Economic development and cultural change, v. 9, no.1, pt.2. Oct. 1960. pp. 1-28.

Taeuber, Irene B. and Frank W. Notestein
The changing fertility of the Japanese. Population studies, v. 1, pt.1. June 1947. pp. 2-28.

White, James, W.
Internal migration in prewar Japan. Journal of Japanese studies, v. 4, no.1. Winter 1978. pp. 81-124.

Yasukawa, Masaaki
Estimates of annual births and of the general fertility rates in Japan, 1890-1920. Keio economic studies, v. 1. 1963. pp. 52-88.

Yasukawa, Masaaki
The population problem of Japan and the trend of its study. Keio economic studies, v. 4. 1966/67. pp. 94-107.

Yasukawa, Masaaki and Keijiro Hirooka
Estimates of the population size and of birth- and death-rates in Japan, 1865-1920. Keio economic studies, v. 11, no.2. 1974. pp. 41-66.

ECONOMIC DEVELOPMENT

GENERAL

I.

Allen, George Cyril
Japan's economic expansion. London, Oxford Univ. Press, 1965. 296p.

Allen, George Cyril
Japan's economic recovery. London, Oxford Univ. Press, 1958. 215p.

Allen, George Cyril
A short economic history of modern Japan, 1868-1937, with a supplementary chapter on economic recovery and expansion, 1954-1960. 2d rev. ed. London, Allen and Unwin, 1962.
237p.

Boulding, Kenneth E. and Alan H. Greason
War as an investment; the strange case of Japan. Washington, External Research Staff, 1964.
20p.

Boulding, Kenneth Ewart and Norman Sun.
The effects of military expenditures upon the economic growth of Japan. Tokyo, International Christian Univ., 1968.
32p.

Broadbridge, Seymour
Industrial dualism in Japan; a problem of economic growth and structural change. Chicago, Aldine Pub. 1966.
105p.

Clark, Colin
Investment and net stock of fixed capital (nonresidential) in Japan. 1972. Submitted to second growth conference held by the Japan Economic Research Center.
Mimeo.

Committee for Translation of Japanese Economic Studies
Translations of Japanese economic studies. Tokyo, International House of Japan, 1959-64.
50 issues.
Contents:
- Excessive dependence of commercial banks on central bank loans in Japanese economic development, by Yoshino Toshihiko, no.6. 33p.
- Capital accumulation and the course of industrialization with special reference to the economic development of Japan, by Kojima Kiyoshi, no.2. 22p.
- Japanese agriculture; productivity trend and development of technique, by Shishido Toshio, no.10. 15p.
- Evolution of wage structure in Japan, by Hotani Rokuro and Hayashi Takashi, no.14. 31p.
- Long-term change in food consumption in Japan, by Nakayama Seiki, no.26. 23p.
- A long-term model of Japanese economy, 1920-1958, by Ueno Hiroya, no.27. 26p.
- An estimation on the actual birth - and death - rates in the early Meiji period of Japan, by Morita Yuzo, no.30. 44p.
- Into the class origins of Meiji enterpreneus, by Tsuchiya Takao, no.32. 25p.
- An approach to the measurement of national savings in Japan (1898-1940), by Emi Koichi, no.35. 32p.
- Production, cost and income distribution of the electric supply industry in pre-war Japan, by Minami Ryoshin, no.39. 20p.
- Conditions for agricultural development in developing Asian countries; an appraisal of the usefulness of Japan's experiences, by Ishikawa Shigeru, no.42. 69p.
- Survey of Japanese literature on the small industry, by Shinohara Miyohei, no.43. 133p. bibl. p.103-133.
- Bank debits and deposit turnover in Japan, by Itoh Masakichi, no.47. 18p.
- An analysis of the population movement from agriculture in Japan, by Minami Ryoshin, no.49. 21p.

Cowan, C. D., ed.
The economic development of China and Japan; studies in economic history and political economy. London, G. Allen & Unwin, 1964.
255p. (Studies on modern Asia and Africa, no.4)
Contents:
- The Kiakhta trade, by Mark Mancall. pp. 19-48.

- British-Chinese steamship rivalry in China, 1873-85, by Kwang-Ching Liu. pp. 49-78.
- China's nineteenth century industrialization; the case of the Hanyehping Coal and Iron Company Limited, by Albert Feuerwerker. pp. 79-110.
- The Chinese labour force in the, first part of the twentieth century, by Jean Chesneaux. pp. 111-127.
- Sino-Soviet economic relations; a pre-appraisal, by Alexander Eckstein. pp. 128-159.
- A Chinese discussion on planning for balanced growth; a summary of the views of Ma Yin-Chu and his critics, by K. R. Walker. pp. 160-191.
- Factors in Japan's economic growth, by G. C. Allen. pp. 192-204.
- Capital formation in pre-war Japan; current findings and future problems, by Henry Rosovsky. pp. 205-219.
- Economic development and foreign trade in pre-war Japan, by Miyohei Shinohara. pp. 220-248.

Haitani, Kanji
The Japanese economic system; an institutional overview.
Lexington, Mass., D. C. Heath, 1976.
190p.

Hicks, J. R. and Nobuko Nosse
The social framework of the Japanese economy; an introduction to economics. Tokyo, Oxford Univ. Press, 1974.
371p.

Kokusai Kaihatsu Senta (International Development Center of Japan)
Papers and proceedings of the conference on Japan's historical development experience and contemporary developing countries; issues of comparative analysis. Feb. 11-16, 1978. Tokyo, 1978.
414p.

Contents:
- Another look at the Tokugawa heritage with special reference to social conditions, by Yasukichi Yasuba. pp. 1-24.
- Initial conditions; economic level and structure, by Kazushi Ohkawa. pp. 25-38.
- On phasing; a preliminary view, by Kazushi Ohkawa & Gustav Ranis. pp. 39-52.
- Agricultural growth against a land resource constraint; a comparative history of Japan, Taiwan, Korea and the Philippines, by Masao Kikuch & Yujiro Hayami. pp. 53-82.
- The supply and demand for quality workers in the cotton textile industries in Japan and India, by Gary Saxonhouse & Yukihiko Kiyokawa. pp. 83-120.
- The place of medium- and small-scale firms in the development of the automobile industry; a study of Japan's experience, by Konosuke Odaka. pp. 121-152.
- Trading companies and the expansion of Japan's foreign trade, by Ippei Yamazawa & Hirohisa Kohama. pp. 153-180.
- Industrialization and external relations; comparative analysis of Japan's historical experience and contemporary developing countries' performance, by Ippei Yamazawa & Akira Hirata. pp. 181-212.
- Production structure and patterns of economic development; Japan and selected LDCs, by Katsuo Otsuka. pp. 213-232.
- Mobilizing slack resources for economic development; the summer-fall rearing technology of sericulture in Japan, by Le Thanh Nghiep & Yujiro Hayami. pp. 233-248.
- Borrowed technology in the iron and steel industry; a comparison between Brazil, India and Japan, by Akira Ono. pp. 249-266.
- Technology choice, adaptation and the quality dimension in the Japanese cotton textile industry, by Gustav Ranis & Gary Saxonhouse. pp. 267-302.
- Relative income share of labor; long-run trend and fluctuations in prewar Japan and their implications, by Ryoshin Minami & Akira Ono. pp. 303-330.

- An aspect of the size distribution of income in prewar Japan, by Toshiyuki Otsuki & Nobukiyo Takamatsu. pp. 331-348.
- The establishment and early development of banking in Japan; phases and policies prior to World War I, by Juro Teranishi & Hugh Patrick. pp. 349-382.
- Agricultural surplus in an overall performance of savings-investment, by Kazushi Ohkawa, Yutaka Shimizu & Nobukiyo Takamatsu. pp. 383-404.
- Prewar Japanese government traditional sector financial investment policy; implications for sectoral growth and welfare, by Bernard Key. pp. 405-414.

Kelley, Allen C. and Jefferey G. Williamson
Lessons from Japanese development; an analytical economic history. Chicago, Univ. of Chicago Press, 1974.
xvi. 285p.

Kelley, Allen C., Jeffrey G. Williamson, and Russell J. Cheetham
Dualistic economic development; theory and history. Chicago, University of Chicago Press, 1972.
xi, 399p.

Klein, Lawrence and Kazushi Ohkawa, ed.
Economic growth; the Japanese experience since the Meiji era; proceedings of the conference of the Japan. Economic Research Center. Homewood, Ill., R. D. Irwin, 1968.
424p.
Contents:
- Postwar Japanese growth in historical perspective; a second look, by Kazushi Ohkawa and Henry Rosovsky. pp. 3-34.
- Construction cycles and their monetary-financial characteristics, by Shozaburo Fujino. pp. 35-68.
- Patterns of industrial development, by Yuichi Shionoya. pp. 69-109.
- Industrialization, technological progress, and dual structure, by Tsunehiko Watanabe. pp. 110-134.
- Technological progress in agriculture, by Yujiro Hayamai and Saburo Yamada. pp. 135-161.
- Foreign trade and economic growth in Japan, 1858-1937, by Masao Baba and Masahiro Tatemoto. pp. 162-196.
- Trends in level and structure of consumption, by Simon Kuznets. pp. 197-242.
- Factors for rapid economic growth; a social accounting approach, by Shinichi Ichimura. pp. 245-277.
- Patterns and some structural changes in Japan's postwar industrial growth by Miyohei Shinohara. pp. 278-302.
- Economic growth and exports, by Hisao Kanamori. pp. 303-325.
- The financing to the public sector in postwar Japan, by Hugh T. Patrick. pp. 326-355.
- The role of the government in the postwar economic development of Japan, by Shuntaro Shishido. pp. 356-381.
- Notes on Japan's economic growth, by Simon Kuznets. pp. 385-422.

Kosobud, Richard F. and Ryoshin Minami, ed.
Econometric studies of Japan. Urbana, Univ. of Illinois Press, 1977.
512p.
Contents:
- The application of alterntive demand models to the Japanese expenditure pattern, by Kunio Yoshihara. pp. 3-48.
- Permanent income and the transaction demand for money by households, by Fujino Shozaburo. pp. 49-74.
- A model of investment behavior; fixed investment and capacity in Japanese manufacturing, 1952-1963, by Kazuo Sato. pp. 75-113.
- Effects of structural change on productivity growth; a long-term measurement by Kazushi Ohkawa pp.114-139.
- Growth in capital stock in the postwar Japanese manufacturing industries, by Fumimasa Hamada. pp. 140-152.

- Scarcity of labor and wage differentials in the Japanese economy, by Tuvia Blumental. pp. 153-177.
- Price changes and the rate of change of money wage earnings in Japan, 1955-1962, by Tsunehiko Watanabe. pp. 178-197.
- An econometric analysis of Japanese exports and imports, by Shinichi Ichimura. pp. 198-220.
- Price elasticities of Japanese exports: a cross-section study, by Yoichi Shinkai, pp. 221-236.
- Japan's balance of payments and its adjustment; a quarterly econometric model, 1961-1967, by Akihiro Amano. pp. 237-275.
- The pattern of Japanese growth, 1914-1954, by Hollis B. Chenery, Shuntaro Shishido, and Tsunehiko Watanabe. pp. 276-337.
- An econometric model of Japan, 1930-1959, by L. R. Klein and Y. Shinkai. pp. 338-373.
- A long-term model of Japanese economic growth, 1906-1968, by Hiroya Ueno. pp. 374-413.
- A stabilization model for postwar Japanese economy, 1954-1962, by Masahiro Tatemoto, Tadao Uchida, and Tsunehiko Watanabe. pp. 414-454.
- Use of national accounts for a short-term econometric model, 1966, by S. Shishido, A. Kohno, S. Nagaya, and S. Tanaka, pp. 455-502.
- Contributors, p. 503-504.
- Index. p. 505.

Kuznets, Simon, Wilbert E. Moore, and Joseph J. Spengler, ed.
Economic growth; Brazil, India, Japan. Durham, N.C., Duke Univ. Press, 1955.
613p.
Contents:
- Problems in comparisons of economic trends, by Simon Kuznets. pp. 3-28.
- Brazil; trends in industrial development, by George Wythe. pp. 29-77.
- Brazilian agriculture development, by Preston E. James. pp. 78-102.
- Long-term trends in output in India, by Daniel Thorner. pp. 103-128.
- The scale of economic growth in Japan, 1868-1938, by William W. Lockwood. pp. 129-178.
- Foreign capital and domestic development in Japan, by Edwin P. Reubens. pp. 179-230.
- Population and labor force in relation to economic growth, by Wilbert E. Moore. pp. 231-240.
- Demographic factors related to economic growth in Brazil, by T. Lynn Smith. pp. 241-262.
- Social and demographic aspects of economic development in India, by Kingsley Davis. pp. 263-315.
- Population and labor force in the industrialization of Japan, 1850-1950, by Irene B. Taeuber. pp. 316-362.
- Social structure, the state, and economic growth, by Joseph J. Spengler. pp. 363-387.
- Social structure and economic change in Brazil, by Bernard J. Siegel. pp. 388-411.
- Brazil; the state and economic growth, by Henry William Spiegel. pp. 412-429.
- Brazilian cotton textile industry, 1850-1950, by Stanley J. Stein. pp. 430-447.
- Indian economic organization, by D. R. Gadgill. pp. 448-463.
- The 'state' and economic development in India, by Helen B. Lamb. pp. 464-495.
- Contrasting factors in the modernization of China and Japan, by Marion J. Levy, Jr. pp. 496-536.
- The state and economic enterprise in modern Japan, by William W. Lockwood. pp. 537-602.
- Index, p. 603.

Lockwood, William W.
The economic development of Japan; growth and structural change 1868-1938. Princeton, Princeton Univ. Press, 1954.
603p. map.
Expanded ed. 1968, 686p.

Lockwood, William W.
The political consequences of economic development in Japan. Tokyo, International House of Japan, 1962.
63p.

Lockwood, William W, ed.
The state and economic enterprise in Japan; essays in the political economy of growth. Princeton, Princeton Univ. Press, 1965.
753p (Studies in the modernization of Japan)
Contents:
- The Tokugawa heritage, by E. Sydney Crawcour. pp. 17-44.
- A century of Japanese economic growth, by Kazushi Ohkawa, Henry Rosovsky. pp. 47-92.
- Japan and Europe; contrasts in industrialization, by David S. Landes. pp. 93-182.
- Modern entrepreneurship in Meiji Japan, by Yasuzo Horie. pp. 183-208.
- Shibusawa Eiichi; industrial pioneer, by Johannes Hirshmeier. pp. 209-247.
- Growth of Japanese agriculture, 1875-1920, by James J. Nakamura. pp. 249-324.
- Innovation in Japanese agriculture, 1880-1935, by Shujiro Sawada. pp. 325-351.
- Meiji fiscal policy and economic progress, by Harry T. Oshima. pp. 353-389.
- Economic growth and consumption in Japan, by Alan H. Gleason. pp. 391-444.
- Japan's new capitalism, by William W. Lockwood. pp. 447-522.
- Economic miracles and Japan's income-doubling plan, by Martin Bronfenbrenner. pp. 523-553.
- Cyclical instability and fiscal-monetary policy in post-war Japan, by Hugh T. Patrick. pp. 555-618.
- Regional planning in Japan today, by Saburo Okita. pp. 619-631.
- Labor markets and collective bargaining in Japan, by Solomon B. Levine. pp. 633-667.
- Labor and politics in post-war Japan, by Robert A. Scalapino. pp. 669-720.

Maddison, Angus
Economic growth in Japan and the USSR. London, G. Allen and Unwin, 1969.
174p. (Unwin University books).
Contents:
- Tokugawa Japan - a fossilized and closed society. pp. 3-8.
- The Meiji period. 9-34.
- Accelerated growth 1913-38. pp. 35-44.
- The impact of war and occupation 1938-53. pp. 45-49.
- 'Explosive' growth since 1953. pp. 50-72.
- The significance of Japanese growth experience. pp. 73-82.
- Tsarist agrarian reform and industrialization. pp. 83-92.
- The revolution and the search for an economic policy. pp. 93-98.
- Stalinism and primitive accumulation 1928-53. pp. 99-107.
- The liberalization of the Soviet economy. pp. 108-130.
- The significance of Soviet growth experience. pp. 131-136.
- Bibliography. pp. 137-142.
- Appendices.
- Comparative levels of real G.N.P., population, employment output per head, productivity and real consumption per head in 1965. pp. 143-148.
- The growth of total output 1870-1965. pp. 149-156.
- Population 1870-1965. pp. 157-158.
- Output per head of population 1870-1965. p. 159.
- Agricultural output 1870-1965. pp. 160-162.
- Manufacturing output 1870-1965. pp. 163-165.
- Foreign trade 1870-1965. pp. 166-168.
- Index. p. 169.

Mahajan, V. S.
Development planning; lessons from the Japanese model. Calcutta, Minerva, 1976.
122p.

Minami, Ryoshin
The turning point in economic development; Japan experience. Tokyo, Kinokuniya. 1973.
330p. (Hitotsubashi Univ. Institute of Economic Research economic research series, no.14)

Morley, James William, ed.
Dilemmas of growth in prewar Japan. Princeton, Princeton University Press, 1971.
527p. (Studies in the modernization of Japan)
Published for the Conference on Modern Japan of the Association for Asian Studies.
Contents:
- The bureaucracy as a political force, 1920-45, by Robert M. Spaulding, Jr. pp. 33-80.
- Retrogression in Japan's foreign policy decision-making process, by Chihiro Hosoya. pp. 81-105.
- The failure of military expansionism, by Akira Iriye. pp. 107-138.
- The radical left and the failure of communism, by George M. Beckmann. pp. 139-178.
- Rural origins of Japanese fascism, by R. P. Dore and Tsutomu Ouchi. pp. 181-209.
- The economic muddle of the 1920's, by Hugh T. Patrick. pp. 211-266.
- Big business and politics in prewar Japan, by Arthur E. Tiedemann. pp. 267-316.
- Intellectuals as visionaries of the new Asian order, by James B. Crowley. pp. 319-373.
- Nakano Seigo and the spirit of Meiji restoration in twentieth-century Japan, by Tetsuo Najita. pp. 375-421.
- Oyama Ikuo and the search for democracy, by Peter Duns. pp. 423-458.
- Japan and Germany in the interwar period, by Kentaro Hayashi. pp. 461-488.
- What went wrong, by Edwin O. Reischauer. pp. 489-510.

Nakayama, Ichiro
Industrialization of Japan. Tokyo, Centre for East Asian Cultural Studies, 1963.
73p. (East Asian cultural studies series)

Nihon Ginko (Bank of Japan)
Outline of Japanese economy and finance. Tokyo, 1964.
69p. illus. maps.

Ohkawa, Kazushi
The growth rate of the Japanese economy since 1878. Tokyo, Kinokuniya, 1957.
250p. (Hitotsubashi Univ. economic research series v. 1)

Ohkawa, Kazushi and Yujiro Hayami, ed.
Economic growth; the Japanese experience since the Meiji era; proceedings of the second conference held by the Japan Economic Research Center, June 26-July 1, 1972 in Japan. Tokyo, Japan Economic Research Center, 1973.
2 vols. (Center paper no.19)
Contents:
Vol. 1: Session A.
Summary of statistical estimates, findings.
- A general presentation, by Kazushi Ohkawa. pp. 1-6.
- Agriculture, by Saburo Yamada and Yujiro Hayami. pp. 7-25.
- Manufacturing, by Miyohei Shinohara. pp. 26-37.
- Railroads and electric utilities, by Ryoshin Minami. pp.38-50.
- Personal consumption expenditures, by Miyohei Shinohara. pp. 51-66.
- Long term movements of gross domestic fixed capital formation in Japan, 1869-1940, by Koichi Emi. pp. 67-79.
- Government expenditure, by Koichi Emi. pp. 80-94.
- Gainful workers, by Mataji Umemura. pp. 95-100.
- Capital stocks, by Shigeru Ishiwata. pp. 101-112.

- Commodity prices and wages, by Tsutomu Noda. pp. 113-132.
- National product and expenditure, by Kazushi Ohkawa. pp. 133-153.
- Textile industry, by Akira Ono and Shiro Fujino. pp. 154-164.

Session B.

Growth, swings and structure-analyses.
- Note on economic development in agriculture in the Tokugawa period, by Mataji Umemura. pp. 175-183.
- Sources of agricultural growth in Japan, 1880-1965, by Masakatsu Akino and Yujiro Hayami. pp. 184-212.
- Kuznets and Juglar cycles during the industrialization of 1874-1940, by growth cycle approach, by Miyohei Shinohara. pp. 237-252.
- Productivity change in the manufacturing sector, 1906-1965, by Kunio Yoshihara, pp. 269-285.
- The measurement of macroeconomic performance in Japan, 1951-1968, by Mitsuo Ezaki and Dale W. Jorgenson. pp. 286-361.

Vol. 2:
- The government sector in Japan's development and growth, by Koichi Emi. pp. 375-388.
- Simple parables of Japanese economic progress; report on early findings, by Allen C. Kelley and J. G. Williamson. pp. 400-464.
- Economic growth with a dual structure; an econometric model of the prewar Japanese economy, by Ryoshin Minami and Akira Ono. pp. 474-507.
- Industrial growth and foreign trade in pre-war Japan, by Yuichi Shionoya and Ippei Yamazawa. pp. 515-548.
- Effective demand and cyclical growth of the Japanese economy, 1906-1938, by Konosuke Odaka and Shigeru Ishiwata. pp. 556-611.
- Session C. General Remarks

Ohkawa, K. and H. Rosovsky
Japanese economic growth; trend acceleration in the twentieth century. Stanford, Stanford University Press, 1973. 327p.

Ohkawa, K. and M. Shinohara, ed.
Patterns of Japanese economic development, a quantitative appraisal. New Haven, Yale Univ. Press, 1979. 411p. (A publication of the Economic Growth Center and the Council on East Asian Studies, Yale Univ.)

Contents:
- Part 1: Overall patterns: 1. Aggregate growth and product allocation, by Kazushi Ohkawa. pp. 3-33. 2. Production structure, by Kazushi Ohkawa. pp. 34-58. - 3. Data and methods, by Miyohei Shinohara. pp. 59-68.
- Outline of differences with other estimates of national product data, by Miyohei Shinohara and Nobukiyo Takamatsu. pp. 69-71.
- Linking the prewar and postwar series, by Miyohei Shinohara. pp. 72-73.
- A historical framework for appraising the reliability of estimates, by Kazushi Ohkawa. pp. 74-79.
- References for Part 1. pp. 80-84.

Part 2: Production and trade - 4. Agriculture, by Saburo Yamada and Yujiro Hayami. pp. 85-103. - 5. Manufacturing, by Miyohei Shinohara. pp. 104-121. - 6. Services, by Kazushi Ohkawa and Nobukiyo Takamatsu. pp. 122-133. - 7. Trade and balance of payments, by Ippei Yamazawa and Yuzo Yamamoto. pp. 134-158.

Part 3: Product allocation - 8. Consumption, by Miyohei Shinohara. pp. 159-176. - 9. Capital formation and capital stock. p. 177.
- Capital formation, by Koichi Emi. pp. 177-180.
- Capital stock, by Shigeru Ishiwata. pp. 181-194. - 10. Government accounts. p. 195.
- Expenditure, by Koichi Emi. pp. 196-198.
- Revenue, by Hiromitsu Ishi. pp. 199-204.

Part 4: Factor shares, prices, and population - 11. Factor incomes and shares, by Ryoshin Minami and Akira Ono. pp. 205-218. - 12. Prices, by Tsutomu Noda. pp. 219-228. - 13. Wages, by Ryoshin Minami and Akira Ono. pp. 229-240. - 14. Population and labor force, by Mataji Umemura. pp. 241-250. Appendix tables. pp. 251-396.
- Index. p. 397.

Patrick, Hugh, ed.
Japanese industrialization and its social consequences. Berkeley, University of California Press, 1976.
505p.
Contents:
- Historical changes in the life style of industrial workers, by Hiroshi Hazama. pp. 21-51.
- Japan's changing occupational structure and its significance, by Robert E. Cole and Kenichi Tominaga. pp. 53-95.
- Country girls and communication among competitors in the Japanese cotton-spinning industry, by Gary R. Saxonhouse. pp. 97-125.
- The Japanese shipbuilding industry, by Tuvia Blumenthal. pp. 129-160.
- General trading companies in Japan; their origins and growth, by Kozo Yamamura. pp. 161-199.
- Firm size and Japan's export structure; a microview of Japan's changing export competitiveness since Meiji, by William V. Rapp. pp. 201-248.
- Evolution of dualistic wage structure, by Yasukichi Yasuba. pp. 249-298.
- The introduction of electric power and its impact on the manufacturing industries; with special reference to smaller scale plants, by Ryoshin Minami. pp. 299-325.
- Demographic transition in the process of Japanese industrialization, by Hiroshi Ohbuchi. pp. 329-361.
- Changes in income inequality in the Japanese economy, by Akira Ono and Tsunehiko Watanabe. pp. 363-389.
- Poverty in modern Japan; perceptions and realities, by Masayoshi Chubachi and Koji Taira. pp. 391-437.
- Industrialization and social deprivation; welfare, environment, and the postindustrial society in Japan, by John W. Bennett and Solomon B. Levine. pp. 439-492.

Rosovsky, Henry
Capital formation in Japan, 1868-1940. Glencoe, Ill., Free Press, 1961.
358p.

Sapir, H. Michael
Japan, China and the West. Washington, National Planning Association, 1959.
70p. (The economics of competitive coexistence)

Shinohara, Miyohei
Growth and cycles in the Japanese economy. Tokyo, Kinokuniya, 1962.
349p. (Hitotsubashi Univ. economic research series v. 5)

Shinohara, Miyohei
Structural changes in Japan's economic development. Tokyo, Kinokuniya, 1970.
445p. (Hitotsubashi Univ. economic research series)

Takahashi, Chotaro, Ryotaro Iochi, and Koichi Emi.
Dynamic changes of income and distribution in Japan. Tokyo, Kinokuniya, 1959.
182p. (Hitotsubashi Univ. economic research series v. 3)

Takahashi, Kamekichi
The rise and development of Japan's modern economy; the basis for 'miraculous' growth. Tokyo, Jiji Tsushinsha, 1969.
389p.

Takahashi, Masao.
Introduction to the Japanese economy. Fukuoka, Kyushu Univ., 1963.
178p.

Takahashi, Masao
Modern Japanese economy since the Meiji Restoration. Tokyo, Kokusai Bunka Shinkokai, 1967.
170p. (Series on Japanese life and culture)

Tsuchiya, Takao
An economic history of Japan, tr. by Michitaro Shidehara, rev. by Neil Shene Smith, ed. by Kurt Singer. Philadelphia, Porcupine Press, 1977. 269, xl p. (Perspectives in Asian history series, no.10)
first pub. in 1937.

Tsunoyama, Sakae
A concise economic history of modern Japan. Bombay, Vora, 1965.
132p. map.

Tsuru, Shigeto
Essays on economic development. Tokyo, Kinokuniya, 1968.
257p. (Hitotsubashi Univ. economic research series v. 9)

Tsuru, Shigeto
Essays on Japanese economy. Tokyo, Kinokuniya, 1958.
241p. (Hitotsubashi Univ. economic research series v. 2)

Yamamoto, Noboru.
The modernization of the economy and postwar expansion. Tokyo, International Society for Educational Information, 1973.
81p. (Changing Japan series)

Yoshihara, K.
Japanese economic development; a short introduction. London, Oxford Univ. Press, 1979.
153p. (Oxford in Asian paperbacks)

Zepke, Nick
The hundred year miracle; economic development, Japan, 1918-1970. London, Heinemann Educational Books, 1976.
43p.

II.

Allen, G. C.
Factors in Japan's economic growth. (Charles Donald Cowan, ed. The economic development of China and Japan; studies in economic history and political economy. London, George Allen and Unwin, 1964. pp. 192-204)

Chenery, Hollis B., Shuntaro Shishido, and Tsunehiko Watanabe.
The pattern of Japanese growth, 1914-1954. (Richard F. Kosobud and Ryoshin Minami, ed. Edonometric studies of Japan. Urbana, University of Illinois Press, 1977. pp. 276-337)

Conroy, Hilary
A rebuttal to economic determinism. (Marlene J. Mayo, ed. The emergence of imperial Japan; self-defense or calculated aggression? Lexington, Mass., Heath, 1970. pp. 83-88)

Crawcour, E. S.
Japanese economic experience and Southeast Asia.
(Australian National University, Papers on modern Japan, v. 1. Camberra, 1965. pp. 70-82)

Crawcour, E. S.
The modern economy. (Arthur E. Tiedemann, ed. An introduction to Japanese civilization. New York, Columbia Univ. Press, 1974. pp. 487-514)

Emi, Koichi
An approach to the measurement of national saving in Japan (1878-1940) (Committee for Translation of Japanese Economic Studies. Translations of Japanese economic studies. no.35. Tokyo, International House of Japan, 1959-64.
32p.)

Emi, Koichi
Long term movements of gross domestic fixed capital formation in Japan, 1869-1940. (Kazushi Ohkawa, and Yujiro Hayamai, ed. Economic growth; the Japanese experience since the Meiji era; proceedings of the second conference held by the Japan Economic Research Center, June 26-July 1, 1972 in Japan. Tokyo, Japan Economic Research Center, 1973. v. 1 pp. 67-79)

Emi, Koichi
Product allocation; capital formation and capital stock; capital formation. (K. Ohkawa and M. Shinohara, ed. Patterns of Japanese economic development; a quantitative appraisal. New Haven, Yale Univ. Press, 1979. pp. 177-180)

Fujii, Shoichi.
Capitalism, international politics, and the emperor system. (Marlene J. Mayo, ed. The emergence of imperial Japan; self-defense or calculated aggression? Lexington, Mass., Heath, 1970. pp. 75-82)

Fujino, Shozaburo
Construction cycles and their monetary-financial characteristics. (L. Klein and K. Ohkawa, ed., Economic growth; the Japanese experience since the Meiji era. Homewood, R. D. Irwine, 1968. pp. 35-68)

Fusé, Toyomasa
Japan's economic development; success, stress and prospects for the future. (Toyomasa Fusé, ed. Modernization and stress in Japan, Leiden, E. J. Bill. 1975. pp. 24-40)

Gleason, Alan H.
Economic growth and consumption in Japan. (W. W. Lockwood, ed. The state and economic enterprise in Japan. Princeton, Princeton Univ. Press, 1965. pp. 391-444)

Horie, Yasuzo
The transformation of national economy; a chapter in Japan's economic history. (Seiichi, Tobata ed. The modernization of Japan - I. Tokyo, Institute of Asian Economic Affairs, 1966. pp. 67-90)

Ichimura, Shinichi
Factors for rapid economic growth; a social accounting approach. (Lawrence Klein and Kazushi Ohkawa, ed. Economic growth; the Japanese experience since the Meiji era. Homewood, Ill., R. D. Irwin, 1968. pp. 245-277)

Ishiwata, Shigeru
Capital stocks. (Kazushi Ohkawa, and Yujiro Hayami, ed. Economic growth; the Japanese experience since the Meiji era; proceedings of the second conference held by the Japan Economic Research Center, June 26-July 1, 1972 in Japan. Tokyo, Japan Economic Research Center, 1973. v. 1. pp. 101-112)

Ishiwata, Shigeru
Product allocation; capital formation and capital stock; capital stock. (K. Ohkawa and M. Shinohara, ed. Patterns of Japanese economic development; a quantitative appraisal. New Haven, Yale Univ. Press, 1979. pp. 181-194)

Kelley, Allen C. and J. G. Williamson
Simple parables of Japanese economic progress; report on early findings. (Kazushi Ohkawa and Yujiro Hayami, ed. Economic growth; the Japanese experience since the Meiji era; proceedings of the second conference held by the Japan Economic Research Centre, June 26-July 1, 1972 in Japan. Tokyo, Japan Economic Research Centre, 1973. v. 2. pp. 400-464)

Klein, L. R. and Y. Shinkai
An econometric model of Japan, 1930-1959. (Richard F. Kosobud and Ryoshin Minami, ed. Econometric studies of Japan. Urbana, University of Illinois Press, 1977. pp. 338-373)

Kojima, Kiyoshi
Capital accumulation and the course of industrialization with special reference to the economic development of Japan. (Committee for Translation of Japanese Economic Studies. Translation of Japanese economic studies. no.2. Tokyo, International House of Japan, 1959-64. 22p.)

Kuznets, Simon
Trends in level and structure of consumption. (L. Klein and K. Ohkawa, ed. Economic growth; the Japanese experience since the Meiji era. Homewood, Ill., R. D. Irwin, 1968. pp. 197-242)

Lockwood, William W.
The scale of economic growth in Japan, 1868-1938. (Simon Kuznets, W. F. Moore, and J. J. Spengler, ed. Economic growth; Brazil, India, Japan. Durham, N.C., Duke Univ. Press, 1955. pp. 129-178)

Minami, Ryoshin
Economic growth with a dual structure; an econometric model of the prewar Japanese economy. (Kazushi Ohkawa and Yujiro Hayami, ed. Economic growth; the Japanese experience since the Meiji era; proceedings of the second conference hled by the Japan Economic Research Center, June 26-July 1, 1972 in Japan. Tokyo, Japan Economic Research Center, 1973. v. 2. pp. 474-507)

Minami, Ryoshin and Akira Ono
Factor shares, prices, and population; factor incomes and shares. (K. Ohkawa and M. Shinohara, ed. Patterns of Japanese economic development; a quantitative appraisal. New Haven Yale Univ. Press, 1979. pp. 205-218)

Noda, Tsutomu
Factor shares, prices, and population; prices. (K. Ohkawa and M. Shinohara, ed. Patterns of Japanese economic development; a quantitative appraisal. New Haven, Yale Univ. Press, 1979. pp. 219-228)

Odaka, Konosuke and Shigeru Ishiwata
Effective demand and cyclical growth of the Japanese economy, 1906-1938. (Kazushi Ohkawa and Yujuro Hayami, ed. Economic growth ; the Japanese experience since the Meiji era; proceedings of the second conference held by the Japan Economic Research Center, June 26-July 1, 1972 in Japan. Tokyo, Japan Economic Research Center, 1973. v. 2. pp. 556-611)

Ohkawa, Kazushi
Effects of structural change on productivity growth; a long-term measurement. (Richard F. Kosobud and Ryoshin Minami, ed. Econometric studies of Japan. Urbana, Univ., Illinois Press 1977. pp. 114-139)

Ohkawa, Kazushi
Initial conditions; economic level and structure. (International Development Center of Japan. Papers and proceedings of the conference on Japan's historical development experience and contemporary developing countries; issues for comparative analysis. Feb. 11-16, 1978. Tokyo, 1978. pp. 25-38)

Ohkawa, Kazushi
National product and expenditure. (Kazushi Ohkawa, and Yujiro Hayami, ed. Economic growth; the Japanese experience since the Meiji era; proceedings of the second conference held by the Japan Economic Research Center, June 26-July 1, 1972 in Japan. Tokyo, Japan Economic Research Center, 1973. v. 1. pp. 133-153)

Ohkawa, Kazushi
Overall patterns; aggregate growth and product allocation. (K. Ohkawa and M. Shimohara, ed. Patterns of Japanese economic development; a quantitative appraisal. New Haven, Yale Univ. Press, 1979. pp. 3-33)

Ohkawa, Kazushi
Overall patterns; a historical framework for appraising the reliability of estimates. (K. Ohkawa and M. Shinohara, ed. Patterns of Japanese economic development; a quantitative appriasal. New Haven, Yale Univ. Press, 1979. pp. 74-79)

Ohkawa, Kazushi
Overall patterns; production structure. (K. Ohkawa and M. Shinohara, ed. Patterns of Japanese economic development; a quantitative appraisal. New Haven, Yale Univ. Press, 1979. pp. 34-58)

Ohkawa, Kazushi
The pattern of Japanese long-term economic growth. (Asian Conference on Income and Wealth, 1st Aug. 1960, Hong Kong. Asian studies in income and wealth; papers. London, Asia Pub. House, 1965. pp. 48-70)

Ohkawa, Kazushi and Gustav Ranis
On phasing; a preliminary view. (International Development Center of Japan. Papers and proceedings of the conference on Japan's historical development experience and contemporary developing countries; issues for comparative analysis. Feb. 11-16, 1978. Tokyo, 1978. pp. 39-52)

Ohkawa, Kazushi and Henry Rosovsky
A century of Japanese economic growth. (W. W. Lockwood, ed. The state and economic enterprise in Japan. Peinceton, Princeton Univ. Press, 1965. pp. 47-92)

Ohkawa, Kazushi and Miyohei Shinohara
Overall patterns; data and methods. (K. Ohkawa and M. Shinohara, ed. Patterns of Japanese economic development; a quantitative appraisal. New Haven, Yale Univ. Press, 1979. pp. 59-68)

Ohkawa, Kazushi and Nobukiyo Takamatsu
Production and trade; services. (K. Ohkawa and M. Shinohara, ed. Patterns of Japanese economic development; a quantitative appraisal. New Haven, Yale Univ. Press, 1979. pp. 122-133)

Ono, Akira and Tsunehiko Watanabe
Changes in income inequality in the Japanese economy. (Hugh Patrick, ed. Japanese industrialization and social consequences. Berkeley, Univ. of California Press, 1976. pp. 363-390)

Otsuka, Katsuo
Production structure and patterns of economic development; Japan and selected LDCs. (International Development Center of Japan. Papers and proceedings of the conference on Japan's historical development experience and contemporary developing countries; issues for comparative analysis. Feb. 11-16, 1978. Tokyo, 1978. pp. 213-232)

Otsuki, Toshiyuki and Nobukiyo Takamatsu
An aspect of the size distribution of income in prewar Japan. (International Development Center of Japan. Papers and proceedings of the conference on Japan's historical development experience and contemporary developing countries; issues for comparative analysis. Feb. 11-16, 1978. Tokyo, 1978. pp. 331-348)

Rosovky, Henry
Capital formation in pre-war Japan; current findings and future problems. (Charles Donald Cowan, ed. The economic development of China and Japan; studies in economic history and political economy. London, George Allen and Unwin, 1974. pp. 205-219)

Shinohara, Miyohei
Kuznets and Juglar cycles during the industrialization of 1874-1940. (Economic growth; the Japanese experience since the Meiji era; proceedings of the second conference held by the Japan Economic Research Center, June 26-July 1, 1972 in Japan. Tokyo, Japan Economic Research Center, 1973. v. 1. pp. 237-252)

Shinohara, Miyohei
Overall patterns; linking the prewar and postwar series. (K. Ohkawa and M. Shinohara, ed. Patterns of Japanese economic development; a quantitative appraisal. New Haven, Yale Univ. Press, 1979. pp. 72-73)

Shinohara, Miyohei
Personal consumption expenditures. (Kazushi Ohkawa and Yujiro Hayami, ed. Economic growth; the Japanese experience since the Meiji era; proceedings of the second conference held by the Japan Economic Research Center, June 26-July 1, 1972 in Tokyo. Tokyo, Japan Economic Research Center, 1973. v. 1. pp. 51-66)

Shinohara, Miyohei
Product allocation; consumption. (K. Ohkawa and M. Shinohara, ed. Patterns of Japanese economic development; a quantitative appraisal. New Haven, Yale Univ. Press, 1979. pp. 159-176)

Shinohara, Miyohei
Production and trade; manufacturing. (K. Ohkawa and M. Shinohara, ed. Patterns of Japanese economic development; a quantitative appraisal. New Haven, Yale Univ. Press, 1979. pp. 104-121)

Shinohara, Miyohei and Nobukiyo Takamatsu
Overall patterns; outline of differences with other estimates of national product data. (K. Ohkawa and M. Shinohara, ed. Patterns of Japanese economic development; a quantitative appraisal. New Haven, Yale Univ. Press, 1979. pp. 59-68)

Shionoya, Yuichi
Patterns of industrial development. (L. Klein and K. Ohkawa, ed. Economic growth; the Japanese experience since the Meiji era. Homewood, Ill., R. D. Irwin, 1968. pp. 69-109)

Tanin, O. and E. Yohan
Capitalism and imperialism. (Marlene J. Mayo, ed. The emergence of imperial Japan; self-defense or calculated aggression? Lexington, Mass., Heath, 1970. pp. 69-74)

Tsuru, Shigeto
The take-off in Japan, 1868-1900. (W. E. Rostow, ed. The economics of take-off into sustained growth; proceedings of a conference held by the International Economic Association. London, Macmillan, 1963. pp. 139-150)

Tsuru, Shigeto and Kazushi Ohkawa
Long term changes in the national income of Japan since 1878. (Milton Gilbert, ed. Income and wealth, series 3. Cambridge, Mass., Bows and Bows, 1953. pp. 19-44)

Ueno, Hiroya
A long-term model of Japanese economic growth, 1906-1968. (Richard F. Kosobud and Ryoshin Minami, ed. Econometric studies of Japan. Urbana, Univ. of Illinois Press, 1977. pp. 374-413)

Ueno, Hiroya
A long-term model of Japanese economy, 1920-1958. (Committee for Translation of Japanese Economic Studies. Translations of Japanese economic studies. no. 27. Tokyo, International House of Japan, 1959-64. 36p.)

Watanabe, Tsunehiko
Industrialization, technological progress, and dual structure. (L. Klein and K. Ohkawa, ed. Economic growth; the Japanese experience since the Meiji era. Homewood, Ill., R. D. Irwin, 1968. pp. 110-134)

Yamazawa, Ippei and Akira Hirata
Industrialization and external relations; comparative analysis of Japan's historical experience and contemporary developing countries' performance. (International Development Center of Japan. Papers and proceedings of the conference on Japan's historical development experience and contemporary developing countries; issues for comparative analysis. Feb. 11-16, 1978. Tokyo, 1978. pp. 181-212)

III.

Burgess, Giles Harold
A study of modern economic growth using estimates of aggregate production functions of six nations, 1870 to 1914. Ph.D. 1973. University of Oregon, 105p.

De Bever, Leonardus J.
The role of the state in early Japanese growth. Ph.D. 1976. The University of Wisconson, Madison. 339p.

Hoekendorf, W. C.
The Secular trend of income velocity in Japan, 1879-1940. Ph.D. 1961. University of Washington.

Niho, Yoshio
Population growth and the development of dual economy; analysis and some testing. Ph.D. 1973. Brown University 237p.

Zahn, Frank
A long-run growth model for Japan and a test of the low level equibrium trap hypothesis. Ph.D. 1969. University of California. 102p.

IV.

Blumenthal, Tuvia
A test of the Klein-Shinkai economic model of Japan. International economic review, v. 6, no.2. May 1965. pp. 211-228.

Bronfenbrenner, M.
Some lessons of Japan's economic development, 1853-1938. Pacific affairs, v. 34, no.1. Spring 1961. pp. 7-27.

Caldarola, Carlo
Socio-economic dualism in Japan. Monumenta Nipponica, v. 20, nos3/4. 1965. pp. 359-373.

Chenery, H. B., S. Shishido, and T. Watanabe
The pattern of Japanese growth, 1914-1953. Econometrica, vol. 30, no.1. Jan. 1962. pp. 98-139.

Duxbury, D.
Economic crisis in Japan. Royal central Asian journal, v. 42, pt. 1. Jan. 1955. pp. 7-20.

Emi, Koichi
An approach to the measurement of national saving in Japan (1878-1940) Hitotsubashi journal of economics, v. 6, no.1. June 1965. pp. 1-19.

Emi, Koichi
Capital formation in residential real estate in Japan, 1887-1940. Annals of the Hitotsubashi academy, v. 9, no.2. Apr. 1959. pp. 218-232.

Emi, Koichi
Long-term movement of capital formation; the Japanese case, 1868-1940. Developing economies, v. 5, no.2. June 1967. pp. 247-273.

Fujino, Shozaburo
Business cycles in Japan, 1868-1962. Hitotsubashi journal of economics, v. 7, no.1. June 1966. pp. 56-79.

Fujino, Shozaburo
A simple model of economic development in the early stage of industrialization. Hitotsubashi journal of economics, v. 5, no.2. Jan. 1965. pp. 84-96.

Fukuhara, Gyōzō
On the development of economic planning in Japan. Bulletin of University of Osaka Prefecture, series D, v. 5. 1961. pp. 22-33.

Gregory, Gene
Japanese economic growth; the human equation. Asian survey, v. 15, no.10. Oct. 1975. pp. 851-869.

Hayakawa, Miyoji
The application of Pareto's law of income to Japan data. Econometrica, v. 19, no.2. Apr. 1951. pp. 174-183.

Hayakawa, Miyoji
Distribution of income in Japan, 1905-1956. Waseda economic papers, no. 4. 1959. pp. 19-35.

Horie, Yasuzo
The transformation of the national economy; a chapter in Japan's economic history. Developing economies, v. 3, no.4. Dec. 1965. pp. 404-426.

Klein, Lawrence R.
A model of Japanese economic growth, 1878-1937. Econometrica, v. 29, no.3. July 1961. pp. 277-292.

Klein, Lawrence R. and Y. Shinkai
The economic model of Japan, 1930-1959. International economic review, v. 4, no.1. Jan. 1963. pp. 1-28.

Lee, Pong S.
Unbalanced growth; a case of Japan 1878-1918. Yale economic essays, v. 6, no.2. Fall 1966. pp. 479-526.

Lindsay, Lord
Japan, China and the West. Japan quarterly, v. 2, no.1. Jan./Mar. 1955. pp. 6-13.

Lockwood, William W.
The state and economic growth in Japan. Far eastern survey, v. 20, no.10. May 16, 1951. pp. 93-99.

Matsumura, Koichi
The transformation of feudal landlord economy into capitalism. Keio University economic review, v. 34, no.1. Apr. 1964. pp. 36-61.

Minami, Ryoshin
Further considerations on the turning point in the Japanese economy (I) (II). Hitotsubashi journal of economics, I, v. 10, no.2. Feb. 1970. pp. 18-60. II, v. 11. no.1. June 1970. pp. 58-112. Bibl. pp. 110-112.

Minami Ryoshin and Akira Ono
Modeling dualistic development in Japan. Hitotsubashi journal of economics, v. 18, no.2. Feb. 1978. pp. 18-32.

Morita, Yūzō
The national income and the standard of living of Japan. Japan quarterly, v. 3, no.1. Jan./Mar. 1956. pp. 107-117.

Nakamura, Takafusa
A long-term survey of Japan's prewar growth process. Japanese economic studies, v. 1. no.1. Fall 1972. pp. 49-98. Bibl. pp. 95-98.

Nelson, Richard R.
Growth models and the escape from the low-level equilibrium trap; the case of Japan. Economic development and cultural change, v. 8, no.4. pt. 1. July 1960. pp. 378-388.

Nose, Nobuko
Japanese economic growth since the Meiji Restoration; a social accounting approach. Kobe economic and business review, v. 17. 1970. pp. 9-34.

Ohkawa, Kazushi
A note on "long term changes in the national product of Japan". Annals of the Hitotsubashi academy, v. 3, no.2. Apr. 1953. pp. 165-178.

Ohkawa, Kazushi and Henry Rosovsky
Economic fluctuations in prewar Japan; a preliminary analysis of cycles and long swings. Hitotsubashi journal of economics, v. 3, no.1. Oct. 1962. pp. 10-33.

Ohkawa, Kazuhsi and Henry Rosovský
On the industrial distribution of national product and labor force during economic growth. Keizai kenkyu, (Hitotsubashi Univ.) v. 12, no.2. Apr. 1961. pp. 126-132.

Oishi, Kaichiro
Japan's industrial revolution; its evolution and characteristic features. Annals of the Institute of Social Science, no.17. 1976. pp. 141-161.

Okita, Saburo
A reappraisal of Japan's economy. Japan quarterly, v. 6, no.3. July/ Sept. 1959. pp. 282-290.

Okita, Saburo
Saving and economic growth in Japan. Economic development and cultural change, v. 6. 1957/58. pp. 32-41.

Oshima, Harry T.
Notes on an alternative method of estimating the national income and expenditure of Japan, 1881. Keizai kenkyu, (Hitotsubashi Univ.) v. 8, no.3. July 1957. pp. 242-251.

Oshima, Harry T.
Rejoinder to Henry Rosovsky. Keizai kenkyu, (Hitotsubashi Univ.) v. 9, no.1. Jan. 1958. pp. 72-73.

Patrick, Hugh T.
Lessons for underdeveloped countries from the Japanese experience of economic development. Indian journal of economics, v. 1, no.2. Oct. 1961. pp. 150-166.

Pertot, Vladimir
Japan seen from the focus of her economic policy. Hitotsubashi journal of economics, v. 19, nos.1/2. Dec. 1978. pp. 62-74.

Ranis, Gustav
The capital-output ratio in Japanese economic development. Review of economic studies, 26. Oct. 1958. pp. 23-32.

Ranis, Gustav
Factor proportions in Japanese economic development. American economic review, v. 47, no.5. Sept. 1957. pp. 594-607.

Ranis, Gustav
The financing of Japanese economic development. Economic history review, v. 11, no.3. Apr. 1959. pp. 440-454.

Rapp, William V.
The many possible extensions of product cycle analysis. Hitotsubashi journal of economics, v. 16, no.1. June, 1975. pp. 22-29.

Rosovsky, Henry
Some thoughts on Mr. Oshima's benchmark for 1881. Keizai kenkyu, (Hitotsubashi Univ.) v. 8, no.3. July 1957. pp. 252-253.

Rosovsky, Henry
The statistical measurement of Japanese economic growth. Economic development and cultural change, v. 7, no.1. Oct. 1958. pp. 75-84.

Shinohara, Miyohei
Capital formation in Japan. Keizai kenkyu (Hitotsubashi Univ.) v. 4, no.1, Jan. 1953. pp. 85-88.

Shinohara, Miyohei
An estimate of capital formation in Japan by "commodity flow" method. Annals of the Hitotsubashi academy, v. 5, no.2. Apr. 1955. pp. 116-139.

Shinohara, Miyohei
Formation and transition of the dual economy in Japan. Hitotsubashi journal of economics, v. 8, no.2. Feb. 1968. pp. 1-38.

Shinohara, Miyohei
Growth and the long swing in the Japanese economy. Hitotsubashi journal of economics, v. 1, no.1 Oct. 1960. pp. 59-83.

Shinohara, Miyohei
Long-term changes of consumption expenditures in Japan, 1874-1940. Developing economies, v. 5, no.2. June 1967. pp. 217-246.

Takahashi, Chotaro
Changes of income distribution in Japan. Annals of the Hitotsubashi academy, v. 6, no.1. Oct. 1955. pp. 16-26.

Takenaka, Yasukazu
Endogenous formation and development of capitalism in Japan. Journal of economic history, v. 29, no.1. Mar. 1969. pp. 141-162.

Tanaka, Kisuke
Measurement of the business cycles in Japan. Waseda business and economic studies, no. 9. 1973. pp. 1-12.

Tanaka, Osamu
The income disparity of a dual economy; Japan's case. Kobe University economic review, no. 11. 1965. pp. 27-44.

Temin, Peter
A time-series test of patterns of industrial growth. Economic development and cultural change, v. 15, no.2, pt. 1. Jan. 1967. pp. 174-182.

Ueno, Hiroya
A long-term model of economic growth of Japan, 1906-1968. International economic review, v. 13, no.3. Oct. 1972. pp. 619-643. Bibl. p.643.

Ueno, Hiroya
A long-term model of the Japanese economy, 1920-1958. International economic review, v. 4, no.2. May 1963. pp. 171-193.

Ueno, Hiroya and Soshichi Kinoshita
A simulation experiment for growth with a long-term model of Japan. International economic review, v. 9, no.1. Feb. 1968. pp. 14-48.

Watanabe, Tsunehiko
Economic aspects of dualism in the industrial development of Japan. Economic development and cultural change, v. 13, no.3. Apr. 1965. pp. 293-312.

Williamson, J. G. and Leo J. de Bever
Saving, accumulation and modern economic growth; the contemporary relevance of Japanese history. Journal of Japanese studies, v. 4, no.1. Winter, 1978. pp. 128-148.

Yamada, Yūzo
The conditions of stability and progress in the Japanese economy (main report) Japan science review, economic sciences, v. 4. 1957. pp. 21-30.

Yamada, Yūzo
The income growth and the rate of saving in Japan. Annals of the Histotsubashi academy, v. 4, no.2. Apr. 1954. pp. 79-97.

Yamada, Yūzo
The national income and industrial structure in Japan. Annals of the Hitotsubashi academy, v. 1, no.1. Oct. 1950. pp. 15-33.

Yamaguchi, Mitoshi
Population growth, agricultural and economic develoooment of Japan since the Meiji period. Kobe University economic review, no.20. 1974. pp. 71-92.

Yamaguchi, Mitoshi and Hans P. Binswanger
The role of sectoral technical change in development; Japan 1880-1965. American journal of agricultural economics, v. 57, no.2. May 1975. pp. 269-278.

Yasuba, Yasukichi
Anatomy of the debate on Japanese capitalism. Journal of Japanese studies, v. 2, no.1. Autumn 1975. pp. 63-82.

Yasuba, Yasukichi
A revised index of industrial production for Japan, 1905-1935. Osaka economic papers, v. 19, no.1/2. Mar. 1971. pp. 19-41.

Yoshihara, Kunio
Demand functions; an application to the Japanese expenditure pattern. Econometrica, v. 37, no.2. Apr. 1969. pp. 257-274.

Yoshihara, Kunio
Long-term models of the Japanese economy. Riron keizaigaku, v. 20, no.3. Dec. 1969. pp. 41-64.

MEIJI PERIOD

II.

Rosovsky, Henry
Japan's transition to modern economic growth, 1868-1885. (H. Rosovsky, ed. Industrialization in two systems. N.Y., Wiley, 1966. pp. 91-139)

IV.

Emi, Koichi
The growth of the Japanese economy in the first half of the Meiji period; in terms of problems of underdeveloped nations. Hitotsubashi journal of economics, v. 3, no.2. June 1963. pp. 6-15.

Fujita, Masahiro
Fundamental features of the accumulation of capital in the late Meiji era. Kobe economic and business review, v. 5. 1958. pp. 23-42.

Furushima, Toshio
Trends in investment in the second decade of the Meiji era 1877-86. Rural economic problems, v. 2, no.1. May 1965. pp. 1-23.

Harootunian, H. D.
The economic rehabilitation of the Samurai in the early Meiji period. Journal of Asian studies, v. 19, no.4. Aug. 1960. pp. 433-444.

Horie, Hideichi
The agricultural structure of Japan in the period of Meiji Restoration (1), (2) Keio University economic review, v. 31, no.2. Oct. 1961. pp. 1-16; v. 32, no.1. Apr. 1962. pp. 1-23.

Inukai, Ichirou and Arlon R. Tussing
Kōgyō iken; Japan's ten year plan, 1884. Economic development and cultural change, v. 16, no.1. Oct. 1967. pp. 51-71.

Miyamoto, M., Y. Sakudo, and Y. Yasuba
Economic development in pre-industrial Japan, 1859-1894. Journal of economic history, vo. 25, no.4. Dec. 1965. pp. 541-564.

Miyata, Kiyozo
Reparations and Japan's economy. Asian affairs, v. 1, no.3. Sept. 1956. oo. 233-245.

Morris, Morris David
The problem of peasant agriculturist in Meiji Japan, 1873-1885. Far Eastern quarterly, v. 15, no.3. May 1956. pp. 357-371.

Niwa, Kunio
The reform of the land tax and the government programme for the encouragement of industry. Developing economies, v. 4, no.4. Dec. 1966. pp. 447-471.

Ono, Kikunosuke
Inflation in the early era of Meiji. Kobe University economic review, no.2. 1956. pp.79-102.

Shindo, Motokazu
The inflation in the early Meiji era. Kyoto University economic review, v. 24, no.2. Oct. 1954. pp. 39-59.

Takahashi, Chotaro
Capital accumulation in early Meiji era. Asian affairs, v. 1, no.2. June 1956. pp. 130-148.

TAISHO-SHOWA PERIOD

I.

Cohen, Jerome B.
Japan's economy in war and reconstruction. Minneapolis, Univ. of Minnesota Press, 1949. 545p.

II.

Allen, G. C.
Political economy, 1929-1936; the concentration of economic control. (Jon Livingston, ed. Imperial Japan, 1800-1945. N.Y., Pantheon Books, 1973. pp. 378-383)

Crowley, James
Political economy, 1929-1936; Japan's quest for autonomy. (Jon Livingston, ed. Imperial Japan, 1800-1945. N.Y., Pantheon Books, 1973. pp. 368-370)

Iriya, Akira
The failure of economic expansion, 1918-1931. (Bernard S. Silberman, ed. Japan in crisis; essays on Taisho democracy. Princeton, Princeton Univ. Press, 1974. pp. 237-269)

Lockwood, William
Political economy, 1929-1936; trade, armament, industrial expansion, 1930-1938. (Jon Livingston, ed. Imperial Japan, 1800-1945. N.Y., Pantheon Books, 1973. pp. 371-377)

Lockwood, William
The twentieth and beyond; Japan's economy in transition. (Jon Livingston, ed. Imperial Japan, 1800-1945. N.Y., Pantheon Books, 1973. pp. 336-341)

Morley, James W.
Dilemmas of growth; the experience of Japan, 1905-1945. (International Conference on the Problems of Modernization in Asia, Seoul, 1965. Report. Seoul, Korea University Asiatic Research Center, 1966. pp. 300-308)

Orchard, John
Labor and industry; the effects of the World War on industrialization. (Jon Livingston, ed. Imperial Japan, 1800-1945. New York, Pantheon Books, 1973. pp. 318-321)

Patrick, Hugh T.
The economic muddle of the 1920's. (J. W. Morley, ed. Dilemmas of growth in prewar Japan. Princeton, Princeton University Press, 1971. pp. 211-266)

Yamamura, Kozo
Then came the great depression; Japan's interwar years. (Herman van de Wee, ed., The great depression revisited. The Hague, Martinus Nijhoff, 1974. pp. 182-212)

Yamamura, Kozo
The Japanese economy, 1911-1930; concentration, conflicts and crises. (B. Silberman and H. Harootunian, ed. Japan in crisis. Princeton, Princeton University Press, 1974. pp. 299-328)

IV.

Aoyama, Hideo, and Toru Hishikawa
Business fluctuations in Japanese economy during the inter-war period. <u>Kyoto University economic review</u>, v. 28, no.1. Apr. 1958. pp. 14-39.

Cho, Yukio
From the Showa economic crisis to military economy, with special reference to the Inoue and Takahashi financial policies. <u>Developing economies</u>, v. 5, no.4. Dec. 1967. pp. 568-596.

Cohen, Jerome B.
The Japanese war economy, 1940-1945. <u>Far eastern survey</u>, v. 15, no.24. Dec. 4. 1946. pp. 361-370.

Fujita, Masahiro
Two deflations in the Showa era. <u>Kobe economic and business review</u>, v. 2. 1955. pp. 53-76.

Klein, Lawrence and Y. Shinkai
An economic model of Japan, 1930-1959. <u>International Economic Review</u>, v. 4, no.1. Jan. 1963. pp. 1-28.

Morgan, Alfred P.
The Japanese war economy; a review. <u>Far Eastern quarterly</u>, v. 8, no.1. Nov. 1948. pp. 64-71.

Nonomura, Kazuo
The development of wartime reproduction theories in Japan. <u>Annals of the Hitotsubashi academy</u>, v. 3, no.2. Apr. 1953. pp. 179-190.

Rice, Richard
Economic mobilization in wartime Japan; business, bureaucracy and military in conflict. Journal of Asian studies, v. 38, no.4. Aug. 1979. pp. 689-719.

Takahashi, Makoto
The development of war-time economic controls. Developing economies, v. 5, no.4. Dec. 1967. pp. 648-665.

TECHNOLOGICAL DEVELOPMENT

II.

Okochi, A.
A comparison of choice of technology among three nations; Great Britain, United States, and Japan. (Keiichiro Nakagawa, ed. Strategy and structure of big business; proceedings of the 1st Fuji Conference. Tokyo, Univ. of Tokyo Press. pp. 153-170)

Ono, Akira
Borrowed technology in the iron and steel industry; a comparison between Brazil, India and Japan. (International Development Center of Japan. Papers and proceedings of the conference on Japan's historical development experience and contemporary developing countries; issues for comparative analysis. Feb. 11-16, 1978. Tokyo, 1978. pp. 249-266)

Ranis, Gustav, and Gary Saxonhouse
Technology choice, adaptation and the quality dimension in the Japanese cotton textile industry. (International Development Center of Japan. Papers and proceedings of the conference on Japan's historical development experience and contemporary developing countries; issues for comparative analysis. Feb. 11-16, 1978. Tokyo, 1978. pp. 267-302)

III.

Sen, Asim
The role of technological change in economic development; the lessons of Japan for presently developing countries. Ph.D. 1979. Rutgers University, the State Univ. of New Jersey. 357p.

Yamaguchi, Mitoshi
Technical change and population growth in the economic development of Japan. Ph.D. 1973. University of Minnesota. 246p.

IV.

Ishikawa, Shigeru
Choice of techniques and choice of industries. Hitotsubashi journal of economics, v. 6, no.2. Feb. 1966. pp. 13-44.

Saito, Masaru
Introduction of foreign technology in the industrialization process - Japanese experience since the Meiji restoration (1868). Developing economies, v. 13, no.2. June 1975. pp. 168-186.

Sato, Kazuo
Growth and technical change in Japan's non-primary economy, 1930-1967. Japanese economic studies, v. 1, no.4 Summer 1973. pp. 63-103.

Sato, Ryuzo
Technical progress and the aggregate production function of Japan, 1930-1960. Riron keizaigaku, v. 19, no.1. Mar. 1968. pp. 15-24.

Saxonhouse, Gary R.
A tale of Japanese technological diffusion in the Meiji period. Journal of economic history, v. 1. 34, no.1. Mar. 1974. pp. 149-165.

AGRICULTURE AND FISHING INDUSTRY

AGRICULTURAL DEVELOPMENT

I.

Grad, Andrew J.
Land and peasant in Japan; an introductory survey. N.Y., Institute of Pacific Relations, 1952.
262p. illus. maps.

Havens, Thomas R. H.
Farm and nation in modern Japan; agrarian nationalism, 1870-1940. Princeton, Princeton Univ. Press, 1974.
xi, 358p.

Hemmi, Kenzo
Japanese agriculture. Tokyo, Ministry of Foreign Affairs. Economic Affairs Bureau, 1968.
36p.

Hoynden, Yoshio
Cooperative movement in Japan. 1. Ed. by Asia Kyokai. Tokyo, Maruzen, 1958.
ix, 311p.

Iso, Eikichi
Rice and crops in its rotation in subtropical zones. Tokyo, Japan FAO Association, 1954.
611p. illus.

Johnston, Bruce F., Mosaburo Hosoda, and Yoshio Kusumi.
Japanese food management in world war II. Stanford, Stanford Univ. Press, 1953.
283p. illus. (Food, agriculture, and world war II)

Kokusai Shokuryo Nogyo Kyokai (Japan FAO Association)
A century of technical development in Japanese agriculture. Tokyo, 1959.
127p.

Morita, Shiro
The development of agricultural cooperative associations in Japan. Tokyo, Japan FAO Association, 1960.
99p. illus.

Nakamura, James I.
Agricultural production and the economic development of Japan 1873-1922. Princeton, Princeton Univ. Press, 1966.
257p. map. (Studies of the East Asian Institute, Columbia Univ.)

Ogura, Takekazu, ed.
Agricultural development in modern Japan. Tokyo, Japan FAO Association, 1963.
688p.
also published by Fuji Pub. Co., 1967.
Contents:
- Part I. Agriculture and economy; Chapter 1. The Meiji restoration and agriculture (1868-1912). pp. 3-26.
- Chapter 2. Japanese agriculture from the pre-World War I period to the post-depression period of the Showa era (1913-40) pp. 27-45.
- Chapter 3. Wartime Japanese agriculture (1941-45) pp. 46-62.
- Chapter 4. Economic rehabilitation and agriculture after the War (1946-54). pp. 63-87.
- Chapter 5. Agricultural problems in a rapidly growing economy (1955-62) pp. 88-104.
- Part II. Agriculture and legislation; Chapter 6. Introduction and summary review of agricultural policies in Japan. pp. 107-118.
- Chapter 7. Modernization of the land tenure system. pp. 119-148.
- Chapter 8. Measures for the encouragement, control, and protection of agriculture. pp. 149-180.
- Chapter 9. Food problem and rice policies. pp. 181-210.
- Chapter 10. The policy for marketing and pricing of silk. pp. 211-221.
- Chapter 11. The policy for marketing and pricing of fertilizer. pp. 222-231.
- Chapter 12. Local government and systems of water utilization and land improvement. pp. 232-246.

- Chapter 13. The system of finance and insurance and agricultural organization. pp. 247-285.
- Chapter 14. The enactment of the agricultural basic law. pp. 286-298.
- Part III. Agriculture and technique; Chapter 15. Instruction and encouragement in agriculture. pp. 299-317.
- Chapter 16. The development of research institutions. pp. 318-330.
- Chapter 17. The establishment and development of agricultural education. pp. 331-345.
- Chapter 18. Improvement of rice cultural techniques. pp. 346-364.
- Chapter 19. Development of a fertilizer-consuming rice culture. pp. 365-387.
- Chapter 20. Land improvement projects. pp. 388-409.
- Chapter 21. Improvement in farm machinery and farm implements and their popularization. pp. 410-422.
- Chapter 22. Disease and insect pest control. pp. 423-434.
- Chapter 23. The northward expansion of rice cultivation - development of rice growing in Hokkaido. pp. 435-447.
- Chapter 24. Development of paddy rice productivity. pp. 448-478.
- Chapter 25. Changes in upland crop growing. pp. 479-508.
- Chapter 26. Progress of fruit farming techniques. pp. 509-527.
- Chapter 27. The development of tea industry. pp. 528-540.
- Chapter 28. The technical developments in the raw silk industry. pp. 541-565.
- Chapter 29. The development of the livestock industry and its bottlenecks. pp. 566-590.
- Part IV. The significance of the Japanese experience. pp. 613-684.
- Literature cited. p. 685.

Ogura, Takekazu
Can Japanese agriculture survive?; a historical approach. Tokyo, Agricultural Policy Research Centre, 1979.
850p.

Ohkawa, Kazushi
Differential structure and agricultures; essays on dualistic growth, Tokyo, Kinokuniya, 1972. 298p. (Hitotsubashi Univ. economic research series, no.13)

Ohkawa, Kazushi, Bruce F. Johnston and Hiromitsu Kaneda., ed.
Agriculture and economic growth; Japan's experience. [Tokyo] Univ. of Tokyo Press, 1969. Princeton, Princeton Univ. Press, 1970.
433p.
Contents:
- Phases of agricultural development and economic growth, by Kazushi Ohkawa. pp. 3-36. bibl. pp. 35-36.
- The financing of Japanese economic development, by Gustav Raniz. pp. 37-57. bibl. pp. 57.
- The Japanese model of agricultural development; its relevance to developing nations, by Bruce F. Johnston. pp. 58-104. bibl. 99-104.
- Agricultural productivity at the beginning of industrialization, by Yujiro Hayami and Saburo Yamada. pp. 105-135. bibl. 126-127.
- Technological change in Japanese agriculture; a long-term analysis, by Shujiro Sawada. pp. 136-154. bibl. pp. 153-154.
- Economics of mechanization in small-scale agriculture, by Keizo Tsuchiya. pp. 155-174. bibl. pp. 168.
- Agriculture and labor supply in the Meiji era, by Mataji Umemura. pp. 175-197. bibl. pp. 196-197.
- The labor force in Meiji economic growth; a quantitative study of Yamanashi prefecture, by Arlon R. Tussing. pp. 198-221. bibl. pp. 221.
- The supply price of labor; farm family workers, by Yukio Masui. pp. 222-249. bibl. pp. 248-249.
- An analysis of part-time farming in the post-war period, by Takeo Misawa. pp. 250-269. bibl. pp. 269.
- The supply of farm labor and the turning point in the Japanese economy, by Ryoshin Minami. pp. 270-299. bibl. pp. 293-295.
- Primary product exports and economic development; the case of silk, by

Kenzo Hemmi. pp. 303-323. bibl. pp. 322-323.
- Development of long-term agricultural credit, by Yuzuru Kato. pp. 324-351. bibl. pp. 347-348.
- Saving of farm households, by Tsutomu Noda. pp. 352-373. bibl. pp. 372-373.
- Effects of the land reform on consumption and investment of farmers, by Shigetō Kawano. pp. 374-397.
- Long-term changes in food consumption patterns in Japan, by Hiromitsu Kaneda. pp. 398-433. bibl. pp. 428-429.

Ozaki, Chujiro
Farm household economy survey in Japan. Tokyo, Agriculture Forestry and Fisheries Productivity Conference, 1960.
60p. map. (Agricultural development series)

Tobata, Seiichi
An introduction to agriculture of Japan. Tokyo, Agriculture Forestry and Fisheries Productivity Conference, 1958.
74p. illus. map.

Tsuchiya, Keizo
Productivity and technological progress in Japanese agriculture. Tokyo, Univ. of Tokyo Press, 1976.
261p.

II.

Akino, Masakatsu and Yujiro Hayami
Sources of agricultural growth in Japan, 1880-1965. (Kazushi Ohkawa and Yujiro Hayami, ed. Economic growth; the Japanese experience since the Meiji era; proceedings of the second conference held by the Japan Economic Research Centre, June 21-July 1, 1972 in Japan. Tokyo, Japan Economic Research Centre, 1973. v. 1. pp. 184-212)

Crawcour, E. Sydney
Japan, 1868-1920. (Richard T. Shand, ed. Agricultural development in Asia. Canberra, Australian National Univ. Press, 1969. pp. 1-24)

Dore, Ronald P.
Agricultural improvement in Japan; 1870-1900. (Thomas C. Smith, ed. City and village in Japan. Chicago, University of Chicago Press, 1960. pp. 69-92)

Hayami, Yujiro and Saburo Yamada
Technological progress in agriculture. (L. Klein and K. Ohkawa, ed. Economic growth; the Japanese experience since the Meiji era. Homewood, Ill., R. P. Irwin, 1968. pp. 135-161.)

Ishino, Iwao
Social and technological change in rural Japan; continuities and discontinuities. (Robert J. Smith, ed. Japanese culture; its development and characteristics. Chicago, Aldine Pub. Co., 1962. pp. 100-114)

Kaneda, Hiromitsu
Long-term changes in food consumption patterns in Japan. (Kazushi Ohkawa, ed. Agriculture and economic growth; Japan's experience. Princeton, N.J. Princeton University Press, 1970. pp. 398-433, Bibl. pp. 428-429)

Kato, Yuzuru
Development of long-term agricultural credit. (Kazushi Ohkawa, ed. Agriculture and economic growth; Japan's experience. Princeton, N.J., Princeton University Press, 1970. pp. 324-351. Bibl. pp. 347-348)

Ladejinsky, W. I.
Agriculture. (Hugh Borton, ed. Japan. Ithaca, N.Y., Cornell University Press, 1950. pp. 46-63)

Murakami, Setsutaro
The formation of citrus growing areas in Japan. (International Geographical Union. Regional conference in Japan, 1957; proceedings of IGU regional conference in Japan. Tokyo, 1959. pp. 420-428)

Nakamura, James I.
Growth of Japanese agriculture, 1875-1920. (W. W. Lockwood, ed. The state and economic enterprise in Japan. Princeton, Princeton Univ. Press, 1965. pp. 249-324)

Nakayama, Seiki
Long-term change in food consumption in Japan. (Committee for Translation of Japanese Economic Studies. Translations of Japanese economic studies. no.26. Tokyo, International House of Japan, 1959-64. 23p.)

Namiki, Masayoshi
The farm population in the national economy before and after World War II. (Thomas C. Smith, ed. City and village in Japan. Chicago, Univ. of Chicago Press, 1960. pp. 29-42)

Nghiep, Le Thanh and Yujiro Hayami
Mobilizing slack resources for economic development; the summer-fall rearing technology of sericulture in Japan. (International Development Center of Japan. Papers and proceedings of the conference on Japan's historical development experience and contemporary developing countries; issues for comparative analysis. Feb. 11-16, 1978. Tokyo, 1978. pp. 233-248)

Noda, Tsutomu
Savings of farm households. (K. Ohkawa, ed. Agriculture and economic growth; Japan's experience. Princeton, Princeton University Press, 1970. pp. 352-373, Bibl. pp. 372-373)

Ohkawa, Kazushi
Agriculture and turning-points in the economic growth. (Seiichi, Tobata. The modernization of Japan - I. Tokyo, Institute of Asian Economic Affairs, 1966. pp. 136-154)

Ohkawa, Kazushi
Concurrent growth of agriculture with industry; a study of the Japanese case. (Roger N. Diey, ed. International exploration of agricultural economics. Ames, Iowa, State University Press, 1964. pp. 201-212)

Ohkawa, Kazushi
Phases of agricultural development and economic growth. (Kazushi Ohkawa, ed. Agriculture and economic growth; Japan's experience. Princeton, N.J., Princeton University Press, 1970. pp. 3-36. Bibl. pp. 35-36)

Ohkawa, Kazushi and Henry Rosovsky
The role of agriculture in modern Japanese economic development. (Thomas C. Smith, ed. City and village in Japan. Chicago, University of Chicago Press, 1960. pp. 43-68)

Ohkawa, Kazushi, Yutaka Shimizu, and Nobukiyo Takamatsu
Agricultural surplus in an overall performance of savings-investment. (International Development Center of Japan. Papers and proceedings of the conference on Japan's historical development experience and contemporary developing countries; issues for comparative analysis. Feb. 11-16, 1978. Tokyo, 1978. pp. 383-404)

Sawada, Shujiro
Innovation in Japanese agriculture, 1880-1935. (W. W. Lockwood, ed. The state and economic enterprise in Japan. Princeton, Princeton Univ. Press, 1965. pp. 325-351)

Sawada, Shujiro
Technological change in Japanese agriculture; a long-term analysis. (Kazushi Ohkawa, ed. Agriculture and economic growth; Japan's experience. Princeton, N.J., Princeton University Press, 1970. pp. 136-154. Bibl. pp. 153-154)

Shishido, Toshio
Japanese agriculture; productivity trend and development of technique. (Committee for Translation of Japanese Economic Studies. Translations of Japanese economic studies. no.10. Tokyo, International House of Japan, 1959-64. 15p.)

Toyoji, Tanaka
Maki-Hara; the four-field system in Japan. (International Geographical Union. Regional conference in Japan, 1957 ; proceedings of IGU regional conference in Japan. Tokyo, 1959. pp. 497-502)

Tsuchiya, Keizo
Economics of mechanization in small-scale agriculture. (Kazushi Ohkawa, ed. Agriculture and economic growth; Japan's experience. Princeton, N.J., Princeton University Press, 1970. pp. 155-174. Bibl. pp. 168)

Umemura, Mataji
Agriculture and labor supply in the Meiji era. (Kazushi Ohkawa, ed., Agriculture and economic growth; Japan's experience. Princeton, N.J., Princeton University Press, 1970. pp. 175-197. Bibl. pp. 196-197)

Yamada, Saburo and Yujiro Hayami
Agricultural productivity at the beginning of industrialization. (Kazushi Ohkawa, ed. Agriculture and economic growth; Japan's experience. Princeton, N.J., Princeton University Press, 1970. pp. 105-135. Bibl. 126-127)

Yamada, Saburo, and Yujiro Hayami
Agriculture. (Kazushi Ohkawa, and Yujiro Hayami, ed. Economic growth; the Japanese experience since the Meiji era; proceedings of the second conference held by the Japan Economic Research Centre, June 26-July 1, 1972 in Japan. Tokyo, Japan Economic Research Centre, 1973. v. 1. pp. 7-25)

Yamada, Saburo and Yujiro Hayami
Production and trade; agriculture. (K. Ohkawa and M. Shinohara, ed. Patterns of Japanese economic development; a quantitative appraisal. New Haven, Yale Univ. Press, 1979. pp. 85-103)

IV.

Akino, Masakatsu and Yujiro Hayami
Agricultural growth in Japan, 1868-1965. Quarterly journal of economics, v. 88, no.3. Aug. 1974. pp. 454-479.

Akino, Masakatsu and Yujiro Hayami
Efficiency and equity in public research rice breeding in Japan's economic development. American journal agricultural economics, v. 57. no.1. Feb. 1957. pp. 1-10.

Danno, Nobuo
Rice cultivation. Japan quarterly, v. 6, no.1. Jan./Mar. 1959. Changing Japan 7. pp. 111-119.

Dore, Ronald P.
Agricultural improvement in Japan; 1870-1900. Economic development and cultural change, v. 9, no.1. Oct. 1960. pp. 69-91.

Fujii, Sadayoshi
On "Makihata" on Oki Island. Bullein of University of Osaka Prefecture, series D. v. 2, 1958. pp. 124-132.

Harano, Kazumasa
The structural and technological changes in the pre-war Japanese agriculture. Bulletin of University of Osaka Prefecture, series D, v. 10. 1966. pp. 34-51.

Havens, Thomas R. H.
Kato Knaji (1884-1965) and the spirit of agriculture in modern Japan. Monumenta Nipponica, v. 25, nos.3/4. pp. 249-266.

Hayami, Yujiro
A critical note on professor Tang's model of Japanese agricultural development. Riron keizaigaku, v. 15, no.3. Aug. 1965. pp. 47-54.

Hayami, Yujiro
Demand for fertilizer in the course of Japanese agricultural development. Journal of farm economics, v. 46, no.4. Nov. 1964. pp. 766-779.

Hayami, Yujiro
Elements of induced innovation; a historical perspective for the green revolution. Explorations in entrepreneurial history, v. 8, no.4. Summer 1971. pp. 445-472.

Hayami, Yujiro
Innovation in the fertilizer industry and agricultural development; the Japanese experience. Journal of farm economics, v. 49, no.2. May 1967. pp. 403-412.

Hayami, Yujiro
Japan's rice policy in historical perspective. Food Research Institute studies, v. 14, no.4. 1975. pp. 359-380.

Hayami, Yujiro
On the Japanese experience of agricultural growth. Rural economic problems v. 4, no.2. May 1968. pp. 79-88.

Hayami, Yujiro
Rice policy in Japan's economic development. American journal of agricultural economics, v. 54, no.1. Feb. 1972. pp. 19-31.

Henmi, Kenzo
Japan's agriculture and anticipated trade liberalization. National Research Institute of Agriculture bulletin, no.6. 1961. 36p.

Ito, Akira
The decline of sericulture and related shifts in Japan's dryland field agriculture since 1930. Rural economic problems, v. 1, no.1. May 1964. pp. 25-44.

Ito, Takeo
Permanent appeal of silk. Contemporary Japan, v. 23, no.7/9. 1955. pp. 521-528.

Johnston, Bruce F.
Agricultural development and economic transformation; a comparative study of the Japanese experience. Food Research Institute studies, v. 3, no.3. 1963. pp. 223-276. Bibl. pp. 274-276.

Johnston, Bruce F.
Agricultural productivity and economic development in Japan. Journal of political economy, v. 59, no.6. Dec. 1961. pp. 498-513.

Kajiura, Minoru
Fruit in plenty. Japan quarterly, v. 9, no.2. Apr./June 1962. Changing Japan 19. pp. 227-233.

Kaneda, Hiromitsu
Long-term changes in food consumption patterns in Japan, 1878-1964. Food Research Institute studies, v. 8, no.1. 1968. pp. 3-32.

Kaneda, Hiromitsu
Substitution of labor and non-labor inputs and technological change in Japanese agriculture. Review of economics and statistics, 47. May 1965.

Kato, Yuzuru
Mechanisms for the outflow of funds from agriculture into industry in Japan. Rural economic problems, Dec. 1966. pp. 1-20.

Kawano, Shigeto
Capital accumulation and agriculture. *Annals of the Histotsubashi academy*, v. 3, no.1. Oct. 1952. pp. 102-113.

Kayo, Nobufumi
The characteristics of heavy applications of fertilizers in Japanese agriculture. *Developing economies*, v. 2, no.4. Dec. 1964. pp. 373-396.

Nakayama, Seiki
Lang-term changes in food consumption in Japan. *Developing economies*, v. 7, no.2. June 1969. pp. 220-232.

Namiki, Masayoshi
The farm population in the national economy before and after World War II. *Economic development and cultural change*, v. 9, no.1. pt.2. Oct. 1960. pp. 29-42.

Noda, Tsutomu
Labor's relative share in the Japanese agriculture since 1878. *Annals of the Hitotsubashi academy*, v. 9, no.2. Apr. 1959. pp.233-243.

Ogino, Yoshio
The dairy industry. *Japan quarterly*, v. 10, no.1. Jan./Mar. 1963. Changing Japan 21. pp. 107-114.

Ogura, Takekazu
Recent agrarian problems in Japan. *Developing economies*, v. 4, no.2. June 1966. pp. 151-170.

Ohkawa, Kazushi
Agriculture and the turning-points in economic growth. *Developing economies*, v. 3, no.4. Dec. 1965. pp. 471-486.

Pitts, Forrest R.
Rural prosperity in Japan. *Univ. of Michigan, Center for Japanese studies occasional papers*, no.8. 1964. --. 97-124.

Rosovsky, H. and K. Ohkawa
The indinenous components in the modern Japanese economy. *Economic development and cultural change*, v. 9, no.3. Apr. 1961. pp. 476-506.

Rosovsky, H. and K. Ohkawa
The role of agriculture in modern Japanese economic development. *Economic development and cultural change*, v. 9, no.1. Oct. 1961. pp. 43-67.

Saito, Yukio
Thought in the development modern agriculture science in Japan. *Rural economic problems*, v. 2, no.2. NOv. 1965. pp. 1-21.

Takabe, Yoshito
Some problems in agriculture in the suburban districts of cities. *Bulletin of University of Osaka Prefecture*, series D. v. 2. 1958. pp. 44-53.

Takabe, Yoshito
The transition of agricultural structure in Japan. *Bulletin of University of Osaka Prefecture*, series D. V. 5. 1961. pp. 16-21.

Tang, Anthony M.
Research and education in Japanese agricultural development, 1880-1938. I-II. *Rironkeizaigaku*,
I: v. 13, no.2. Feb. 1963. pp. 27-41.
II: v. 13, no.3. May, 1963. pp. 91-99.

Teruoka, Shūzō
Japanese capitalism and its agricultural problems, culminating in the rice riots. *Developing economies*, v. 4, no.4. Dec. 1966. pp. 472-498.

Umemura, Mataji
Agriculture and labour supply in Japan in the Meiji era. *Developing economies*, v. 3, no.3. Sept. 1965. pp. 269-285.

Yamada, Saburo
Changes in output and in conventional and non-conventional inputs in Japanese agriculture since 1880. Food Research Institute studies, v. 7, no.3. 1967. pp. 371-413.

Yamauchi, Toyoji
Actuarial structure of crop insurance in Japan and appraisal on its benefits. Bullein of University of Osaka Prefecture, series D. v. 18. 1974. pp. 11-42.

INTERNATIONAL COMPARISON

I.

Hayami, Yujiro
A century of agricultural growth in Japan; its relevance to Asian development. [Tokyo] Univ. of Tokyo Press, [1975]
248p.

Hayami, Yujiro and Vermon W. Ruttan
Agricultural development; an international perspective. Baltimore, Johns Hopkins Press, 1971.
xiv. 367p.

Nair, Kusum
The lonely furrow; farming in the United States, Japan and India. Ann Arbor, Univ. of Michigan Press, 1969.
314p. maps.

Nair, Kusum
Three bowls of rice; India and Japan, a century of effort. East Lansing, Michigan State Univ. Press, 1973.
228p.

II.

Ishikawa, Shigeru
Conditions for agricultural development in developing Asian countries; an appraisal of the usefulness of Japan's experiences. (Committee for Translation of Japanese Economic Studies. Translations of Japanese economic studies. no.42. Tokyo, International House of Japan, 1959-64. 69p.)

Johnston, Bruce F.
The Japanese model of agricultural development; its relevance to developing nations. (Kazushi Ohkawa, ed. Agriculture and economic growth; Japan's experience. Princeton, Princeton University Press, 1970. pp. 58-104. Bibl. 99-102)

Kikuchi, Masao and Yujiro Hayamai
Agricultural growth against a land resource constraint; a comparative history of Japan, Taiwan, Korea and the Philippines. (International Development Center of Japan. Papers and proceedings of the conference on Japan's historical development experience and contemporary developing countries; issues for comparative analysis. Feb. 11-16, 1978. Tokyo, 1978. pp. 53-82)

Nakamura, James I.
Incentives, productivity gaps and agricultural growth rates in prewar Japan, Taiwan and Korea. (B. Silberman and H. Harootunian, ed. Japan in crisis. Princeton, Princeton University Press, 1974. pp. 329-373)

III.

Sawai Boonma (Boonma, Sawai).
Agricultural contributions to economic development; a study of postwar Thailand and Meiji Japan. Ph.D. 1974. Claremont Graduate School.
275p.

IV.

Hayami, Yujiro and V. Ruttan
Factor prices and technical change in agricultural development; the U. S. and Japan, 1880-1960. _Journal of political economy_, v. 78, no.5. Sept./Oct. 1970. pp. 1115-1141.

Hayami, Yujiro and V. Ruttan
Korean rice, Taiwan rice, and Japanese agricultural stagnation; an economic consequence of colonialism. _Quarterly journal of economics_, v. 84, no.4. Nov. 1970. pp. 562-589.

Johnston, Bruce F.
Agriculture and economic development; the relevance of the Japanese experience. _Food Research Institute studies_, v. 6, no.3. 1966. pp. 251-312.

Kato, Yuzuru
Sources of loanable funds of agricultural credit institutions in Asia - Japan's experience. _Developing economies_, v. 10, no.2. June 1972. pp. 126-140.

Kikuchi, Masao and Yujiro Hayami
Agricultural growth against a land resource constraint; a comparative history of Japan, Taiwan, Korea and the Philippines. _Journal of economic history_, v. 37, no.4. Dec. 1978. pp. 839-864.

Ohkawa, Kazushi
International comparisons of productivity in agriculture. _National Research Institute of Agriculture bulletin_, no.1. 1949. 35p.

LAND TENURE SYSTEM

I.

Dore, Ronald Philip
Land reform in Japan. London, Oxford Univ. Press, 1959. 51op. illus. maps.

Ogura, Takekazu
Agrarian problems and agricultural policy in Japan; a historical sketch. Tokyo, Institute of Asian Economic Affairs, 1967. 62p. (I. A. E. A. occasional papers, series no.1)

Waswo, Ann
Japanese landlords; the decline of a rural elite. Berkeley, Univ. of California Press, 1977. viii, 152p.

II.

Dore, Ronald P.
Land reform and Japan's economic development. (Seiichi, Tobata The modernization of Japan - I. Tokyo, Institute of Asian Economic Affairs, 1966. pp. 155-164)

Kawano, Shigetō
Effects of the land reform on consumption and investment of farmers. (K. Ohkawa, ed. Agriculture and economic growth; Japan's experience. Princeton, Princeton Univ. Press, 1970. pp. 374-397)

Scott, J. W. Robertson
The peasants; the most exacting crop in the world. (Jon Livingston, ed., Imperial Japan, 1800-1945. New York, Pantheon Books, 1973. pp. 26-33)

Wakukawa, Seiyei
Agriculture; the tenant movement. (Jon Livingston, ed. Imperial Japan, 1800-1945. New York, Pantheon Books, 1973. pp. 251-255)

Waswo, Ann
The origins of tenant unrest. (B. Silberman and H. Harootunian, ed. Japan in crisis. Princeton, Princeton University Press, 1974. pp. 374-397)

III.

Waswo, Barbara Ann Lardner
Landlords and social change in prewar Japan. Ph.D. 1969. Stanford University.
217p.

IV.

Beaskey, W. G.
Feudal revenue in Japan at the time of the Meiji restoration. Journal of Asian studies, v. 19, no.3. May 1960. pp. 255-272.

Bird, Richard M.
Land taxation and economic development, the model of Meiji Japan. Journal of development studies, v. 13, no.2. Jan. 1977. pp. 162-174. Bibl. pp. 173-174.

Dore, Ronald P.
Land reform and Japan's economic development. Developing economies, v. 3, no.4. Dec. 1965. pp. 487-496.

Dore, Ronald P.
The Meiji landlords; good or bad? Journal of Asian studies, v. 18, no.3. May 1959. pp. 343-355.

Johnson, Erwin H.
Land tax and its impact on use and ownership in rural Japan. Economic development and cultural change, v. 19, no.1. Oct. 1970. pp. 49-71.

Kondo, Yasuo
The landreform in Japan. National Research Institute of Agriculture bulletin, no. 2. 1952.
36p.

Nakamura, James I
Meiji land reform, redistribution of income, and saving from agriculture. Economic development and cultural change, v. 14, no.4. July 1966. pp. 428-439.

Seki, Junya
The historical meaning of the revision of the land tax system. Kyoto University economic review, v. 26, no.2. Oct. 1956. pp. 47-70.

Smith, Thomas C.
Landlords and rural capitalists in the modernization of Japan. Journal of economic history, v. 16, no.2. June 1956. pp. 165-181.

Takigawa, Tsutomu
Historical background of agricultural land reform in Japan. Developing economies, v. 10, no.3. Sept. 1972. pp. 290-328.

VILLAGE STUDIES

I.

Beardsley, Richard K., Joh W. Hall, and Robert E. Ward
Village Japan. Chicago, University of Chicago Press, 1959.
498p. illus. maps.

Dore, Ronald Philip
Shinohata; a portrait of a village. N.Y., Pantheon Books, 1978.
322p.

Embree, John F.
A Japanese village; Suye mura. London, Kegan Paul, 1946.
268p. illus. maps. (The international library of sociology and social reconstruction)

Fukutake, Tadashi
Japanese rural society; China, India, Japan, tr. by R. P. Dore. Seattle, Univ. of Washington Press, 1967.
207p. illus. maps.
also published by Tokyo, Oxford Univ. Press.

Keio Daigaku Kujukuri Shakai-chosa Iinkai. (Keio University, Kujukuri Research Committee)
Kujukurihama; study of fishing community in Japan. Tokyo, 1958.
166p. maps.

Kokusai Kirisutokyo Daigaku (International Chritian Univ.),
The power structure in a rural community; the case of Matsuzawa Mura. Tokyo, 1960.
45p.

Nakane, Chie
Kinship and economic organization in rural Japan. London, Univ. of London Press, 1967.
203p. illus. maps. (London School of Economics monographs on social anthropology)

Norbeck, Edward
Takashima; a Japanese fishing community. Salt Lake City, Univ. of Utah Press, 1954.
232p. illus. maps.

Shimpo, Mitsuru
Three decades in Shiwa; economic development and social change in a Japanese farming community. Vancouver, Univ. of British Columbia Press, 1976.
141p.

Supreme Commander for the Allied Powers.
Natural Resources Section
The Japanese village in transition, by Arthur F. Raper and others. Tokyo, 1950.
272p. illus.

Ushiomi, Toshitaka
Forestry and mountain village communities in Japan; a study of human relations. Tokyo, Kokusai Bunka Shinkokai, 1964.
107p. illus. (Series on Japanese life and culture).

II.

Embree, John
Labor, peasants, women, conscription, repression; Suye mura, the life history of the individual. (Jon Livingston, ed. Imperial Japan, 1800-1945. New York, Pantheon Books, 1973. pp. 439-444)

Fukutake, Tadashi
Agriculture; landlords and village society. (Jon Livingston, ed. Imperial Japan, 1800-1945. New York, Pantheon Books, 1973. pp. 240-244)

Fukutake, Tadashi
Agriculture; the power structure of the hamlet. (Jon Livingston, ed. Imperial Japan, 1800-1945. New York, Pantheon Books, 1973. pp. 245-250)

Fukutake Tadashi
Village community ("Buraku") in Japan and its democratization. (Robert J. Smith, ed. Japanese culture; its development and characteristics. Chicago, Aldine Pub. Co., 1962. pp. 86-90)

Johnson, Erwin H.
Status changes in hamlet structure accompanying modernization. (Ronald P. Dore, ed. Aspects of social change in modern Japan. Princeton, Princeton University Press, 1967. pp. 153-183)

Steiner, Kurt
Popular political participation and political development in Japan; the rural level. (Robert E. Ward, ed. Political development in modern Japan. Princeton, Princeton University Press, 1968. pp. 213-248)

Yanagida, Kunio
The countryside and the cities; from the village to the factory. (Jon Livingston, ed. Imperial Japan, 1800-1945, New York, Pantheon Books, 1973. pp. 132-134)

III.

Bedford, Yukiko Numata
Modernization of a Japanese village; Burakism and its spatial expression. Ph.D. 1978. The University of Michigan.
309p.

IV.

Beardsley, Richard K.
The household in the status system of Japanese villages. Univ. of Michigan, Center for Japanese studies occasional paper, no. 1. 1951. pp. 62-74.

Cornell, John B.
Dozoku; an example of evolution and transition in Japanese village society. Comparative studies in society and history, v. 6, no.4. July 1964. pp. 449-480.

Cornell, John B. and Robert J. Smith
Two Japanese villages; Matsunagi, a Japanese mountain community, Kurusu, a Japanese agricultural community. Univ. of Michigan, Center for Japanese studies occasional papers, no. 5, 1956. 232p.

Davis, Winston
Parish guilds and political culture in village Japan. Journal of Asian studies. v. 36, no.1. Nov. 1976. pp. 25-36.

Ōuchi, Tsutomu
Agricultural depression and Japanese villages. Developing economies, v. 5, no.4. Dec. 1967. pp. 597-627.

Smith, Robert J.
Cooperative forms in a Japanese agricultural community. Univ. of Michigan, Center for Japanese studies occasional papers, no.3, 1952. pp. 59-70.

FISHING INDUSTRY

IV.

Asano, Nagamitsu
Japan's deep-sea fishing industry. Japan quarterly, v. 5, no.2. Apr./June 1958. Changing Japan 4. pp. 236-248.

Comitini, Salvatore
Marine resources exploitation and management in the economic development of Japan. Economic development and cultural change. v. 14, no.4. July 1966. pp. 414-427.

INDUSTRIES

GENERAL

I.

Ajia Kyokai (Society for Economic Cooperation in Asia)
The major industry and its technique in Japan. Tokyo, 1954.
106p. illus.

Hadley, Eleanor M.
Antitrust in Japan. Princeton, N.J., Princeton Univ. Press, 1970.
528p.

II.

Lockwood, William W.
Industrial development. (Hugh Borton ed. Japan. Ithaca, N.Y., Cornell Univetsity Press, 1950. pp. 64-80)

Shinohara, Miyohei
Manufacturing. (Kazushi Ohkawa and Yujiro Hayami, ed. Economic growth; the Japanese experience since the Meiji era: proceedings of the second conference held by the Japan Economic Research Centre, June 26-July 1, 1972 in Japan. Tokyo, Japan Economic Research Centre, 1973. v. 1. pp. 26-37)

Yamazawa, Ippei
Strategy of industrial development; the Japanese experience. (Nagatoshi Suzuki, ed. Asian industrial development. Tokyo, Institute of Developing Economics, 1975. pp. 214-348)

Yoshihara, Kunio
Productivity change in the manufacturing sector, 1906-1965. (Economic growth; the Japanese experience since in the Meiji era; proceedings of the second conference held by the Japan Economic Research Centre, June 26-July 1, 1972 in Japan. Tokyo, Japan Economic Research Centre, 1973. v. 1. pp. 269-285)

III.

Nakamura, Toru
Dual structure reconsidered; structural analysis of firms in Japan's manufacturing. Ph.D. 1976. Claremont Graduate School. 112p.

IV.

Aki, Koichi
Industrial development and technological progress in Japan. Asian affairs, v. 1, no.2. June 1956. pp. 176-188.

Fujii, Shigeru
The development of Japanese industries from standpoint of rate of growth. Kobe University economic review, no. 1. 1955. pp. 29-44.

Imai, Ken-ichi
The growth of firms in the Japanese manufacturing industries. Hitotsubashi journal of commerce and management, v. 4, no.1. Nov. 1966. pp. 59-77. bibl. 76-77.

Nakamura, Takafusa
The modern industries and the traditional industries; at the early stage of the Japanese economy. Developing economies, v. 4, no.4. Dec. 1966. pp. 567-593.

HEAVY INDUSTRIES

I.

Kamiya, Shotaro
My life with Toyota. Toyota Motor Sales Co., Ltd., 1976. 141p.

Yamamura, Kozo
The decade of sowing; absorption of Western technology by the electric machinery and the machine tool industries of Japan during the 1920s; paper presented at the Conference on Japanese-American relations during the 1916-1931 period, held under the auspices of the Social Science Research Council in Kauai, Hawaii, Jan. 1975.

II.

Ando, Yoshio
The formation of heavy industry; one of the processes of industrialization in the Meiji period. (Seiichi, Tobata), ed. The modernization of Japan - I. Tokyo, Institute of Asian Economic Affairs, 1966. pp. 115-135)

Blumenthal, Tuvia
The Japanese shipbuilding industry. (Hugh Patrick, ed. Japanese industrialization and its social consequences. Berkeley, University of California Press, 1976. pp. 129-160)

III.

Burton, William Donald
The origins of the modern Japanese iron and steel industry, with special reference to Mito and Kamaishi, 1853-1901. Ph.D. 1972. University of London.
672p.

Chang, Chan Sup.
The Japanese motor vehicle industry; a study of the history of the Japanese motor vehicle industry and the impact of the Japanese motor vehicles on the U.S. Market. Ph.D. 1974.
255p.

D'Cruz, Joseph Rudolph
Quasi integration in raw material markets; the overseas procurement of coking coal by the Japanese steel industry. D. B. A. 1979, Harvard University.
356p.

Rice, Richard Bruce
Hitachi; Japanese industry in an era of militarism, 1937-1945. Ph.D. 1974. Harvard University.
v, 301p.

IV.

Ando, Yoshio
The formation of heavy industry; one of the processes of industrialization in the Meiji period. Developing economies, v. 3, no.4. Dec. 1965. pp. 450-470.

Azami, Eikichi
The shipbuilding industry; past and present. Japan quarterly, v. 5, no.3. Jul./Sept. 1958. Changing Japan 5. pp. 370-380.

Broadbridge, Seymour
Shipbuilding and the state in Japan since the 1850s. Modern Asian studies, v. 11, pt.4. Oct. 1977. pp. 601-613.

Inoue, Tadakatsu
Rise of modern shipbuilding in Japan and promoters. Kobe economic and business review, v. 15. 168. pp. 29-38.

Kuroda, Chikara
Machine industry of Japan and Southeast Asia. Contemporary Japan, v. 23, no.7/9. 1955. pp. 495-504.

McMaster, John
The Takashima Mine; British capital and Japanese industrialization. Business history review, v. 37, no.3. Autumn 1963. pp. 217-239.

Ono, Kazuichiro and Hitaro Namba
The growth of iron and steel industry in Japan and the problems of raw materials (I) (II). Kyoto University economic review, v. 25, no.1. Apr. 1955. pp. 11-41. no.2. Oct. 1955. pp. 50-69.

Tsuji, Yutaka
Japan's automobile industry. Japan quarterly, v. 6, no.3. July/Sept. 1959. Changing Japan 9. pp. 364-372.

Yamazawa, Ippei
Industry growth and foreign trade; a study of Japan's steel industry. Hitotsubashi journal of economics, v. 12, no.2. Feb. 1972. pp. 41-60.

POWER INDUSTRIES

II.

Minami, Ryoshin
The introduction of electric power and its impact on the manufacturing industries; with special reference to smaller scale plants. (Hugh Patrick, ed. Japanese industrialization and social consequences. Berkeley, University of California Press, 1976. pp. 299-326)

Minami, Ryoshin
Production, cost and income distribution of the electric supply industry in pre-war Japan. (Committee for Translation of Japanese Economic Studies. Translations of Japanese economic studies. no.39. Tokyo, International House of Japan. 1959-64. 20p.)

IV.

Erselcuk, Muzaffer
Electricity in Japan. Far Eastern quarterly, v. 6. no.3. May 1947. pp. 283-293.

Ishimitsu, Tohru
Energy inputs and the economic growth in Japan, 1875-1962. Kobe University economic review, no. 10. 1964. pp. 29-62.

Minami, Ryoshin
Production, const and income distribution of the electric supply industry in pre-war Japan. Hitotsubashi journal of economics. v. 6, no.1. June 1965. pp. 62-73.

Takahashi, Saburō
The electric power industry. Japan quarterly, v. 6, no.2. Apr./June 1959. Changing Japan 8. pp. 240-250.

TEXTILE INDUSTRIES

I.

Aoki, Keizo
The cotton industry of Japan. Tokyo, Japan Society for the Promotion of Science, 1956.

Nihon Boseki Kyokai (All Japan Cotton Spinners' Association)
The story of the Japanese cotton textile industry. Osaka, 1957. 90p.

Seki, Keizo
The cotton industry of Japan. Tokyo, Japan Society for the Promotion of Science, 1956. 417p.

II.

Ono, Akira and Shiro Fujino
Textile industry. (Kazushi Ohkawa and Yujiro Hayami, ed. Economic growth; the Japanese experience since the Meiji era; proceedings of the second conference held by the Japan Economic Research Centre, June 26-July 1, 1972 in Japan. Tokyo, Japan Economic Research Centre, 1973. v. 1. pp. 154-164)

Sugiyama, K.
Trade credit and the development of the cotton spinning industry; its role and background. (Keiichiro Nakagawa, ed. Marketing and finance in the course of industrialization; proceedings of the 3rd Fuji Conference. Tokyo, University of Tokyo Press, 1978. pp. 59-82)

III.

Chung, Young Yang
The origins and historical development of the embroidery of China, Japan and Korea. Ph.D. 1976. New York Univerwity. 307p.

Saxonhouse, Gary Roger
Productivity change in the Japanese cotton spinning industry, 1891-1935. Ph.D. 1971. Yale University. 142p.

IV.

Iyemoto, Hidetaro
A measurement of Douglas production function for Japan's cotton industry during the pre-war period. Kobe University economic review, no. 12. 1966. pp. 1-8.

Nakagawa, Keiichiro, and Henry Rosovsky
The case of the dying Kimono; the influence of changing fashions on the development of the Japanese woolden industry. Business history review, v. 37, no.1/2. Spring/summer 1963. pp. 59-80.

Ōhara, Soichirō
From cotton to vinylon; a short history of the textile industry. Japan quarterly, v. 4. no.4. Oct./Dec. 1957. Changing Japan 2. pp. 519-522.

Saxonhouse, Gary R.
Productivity change and labor absorption in Japanese cotton spinning 1891-1935. Quarterly journal of economics, v. 91. no.2. May 1977. pp. 195-220.

Tagawa, Shin-ichi
Japan's cotton industry. Contemporary Japan, v. 23. no.7/9. 1955. pp. 505-520.

Ueno, Hiroya
Investment behavior in the Japanese cotton spinning industry, 1916-1934. Econometrica, v. 29. no.1. Jan. 1961. pp. 44-57.

OTHERS

I.

Emi, Koichi
Essays on the service industry and social security in Japan. Tokyo, Kinokuniya Book-store Co., Ltd., 1978. xi, 186p.

Narita, Kiyofusa
Japanese paper-making. Tokyo, Hokuseido, 1954. 60p. illus.

II.

Nishimura, Matsuo
Traditional manufacturing industry in Japan. (International Geographical Union. Regional conference in Japan, 1957. Proceedings of IGU regional conference in Japan. Tokyo, 1959. p. 439)

IV.

Ina, Nobuo
Japan's photographic industry. Japan quarterly, v. 5, no.1. Oct./Dec. 1958. Changing Japan 6. pp. 507-514.

Mishima, Yasuo
The industrial revolution in pottery in Japan - Seto and Nagoya. Keio University economic review, v. 25, no.2. Oct. 1955. pp. 31-49.

Nomura, Torasaburo
Historical development of public warehousing industry in Japan. Annals of the School of Business Administration, Kobe Univ., no. 2. 1958. pp. 57-73.

Ueda, Toshiro
The beer-brewing industry. Japan quarterly, v. 6, no.4. Oct./Dec. 1959. Changing Japan 10. pp. 502-508.

Yamazaki, Teiichi
Cement industry, as an indicator of industrialization in under-developed countries. Kobe University economic review, no. 3. 1957. pp. 67-78.

SMALL-SCALE INDUSTRIES

I.

Ajia Kyokai (Society for Economic Co-operation in Asia)
The smaller industry in Japan. Tokyo. 1954-57. 117p. illus.

Ono, Keinosuke and Odaka Konosuke
Ancillary farm development in the Japanese automobile industries; selected case studies 1. Tokyo, Hitotsubashi University, 1979. 137p. (Institute of Economic Research, Hitotsubashi University, Discussion paper series, no.24)

United Nations. Economic Commission for Asia and the Far East
Report of the study group of small-scale industry experts on their visit to Japan. Tokyo. 1955. 293p. illus. map.

Vepa, Ram R.
Small industries in Japan. Bombay, Vora, 1967. 237p. illus.

Yamanaka, Tokutaro
Small business - in Japan's economic progress. Tokyo, Asahi Evening News, 1971. 140p.

Yamanaka, Tokutaro and Kobayashi Yoshio
The history and structure of Japan's small and medium industries with two specific surveys. Tokyo, Science Council of Japan, 1957. 89p. (Science Council of Japan, economic series, no.15)

II.

Ballon, Robert J.
The formation of an industrial society (1868-1914) (Robert J. Ballon, ed. Doing business in Japan, 2d ed. Tokyo, Sophia Univ., 1968. pp. 37-51)

Fujita, Keizo
Short history of small enterprises in Japan. (Tokutaro, Yamanaka comp. Small business in Japan. Tokyo. Japan Times, 1960. pp. 10-20)

Odaka, Konosuke
The place of medium- and small-scale firms in the development of the automobile industry; a study of Japan's experience. (International Development Center of Japan. Papers and proceedings of the conference on Japan's historical development experience and contemporary developing countries; issues for comparative analysis. Feb. 11-16, 1978. Tokyo, 1978. pp. 121-152)

IV.

Figgess, John
Japanese ceramics; a living tradition. Asian affairs (J. of the Royal Society for Asian Affairs) v. 8, pt. 2. June 1977. pp. 152-156.

Fujii, Shigeru
Characteristics and modernization of match industry - a case of small business in Japan. Kobe University economic review, no.9. 1963. pp. 13-30.

Fujita, Keizo
Management structure of small and medium enterprises. Asia affairs, v. 2, no.2. June 1957. pp. 123-141.

Inaba, Noboru
Development of the problem of medium and small industries in Japan. Annals of the School of Business Administration, Kobe Univ., no. 9. 1965. pp. 45-64.

Kawano, Shigetō
Implementation of the industrial cooperative system in the Meiji era. Developing economies, v. 15, no.4. Dec. 1977. pp. 462-486.

Pelzel, J. C.
The small industrialists in Japan. Explorations in entrepreneurial history, 7. Dec. 1954.

Reubens, Edwin P.
Small-scale industry in Japan. Quarterly journal of economics, v. 61, no.4. Aug. 1947. pp. 577-604.

Yamanaka, Tokutaro
Illogicality in Japanese small business; a comparative survey of earnings of small manufacturing plants in Japan, Britain and the United States. Annals of the Hitotsubashi academy, v. 10. no.2. Dec. 1959. pp. 141-157.

Yamanaka, Tokutaro
Japanese small industries during the industrial revolution. Annals of the Hitotsubashi academy, v. 2. no.1. Oct. 1951. pp. 15-36.

Yamanaka, Tokutaro
The nature of small industries; a survey of the economic interpretation in Japan. Annals of the Hitotsubashi academy, v. 4. no.1 Oct. 1953. pp. 1-14.

Yamanaka, Tokutaro
Prerequisites for Japanese economy and small-medium industry. Annals of the Hitotsubashi academy, v. 7, no.2. Apr. 1957. pp. 91-114.

MANAGEMENT

I.

Abegglen, James G.
The Japanese factory; aspects of its social organization. Glencoe, Ill., Free Press, 1958.
142p. (Book from the Center for International studies, M.I.T.)

Arai, Shunzo
An intersection of East and West; Japanese business management. Tokyo, Rikugei Pub. House, 1971.
212p.

De Mente, Boye
Japanese manners and ethics in business. Tokyo, East Asia Pub. 1961.
179p.

Dore, Ronald P.
British factory - Japanese factory; the origins of national diversity in industrial relations. London, G. Alen & Unwin, Ltd., 1973.
431p.

Hirschmeier, Johannes
The origins of entrepreneurship in Meiji Japan. Cambridge, Mass., Harvard Univ. Press, 1964.
354p. (Harvard East Asian series).

Hirschmeier, Johannes and Tsunehiko Yui
The development of Japanese business, 1600-1973. London, George Allen & Unwin Ltd., 1975.
340p.

Hunsberger, Warren S.
Japan; lessons in enterprise. Chicago, Curriculum Resources, 1963.
72p. illus. maps.

Long, William A. and K. K. Seo
Management in Japan and India; with reference to the United States. N.Y., Praeger Publishers, 1977.
293p.

Mannari, Hiroshi
The Japanese business leaders. Tokyo, Univ. of Tokyo Press, 1974.
291p.

Marsh, Robert M. and Hiroshi Mannari
Modernization and the Japanese factory. Princeton, N.J., Princeton Univ. Press, 1976.
437p.

Marshall, Byron K.
Capitalism and nationalism in prewar Japan; the ideology of the business elite 1868-1941.
Stanford, Standford Univ. Press, 1967.
163p.

Nakagawa, Keiichiro, ed.
Social order and entrepreneurship; proceedings of the 2nd Fuji Conference, Tokyo, Univ. of Tokyo Press, 1977.
330p. (International conference on Business History 2)
Contents:
- Entrepreneurs and the social order; America, Germany and Japan, by J. Hirschmeier. pp. 3-41. (Comments 1, by T. C. Cochran, pp. 42-45. Comments 2, by S. G. Checkland, pp. 46-48. Comments 3, by J. Kocka, pp. 49-52)
- Cultural factor and British business men, 1815-1914, by S. G. Checkland. pp. 53-82. (Comments, by M. Arai. pp. 83-86)
- Gentlemanship and entrepreneurship, by S. Tsunoyama. pp. 87-104. (Comments, by S. G. Checkland 105-110)
- The social basis of enterprise in the United States, by T. C. Cochran, pp. 111-145. (Comments, by T. Inoue. pp. 146-148)
- Entrepreneurship in a late-comer country; the German case, by J. Kocka, pp. 149-190. (Comments, by H. Watanabe. pp. 191-198)
- Industrialization and "groupism", by H. Hazama. pp. 199-223. (Comments, by J. Kocka. pp. 224-230)
- The tradition of Ie (House) and the industrialization of Japan, by Y. Horie, pp. 231-254. (Comments, by S. Yasuoka, pp. 255-256)
- Local culture and business behavior in Japan, by M. Miyamoto, pp. 257-290. (Comments, by M. Kobayashi. pp. 291-292)
- Entrepreneurship and social order in Southeast Asian countries, by Tien-yi Yang. pp. 293-318. (Comments, by K. Toba. pp. 319-324)
- Summary of concluding discussion, by K. Nakagawa. p. 325.

Nishikawa, Kojiro
Origin of "cash method bookkeeping" in Japan. Tokyo, Science Council of Japan, 1956.
23p. (Science Council of Japan, Economic Series, no.11)

Sueno, Akira
Entrepreneur and gentleman; a case study of a Japanese company, tr. by Neal Donner. Tokyo, Charles E. Tuttle, 1977.
245p.

Yoshino, M. Y.
Japan's managerial system; tradition and innovation. Cambridge, Mass., MIT Press, 1968.
292p.

II.

Ballon, Robert J.
The Japanese dimensions of industrial enterprise. (Robert J. Ballon, ed. The Japanese employee. Tokyo, Sophia University, 1969. pp. 3-40)

Chandler, A. D., Jr.
Institutional integratiion; an approach to comparative studies of the history of large-scale business. (Keiichiro Nakagawa, ed. Strategy and structure of big business; proceedings of the 1st Fuji Conference. Tokyo, Univ. of Tokyo Press. pp. 121-147)

Hazama, H.
Industrialization and "groupism." (Keiichiro, Nakagawa, ed. Social order and entrepreneurship; proceedings of the 2nd Fuji Conference. Tokyo, University of Tokyo Press, 1977. pp. 224-230)

Hirschmeier, Johannes
Entrepreneurs and the social order; America, Germany and Japan, 1870-1900. (Keiichiro Nakagawa, ed. Social order and entrepreneurship; proceedings of the 2nd Fuji Conference. Tokyo, University of Tokyo Press, 1977. pp. 3-41)

Hirschmeier, Johannes
Shibusawa Eiichi; industrial pioneer. (W. W. Lockwood, ed. The state and economic enterprise in Japan. Princeton, Princeton Univ. Press, 1965. pp. 209-247)

Horie, Yasuzo
Modern entrepreneurship in Meiji Japan. (W. W. Lockwood, ed., The state and economic enterprise in Japan, Princeton, Princeton Univ. Press, 1965. pp. 183-208)

Johnson, Erwin
The emergence of a self-conscious entrepreneurial class in rural Japan. (Robert J. Smith, ed. Japanese culture; its development and characteristics. Chicago, Aldine, 1962. pp. 91-99)

Kluge, M.
The role of top management in accelerating economic growth. (Ajia Seisansei Kiko. Top management symposium. Tokyo, 1970. pp. 24-30)

Lockwood, William
Labor and industry; the great combines. (Jon Livingston, ed. Imperial Japan, 1800-1945. New York, Pantheon Books, 1973. pp. 285-290)

Miyamoto, M.
Local culture and business behavior in Japan. (Keiichiro Nakagawa, ed. Social order and entrepreneurship; proceedings of the 2nd Fuji Conference. Tokyo, University of Tokyo Press, 1977. pp. 257-290)

Smith, Thomas C.
Landlords' sons in the business elite. (Thomas C. Smith, ed. City and village in Japan. Chicago, University of Chicago Press, 1960. pp. 93-108) reprinted from Economic development and cultural change, v. 9, no.1. Oct. 1960. pp. 93-107.

Takatera, S.
Introduction and diffusion of depreciation accounting in Japan, 1875-1903. (Keiichiro Nakagawa, ed. Marketing and finance in the course of industrialization; proceedings of the 3rd. Fuji Conference. Tokyo, University of Tokyo Press, 1978. pp. 105-115)

Tsuchiya, M.
Management organization of vertically integrated nonzaibatsu business. (Keiichiro Nakagawa, ed. Strategy and structure of big business; proceedings of the 1st Fuji Conference. Tokyo, Univ. of Tokyo Press. pp. 65-78)

Tsuchiya, Takao
Into the class origins of Meiji enterpreneurs. (Committee for Translation of Japanese Economic Studies. Translations of Japanese economic studies. no.32. Tokyo, International House of Japan, 1959-64. 25p.)

III.

Laker, Joseph Alphonse
Entrepreneurship and the development of the Japanese beer industry, 1872-1937. Ph.D. 1975. Indiana University.
365p.

IV.

Abegglen, J. C. and H. Mannari
Leaders of modern Japan; social origins and mobility. Economic development and cultural change. v. 9. no.1. Oct. 1960. pp. 109-134.

Brown, William
Japanese management; the cultural background. Monumenta Nipponica, v. 21, nos.1/2. 1966. pp. 47-60.

Dore, R. P.
The modernizer as a special case; Japanese factory legislation, 1882-1911. Comparative studies in society and history, v. 2, no.4. Oct. 1969. pp. 433-450.

Fruin, W. Mark
The Japanese company controversy; ideology and organization in a historical perspective. Journal of Japanese studies, v. 4. no.2. Summer 1978. pp. 267-300.

Hazama, Hiroshi
Formation of the management system in Meiji Japan; personnel management in large corporations. Developing economies. v. 15, no.4. Dec. 1977. pp. 402-419.

Hirschmeier, Johonnes
The Japanese spirit of enterprise, 1867-1970. Business history review, v. 44, no.1. Spring 1970. pp. 13-38.

Horie, Yasuzo
Business pioneers of modern Japan. Kyoto University economic review. v. 30, no.2. Oct. 1960. pp. 1-16.

Inoue, Tadakatsu
On business history. Kobe economic and business review, v. 1. 1954. pp. 119-125.

Inoue, Tadakatsu and Yoshiro Ikushima
Company histories in Japan, materials for business history. Kobe economic and business review, v. 6. 1959. pp. 157-188.

Katano, Ichiro
Business income during the inflation in Japan. Annals of the Hitotsubashi academy, v. 4, no.2. Apr. 1954. pp. 98-111.

Kimura, Ki
Dawn of modern industry in Japan. Contemporary Japan, v. 23, no.7/9. July-Aug. 1955. pp. 483-494.

Kusakabe, Yoichi
The development of professional accounting in Japan. Waseda business and economic studies, no.2. 1966. pp. 19-32.

Mano, Osamu
On the development of personnel management in Japan. Hokudai economic papers, v. 4. 1974/1975. pp. 1-10.

Mano, Osamu
On the science of business administration in Japan. Hokudai economic papers, v. 1. 1968/1969. pp. 77-93.

Matsumoto, Masao
The development of managerial accounting in Japan. Annals of the Hitotsubashi academy, v. 4, no.1. Oct. 1953. pp. 40-54.

Ranis, Gustav
The community-centered entrepreneur in Japanese development. Explorations in enterepreneurial history, 13, 1955.

Sekiguchi, Misao
The backgrounds of business creed in Japan. Keio business review, no. 2. 1963. pp. 95-124.

Smith, Thomas C.
Landlords' sons in business elite. Economic development and cultural change, v. 9, no.1. Oct. 1960. pp. 93-107.
cf. Thomas C. Smith, ed. City and village in Japan.

Yamamura, Kozo
Introduction. Explorations in entrepreneurial history, v. 15, no.1. (special issue for Japan) Jan. 1978. pp. 1-10.

Yamamura, Kozo
A re-examination of entrepreneurship in Meiji Japan, 1868-1912. Economic history review, v. 21, no.1. Apr. 1968. pp. 144-158.

ZAIBATSU

I.

Mitsubishi Keizai Kenkyujo. (Mitsubishi Economic Research Institute)
Mitsui-Mitsubishi-Sumitomo; present status of the former Zaibatsu enterprises. Tokyo, 1955. 359p. illus. map.

Nakagawa, Keiichiro, ed.
Strategy and structure of big business; proceedings of the 1st Fuji Conference. Tokyo, Univ. of Tokyo Press. 312p. (International Conference on business History 1)
Contents:
- Business strategy and industrial structure in pre-World War II Japan, by K. Nakagawa. pp. 3-38.
(Comments 1, by A. D. Chandler, Jr. pp. 39-41. Comments 2, by Y. Sakudo, pp. 42-44)
- Management structure and control devices for diversified Zaibatsu business, by H. Morikawa. pp. 45-60.
(Comments, by Y. Mishima. pp. 61-64)
- Management organization of vertically integrated nonzaibatsu business, by M. Tsuchiya. pp. 65-78.
(Comments, by T. Inoue. pp. 79-80)
- The tradition of family business in the strategic decision process and management structure of Zaibatsu business; Mitsui, Sumitomo, and Mitsubishi, by S. Yasuoka. pp. 81-101.
(Comments, by Y. Togai. pp. 102-104)
- The traditional system of middlemen and marketing policies of food manufactures, by T. Yui. pp. 105-114.
(Comments, by K. Toba. pp. 115-120)

- Institutional integration; an approach to comparative studies of history of large-scale business enterprise, by A. D. Chandler, Jr. pp. 121-147. (Comments, by K. Shimokawa. pp. 148-152)
- Comparison of choice of technology among three nations; Great Britain, United States, and Japan, by A. Okochi. pp. 153-170. (Comments, by T. Chokki. pp. 171-176)
- Marketing strategy and market structure in three nations; the United States, the United Kingdom, and Japan, by R. Iwata. pp. 177-195. (Comments 1, by Y. Yamashita. pp. 196-197. Comments 2, by A. D. Chandler, Jr. pp. 198-202)
- Organizational innovation in the McCormick and international harvester companies, by K. Kobayashi. pp. 203-213. (Comments, by A. D. Chandler, Jr. pp. 214-216)
- The strategy and structure of cotton and steel enterprises in Britain, 1900-1939, by S. Yonekawa. pp. 217-257. (Comments, by C. Wilson. pp. 258-264)
- The multinational in historical perspective remarks of professor Charles Wilson pertaining to his paper, by C. Wilson. pp. 265-303. (Comments 1, by Y. Kinugasa. pp. 304-305. Comments 2, by S. Yonekawa. pp. 306-308)
- Summary of concluding discussion, by K. Nakagawa. pp. 309-312.

Roberts, John C.
Mitsui; three centuries of Japanese business. Tokyo, Weatherhill, 1973.
564p.

Russel, Oland D.
The house of Mitsui. Westport, Conn., Greenwood Press, 1970 (reprint)
328p.
Originally published in 1939 by Little Brown and Co., Boston.

II.

Bisson, T. A.
Political economy, 1936-1945; increase in Zaibatsu predominance in wartime Japan.
(Jon Livingston, ed. Imperial Japan, 1800-1945. New York, Pantheon Books, 1973. pp. 458-455)

Bisson, T. A.
Political economy, 1936-1945; the Zaibatsu's Wartime role.
(Jon Livingston, ed. Imperial Japan, 1800-1945. New York, Pantheon Books, 1973. pp. 458-464)

Hadley, Eleanor
Political economy, 1936-1945; the Zaibatsu and the War.
(Jon Livingston, ed. Imperial Japan, 1800-1945. New York, Pantheon Books, 1973. pp. 452-455)

Masaki, H.
The financial characteristics of the Zaibatsu in Japan; the old Zaibatsu and their closed finance. (Keiichiro Nakagawa, ed. Marketing and finance in the course of industrialization; proceedings of the 3rd Fuji Conference. Tokyo, Univ. of Tokyo Press, 1978. pp. 33-54)

Morikawa, H.
Management structure and control devices for diversified Zaibatsu business. (Keiichiro Nakagawa, ed. Strategy and structure of big business; proceedings of the 1st Fuji Conference. Tokyo, Univ. of Tokyo Press. pp. 45-60)

Nakase, T.
The introduction of scientific management in Japan and its characteristics; case studies of companies in the Sumitomo Zaibatsu. (Keiichiro Nakawaga, ed. Labor and management; proceedings of the 4th Fuji Conference. Tokyo, Univ. of Tokyo Press, 1979. pp. 171-202)

Tiedemann, Arthur E.
Big business and politics in prewar Japan. (James William Morley, ed. Dilemmas of growth in prewar Japan. Princeton, Princeton University Press, 1971. pp. 267-316)

Yasuoka, S.
The tradition of family business in the strategic decision process and management structure of Zaibatsu business; Mitsui, Sumitomo, and Mitsubishi. (Keiichiro Nakagawa, ed. Strategy and structure of big business; proceedings of the 1st Fuji Conference. Tokyo, Univ. of Tokyo Press. pp. 81-101)

IV.

Bisson, T. A.
Increase of Zaibatsu predominance in wartime Japan. Pacific affairs, v. 18, no.1. Mar. 1945. pp. 55-61.

Inoue, Tadakatsu
Note on the Zaibatsu combines. Kobe economic and business review, v. 3. 1956. pp. 125-134.

Kokoris, James A.
The Ohara Zaibatsu of Okayama. Univ. of Michigan, Center for Japanese studies occasional papers, no. 8. 1964. pp. 39-58.

Masaki, Kenji
Anti-monopoly law and elimination of excessive concentration of economic power law in Japan. Osaka economic papers, v. 2, no.2. Mar. 1954. pp. 18-31.

Morikawa, Hidemasa
The organizational structure of Mitsubishi and Mitsui Zaibatsu, 1868-1922; a comparative study. Business history review, v. 44, no.1. Spring 1970. pp. 62-83.

Noguchi, Tasuku
The formation of the Japanese Zaibatsu; the political merchant in the original accumulation of capital. Keio business review, no. 16. 1979. pp. 169-187.

Shibagaki, Kazuo
The early history of the Zaibatsu. Developing economies, v. 4, no.4. Dec. 1966. pp. 535-566.

Yamamura, Kozo
The founding of Mitsubishi; a case study in Japanese business history. Business history review, v. 41, no.2 . Summer 1967. pp. 141-160.

Yamamura, Kozo
Zaibatsu, prewar and Zaibatsu, postwar. Journal of Asian studies, v. 23, no.4. Aug. 1964. pp. 539-555.

Yasuoka, Shigeaki
Social background of Zaibatsu in Japan. Doshisha shogaku, v. 30, no.2. Sept. 1978. pp. 1-11.

Yui, Tsunehiko
The personality and career of Hikojiro Nakamigawa, 1881-1901. Business history review, v. 44, no.1. Spring 1970. pp. 39-61.

PUBLIC FINANCE AND PUBLIC ENTERPRISES

I.

Emi, Koichi
Government fiscal activity and economic growth in Japan, 1868-1960. Tokyo, Kinokuniya, 1963.
186p. (Hitotsubashi Univ. economic research series, no.6)

Feldman, Robert A.
Financial upheaval and funds re-channeling; the case of Japan from the panic of 1927 to the end of the Takahashi era, 1936. Unpublished discussion paper. Yale Univ., 1976.

Smith, Thomas C.
Political change and industrial development in Japan; government enterprise, 1868-1880. Stanford, Stanford Univ. Press, 1965. 126p.

II.

Emi, Koichi
Government expenditure. (Kazushi Ohkawa, and Yujiro Hayami, ed. Economic growth; the Japanese experience since the Meiji era; proceedings of the second conference held by the Japan Economic Research Centre, June 26-July 1, 1972 in Japan. Tokyo, Japan Economic Research Centre, 1973. v. 1. pp. 80-94)

Emi, Koichi
The government sector in Japan's development and growth. (Japan Economic Research Centre. Economic growth; the Japanese experience since the Meiji era, proceedings of the second conference, June 26-July 1, 1972. Tokyo, 1973. v. 2. pp. 375-388)

Emi, Koichi
Product allocation; government accounts, expenditure. (K. Ohkawa and M. Shinohara, ed. Patterns of Japanese economic development; a quantitative appraisal. New Haven, Yale Univ. Press, 1979. pp. 196-198)

Ishi, Hiromitsu
Product allocation; government accounts, revenue. (K. Ohkawa and M. Shinohara, ed. Patterns of Japanese economic development, a quantitative appraisal. New Haven, Yale Univ. Press, 1979. pp. 199-264)

Key, Bernard
Prewar Japanese government traditional sector financial investment policy; implications for sectoral growth and welfare. (International Development Center of Japan. Papers and proceedings of the conference on Japan's historical development experience and contemporary developing countries; issues for comparative analysis. Feb. 11-16, 1978. Tokyo, 1978. pp. 405-414)

Kim, Byong Kuk
The role of government for economic development in transition to modern industrialism with special reference to Japan. (International conference on the problems of modernization in Asia, Seoul, 1965. Report. Seoul, Korea University Asiatic Research Center, 1966. pp. 573-585)

Lockwood, William W.
The state and economic enterprise in modern Japan, 1868-1938. (Simon Kuznets W. E. Moore and J. J. Spengler, ed. Economic growth; Brazil, India, Japan. Durham, N.C., Duke University Press, 1955. pp. 537-602)

Oshima, Harry T.
Meiji fiscal policy and economic progress. (W. W. Lockwood, ed., The state and economic enterprise in Japan. Princeton, Princeton Univ. Press, 1965. pp. 353-389)

Takeda, Takao
The financial policy of the Meiji government. (Seiichi, Tobata) ed. The modernization of Japan - I. Tokyo, Institute of Asian Economic Affairs, 1966. pp. 91-114)

III.

Stillson, Richard Thomas
An analysis of financial intermediation in the context of financial development. Ph.D. 1970. Stanford University.
160p.

IV.

Asakura, Koichi
The characteristics of finance in the Meiji period, the period of take-off. Developing economies, v. 5, no.2. June 1967. pp. 274-300.

Furuta, Seiji
The incidence of corporation income tax in Japanese industries, 1920-63. Keio economic studies, v. 7, no.1. 1970. pp. 1-27.

Hirota, S.
A study of iron and steel subsidy. Kyoto University economic review, v. 21, no.2. Oct. 1951. pp. 1-47.

Kimura, Motokazu
Fiscal policy and industrialization in Japan 1868-1905. Annals of the Hitotsubashi academy, v. 6, no.2. Apr. 1956. pp. 12-28.

Kimura, Motokazu
Taxation and capital accounting. Annals of the Hitotsubashi academy, v. 4, no.1. Oct. 1953. pp. 15-39.

Matsuno, Kengo
A brief history of Japan's public finance. Kobe University economic review, no. 9. 1963. pp. 31-40.

Nakayama, Ichiro
The Japanese economy and the role of the government. Hitotsubashi journal of economics, v. 1, no.1. Oct. 1960. pp. 1-12.

Ohkawa, Masazo
The armaments expansion budgets and the Japanese economy after the Russo-Japanese War. Hitotsubashi journal of economics, v. 5, no.2. Jan. 1965. pp. 68-83.

Rosovsky, Henry
Japanese capital formation; the role of the public sector. Journal of economic history, v. 19, no.3. Sept. 1959. pp. 350-375.

Shima, Yasuhiko
Some aspects of expenditures of the Japanese self-defence agency. Kyoto University economic review, v. 25, no.2. Oct. 1955. pp. 10-30.

Taira, Koji
Public assistance in Japan. Journal of Asian studies, v. 27, no.1. Nov. 1967. pp. 95-109.

Takeda, Takao
The financial policy of the Meiji government. Developing economies, v. 3, no.4. Dec. 1965. pp. 427-449.

Takenaka, Tatsuo
A mutural approach between the public and the private enterprise. Annals of the School of Business Administration, Kobe Uuiv., no. 5. 1961. pp. 9-29.

MONEY AND BANKING

I.

Adams, Thomas F. M.
Japanese securities markets; a historical survey. Tokyo, Seihei Okuyama, c1953.
142p.

Adams, Thomas F. M. and Iwao Hoshii
A financial history of the new Japan. Tokyo, Kodansha International, 1972.
547p.

Arai, Masao
Development of local banking in Japan; Period of development of industrial capitalism. Tokyo, Science Council of Japan, 1958.
45p. (Science Council of Japan, Economic Series, no.19)

Fuji Ginko. Chosa-bu. (Fuji Bank, Research Division)
Banking in modern Japan. 2d. ed. Tokyo, 1967.
299p.

Sakurai, Kinichiro
Financial aspects of economic development of Japan, 1868-1958. Tokyo, 1964.
155p. (Science Council of Japan. Division of Economics, Commerce and Business Administration economic series, no.34)

Shinjo, Hiroshi
History of the yen; 100 years of Japense money economy. Kobe, Research Institute for Economic and Business Administration, Kobe Univ. c1962.
205p. (Kobe economic and business research series, no.1)

Shiomi, Saburo
Japan's finance and taxation 1940-1956, tr. by Shotaro Hasegawa, N.Y., Columbia Univ. Press, 1957.
190p.

II.

Cohen, Jerome B.
Financial development. (Hugh Borton, ed. Japan. Ithaca, N.Y., Cornell University Press, 1959. pp. 127-143)

Itoh, Masakichi
Bank debits and deposit turnover in Japan. (Committee for Translation of Japanese Economic Studies. Translations of Japanese economic studies. no.47. Tokyo, International House of Japan, 1959-64. 18p.)

Patrick, Hugh T.
Finance, capital markets and economic growth in Japan. (Arnold W. Samertz, ed., Financial development and economic growth. New York, New York University Press, 1972. pp. 109-139)

Patrick, Hugh T.
Japan, 1868-1914. (Rondo Cameron, ed. Banking in the early stages of industrialization. New York, Oxford Univ. Press, 1967. pp. 239-289)

Ranis, Gustav
The financing of Japanese economic development. (Kazushi Ohkawa, ed. Agriculture and economic growth; Japan's experience. Princeton, N.J., Princeton University Press, 1970. pp. 37-57, Bibl. pp. 57)

Teranishi, Juro and Hugh Patrick
The establishment and early development of banking in Japan; phases and policies prior to World War I. (International Development Center of Japan. Papers and proceedings of the conference on Japan's historical development experience and contemporary developing countries; issues for comparative analysis. Feb. 11-16, 1978. Tokyo, 1978. pp. 349-383.)

Yamamura, Kozo
Japan, 1868-1930; a revised view. (Rondo Cameron, ed. Banking and economic development; some lessons of history. New York, Oxford Univ. Press, 1972. pp. 168-198)

Yoshino, Toshihiko
Excessive dependence of commercial banks on central bank loans in Japanese economic development. (Committee for Translation of Japanese Economic Studies. Translations of Japanese economic studies. no.1. Tokyo, International House of Japan, 1959-64. 33p.)

IV.

Fujita, Masahiro
The banking system in the middle Meiji era (1870-1910). Kobe economic and business review, v. 3. 1956. pp. 55-86.

Fujita, Masahiro
The central banking policy in the Meiji era. Kobe economic and business review, v. 6. 1959. pp. 19-28.

Fujita, Masahiro
The development of overseas banking in Japan in the Meiji era. Kobe economic and business review, v. 4. Oct. 1957. pp. 69-90.

Fujita, Masahiro
The gold standard and banking capital in Japan. Kobe economic and business review, v. 7. 1960. pp. 21-38.

Fukuda, Keitaro
An analysis of securities market in Japan. Annals of the School of Business, Administration, Kobe Univ. no. 1. 1957. pp. 39-58.

Inoue, Tadakatsu
Rise of the mutal financing business in Japan. Kobe economic and business review, v. 10. 1963. pp. 35-40.

Ito, Masakichi
Bank deposit turnover in Japan. Hitotsubashi journal of economics, v. 5, no.2. Jan. 1965. pp. 58-67.

Kato, Toshihiko
Development of Japanese banking system. Annals of the Institute of Social Science. no. 7. 1966. pp. 13-33.

Kenneth A. Leuis, and Kozo Yamamura
Industrialization and interregional interest rate structure, the Japanese case; 1889-1925. Explorations in entrepreneurial history, v. 8, no.4. Summer 1971. pp. 473-499.

Matsumura, Zentaro
Introducing Prof. Shinjo's "history of the yen". Kobe economic and business review, v. 10. 1963. pp. 115-119.

Mizushima, Kazuya
Insurance industry in the formative stage of modern industries during the Meiji period of Japan. Annals of the School of Business Administration, Kobe Univ. no. 11. 1967. pp. 28-47.

Nakamura, Saichi
A brief sketch of trading and monetary development in Japan. Waseda economic papers. no. 6. 1961. pp. 1-22.

Niino, Kojiro
The formation of the Japanese finance capital and its characteristics. Kobe University economic review, no. 2. 1956. pp. 53-68.

Noritake, Yasuo
The development of monetary and banking system in Japan, 1932-1945. Kobe University economic review, no. 2. 1956. pp. 69-78.

Ott, David J.
The financial development of Japan, 1878-1958. Journal of political economy, v. 69, no.2. Apr. 1961. pp. 122-141.

Patrick, Hugh T.
External equilibrium and internal convertibility; financial policy in Meiji Japan. Journal of economic history, v. 25, no.2. June 1965. pp. 187-213.

Sakudō, Yōtarō
The reform of the monetary system in the early years of Meiji. Osaka economic papers, v. 6, no.1. Sept. 1957. pp. 32-47.

Shinjo, Hiroshi
History of yen, its developments in the Japanese economy 1-2. Kobe economic and business review, 1: v. 5. 1958. pp. 1-22. 2: v. 6. 1959. pp. 1-18.

Shoda, Kenichiro
Trade and credit in a local industrial area in the early years of the Meiji era. Waseda economic papers, no. 10. 1967. pp. 47-76.

Takatera, Sadao
Early experiment of depreciation accounting in national bank, 1875-1879. Kyoto University economic review, v. 32, no.1. Apr. 1962. pp. 50-70.

Takatera, Sadao
Introduction and diffusion of depreciation accounting in Japan, 1875-1903. Kyoto University economic review, v. 45, no.1/2. Apr./Oct. 1975. pp. 14-22.

Teranishi, Juro
Availability of safe assets and the process of bank concentration in Japan. Economic development and cultural change, v. 25, no.3. Apr. 1977. pp. 447-470.

Yamaguchi, Shigeru
Interrelations between "Ginme" bar silver, the Mexican silver dollar, and foreign exchange rates during the early Meiji era. Annals of the Hitotsubashi academy, v. 3, no.2. Apr. 1953. pp. 209-226.

Yamamura, Kozo
The role of samurai in the development of modern banking in Japan. Journal of economic history, v. 27, no.2. June 1967. pp. 198-220.

Yoshino, Toshihiko
The creation of the bank of Japan; its western origin and adaptation. Developing economies, v. 15. no.4. Dec. 1977. pp. 381-401.

LABOUR AND LABOUR MOVEMENT

I.

Ayusawa, Iwao
A history of labor in modern Japan. Honolulu, East-West Center Press, 1966.
406p.

Ballon, Robert J., ed.
The Japanese employee. Tokyo, Sophia Univ., 1969.
317p.
Contents:
- The Japanese dimensions of industrial enterprise, by Robert J. Ballon. pp. 3-40.
- Motivational forces in Japanese life, by Maurice Bairy. pp. 41-62.
- Participative employment, by Robert J. Ballon. pp. 63-76.
- The Japanese executive, by Herbert Glazer. pp. 77-98.
- Organizational change, by James C. Abegglen. pp. 99-122.
- Lifelong remuneration system, by Robert J. Ballon. pp. 123-166.
- Labor cost accounting, by Iwao Tomita. pp. 167-178.
- Private pension plans, by Motoshi Isomura. pp. 179-200.
- The labor movement, by Paul Timothy Chang, pp. 201-226.
- Enterprise unionism and wage increases, by Makoto Sakurabayashi. pp. 227-240.
- Labor disputes and their settlement, by Tadashi Hanami. pp. 241-250.
- Personnel management in foreign corporations, by Hirono Ryokichi. pp. 251-272.
- Statistical appendix. pp. 273-306.

Cole, Robert E.
Japanese blue collar; the changing tradition. Berkeley, Univ. of California Press, 1971.
300p.

Cole, Robert E.
Work, mobility, and participation; a comparative study of American and Japanese industry. Berkeley, Calif., Univ. of California Press, 1979.
293p.

Evans, Robert, Jr.
The labor economies of Japan and the United States. N.Y., Praeger, 1971.
276p.

Harada, Shuichi
Labour conditions in Japan.
Reprint ed. N.Y., AMS Press, 1968.
293p.

Large, Stephen S.
The rise of labor in Japan; the Yuaikai, 1912-19. Tokyo, Sophia Univ. Press, 1972.
218p.

Nakagawa, Keiichiro, ed.
Labor and management; proceedings of the 4th Fuji Conference. Tokyo, Univ. of Tokyo Press, 1979.
251p. (International Conference on Business history 4)
Contents:
- Management and labor; the evolution of employer-employee relations in the course of industrial development, by E. Daito. pp. 1-25.
- The formation and characteristics of the work group in Japan, by H. Hazama. pp. 29-42.
- Management and labor in Britain during the period of industrialization, by S. Pollard. pp. 45-73.
- United States labor-management relations, 1860-1930, by R. Ozanne. pp. 77-95.
- Labor-management and industrial relations in Germany, 1870-1930, by W. Fischer. pp. 99-123.
- Traditional labor management in Japan, 1710-1890, by Y. Sakudo, pp. 127-140.
- Labor management in the cotton spinning industry, by T. Chokki, pp. 145-167.
- The introduction of scientific management in Japan and its characteristics - case studies of companies in the Sumitomo Zaibatsu, by T. Nakase. pp. 171-202.
- Industrial relations in Great Britain and Japan, from the 1880s to the 1920s, by R. Okayama. pp. 207-237.
- Summary of discussions, by E. Daito. pp. 241-251.

Odaka, Kunio
Toward industrial democracy; management and workers in modern Japan. Cambridge, Mass., Harvard Univ. Press, 1975.
226p.

Okochi, Kazuo
Labor in modern Japan. Tokyo, 1958.
117p. (Science Council of Japan economic series. no.18)

Okochi, Kazuo, Bernard Karsh, and Solomon B. Levine, ed.
Workers and employers in Japan; the Japanese employment relations system. Princeton, N.J., Princeton Univ. Press, 1973. 538p.
Contents:
- Chapter 1 - the concept of a national industrial relations system, by B. Karsh and S. B. Levine. pp. 3-14.
- Chapter 2 - the emergence of modern Japan, by Mikio Sumiya. pp. 15-48.
- Chapter 3 - Contemporary management; an overview, by Mikio Sumiya. pp. 49-88.
- Chapter 4 - the legal framework; past and present, by Toru Ariizumi. pp. 89-132.
- Chapter 5 - the labor market, by Shojiro Ujihara. pp. 133-162.
- Chapter 6 - management and their organizations, by Hideaki Okamoto. pp. 163-216.
- Chapter 7 - workers and their organizations, by Hisashi Kawada. pp. 217-268.

- Chapter 8 - collective bargaining, by Taishiro Shirai. pp. 269-308.
- Chapter 9 - labor disputes, by Wakao Fujita. pp. 309-360.
- Cahpter 10 - the industrial reward system; wages and benefits, by Naomichi Funahashi. pp. 361-398.
- Chapter 11 - personnel administration at the industrial plant level by Masumi Tsuda. pp. 399-440.
- Chapter 12 - social security for workers, by Takeshi Takahashi. pp. 441-484.
- Chapter 13 - the Japanese industrial relations system; a summary, by K. Okochi, B. Karsh, and S. B. Levine. pp. 485-516.
- Contributors. pp. 517-522.
- Index. p. 523.

Shakai Hoshyo Kenkyusho (Social Development Research Institute)
Social security in Japan. Tokyo, 1967.
99p. illus.

Taira, Koji
Economic development and the labor market in Japan. N.Y., Columbia Univ. Press, 1970.
282p. (Studies of the East Asian Institute)

Whitehill, Arthur M. Jr. and Shin-ichi Takezawa.
The other worker; a comparative study of industrial relations in the United States and Japan. Honolulu, East-West Center Press, 1968.
481p.

II.

Ayusawa, Iwao
Labor and industry; labor, repression, and the public police act.
(Jon Livingston, ed. Imperial Japan, 1800-1945. New York, Pantheon Books, 1973. pp. 291-287)

Ballon, Robert J.
Participative employment. (Robert J. Ballon, ed. The Japanese employee. Tokyo, Sophia University, 1969. pp. 63-76)

Chokki, T.
Labor management in the cotton spinning industry. (Keiichiro Nakagawa, ed. Labor and management; proceedings of the 4th Fuji Conference. Tokyo, University of Tokyo Press, 1979. pp. 145-167)

Cole, Robert E. and Kenichi Tominaga
Japan's changing occupational structure and its significance. (Hugh Patrick, ed. Japanese industrialization and its social consequences. Berkeley, University of California Press, 1976. pp. 53-96)

Dore, R. P.
Industrial relations in Japan and elsewhere. (Albert M. Craig, ed. Japan; a comparative view. Princeton, N.J., Princeton Univ. Press, 1979. pp. 324-370)

Farley, Miriam S.
Labor relations. (Hugh Borton, ed. Japan. Ithaca, N.Y., Cornell University Press, 1950. pp. 94-109)

Hazama, Hiroshi
Historical changes in the life style of industrial workers. (Hugh Patrick, ed. Japanese industrialization and its social consequences. Berkeley, University of California Press, 1976. pp. 21-52)

Ishimoto, Shidzue
Labor and industry; are miners human beings? (Jon Livingston, ed. Imperial Japan, 1800-1945. New York, Pantheon Books, 1973. pp. 313-317)

Matsukata, Kōjirō
Labor and industry, Japanese laborers. (Jon Livingston, ed. Imperial Japan, 1800-1945. New York, Pantheon Books, 1973. pp. 311-312)

Minami, Ryoshin
An analysis of the population movement from agriculture in Japan. (Committee for Translation of Japanese Economic Studies. Translations of Japanese economic studies. no.49. Tokyo, International House of Japan, 1959-64. 21p. bibl. 20-21)

Minami, Ryoshin
The supply of farm labor and the turning point in the Japanese economy. (Kazushi Ohkawa, ed. Agriculture and economic growth; Japan's experience. Princeton, Princeton University Press, 1970. pp. 270-299. bibl. pp. 293-295)

Okamoto, Hideaki
Management and their organizations. (Kazuo Okochi, Bernard Karsh, and Solomon B. Levine, ed. Workers and employers in Japan; the Japanese employment relations system. Princeton, Princeton Univ. Press, 1973. pp. 163-216)

Okayama, R.
Industrial relations in Great Britain and Japan, from the 1880s to the 1920s. (Keiichiro Nakagawa, ed. Labor and management; proceedings of the 4th Fuji Conference. Tokyo, University of Tokyo Press, 1979. pp. 207-237)

Orchard, John
Labor and industry; Japan's economic position, the progress of industrialization. (Jon Livingston, ed. Imperial Japan, 1800-1945. New York, Pantheon Books, 1973. pp. 305-310)

Pelzel, John C.
Factory life in Japan and China today. (Albert M. Craig. Japan; a comparative view. Princeton, N.J., Princeton Univ. Press, 1979. pp. 371-432)

Sakudō, Y.
Traditional labor management in Japan, 1710-1890. (Keiichiro Nakagawa, ed. Labor and management; proceedings of the 4th Fuji Conference. Tokyo, University of Tokyo Press, 1979. pp. 127-140)

Sakurabayashi, Makoto and Robert J. Ballon
Labor-management relation in modern Japan. (Joseph Roggendorf, ed., Studies in Japanese culture. Tokyo, Sophia University, 1963. pp. 245-268

Saxonhouse, Gary R.
Country girls and communication among competitors in the Japanese cotton-spinning industry. (Hugh Patrick, ed. Japanese industrialization and its social consequences. Berkeley, University of California Press, 1976. pp. 97-126)

Saxonhouse Gary and Yukihiko Kiyokawa
The supply and demand for quality workers in the cotton textile industries in Japan and India. (International Development Center of Japan. Papers and proceedings of the conference on Japan's historical development experience and contemporary developing countries; issues for comparative analysis. Feb. 11-16, 1978. Tokyo, 1978. pp. 83-120)

Totten, George O.
Collective bargaining and works councils as innovations in industrial relations in Japan during the 1920's. (Ronald P. Dore, ed. Aspects of social change in modern Japan. Princeton, Princeton University Press, 1967. pp. 203-243)

Totten, George O.
Japanese industrial relations at the crossroads; the great Noda strike of 1927-1928. (B. Silberman and H. Harootunian, ed. Japan in crisis. Princeton, Princeton University Press, 1974. pp. 398-436)

Totten, George O.
Labor and agrarian disputes in Japan following World War I. (Thomas C. Smith, ed. City and village in Japan. Chicago, Univ. of Chicago Press, 1960. pp. 187-212)

Tsuda, M.
The formation and characteristics of the work group in Japan. (Keiichiro Nakagawa, ed. Labor and management; proceedings of the 4th Fuji Conference. Tokyo, University of Tokyo Press, 1979. pp. 29-42)

Tussing, Arlon R.
The labor force in Meiji economic growth; a quantitative study of Yamanashi prefecture. (Kazushi Ohkawa, ed. Agriculture and economic growth; Japan's experience. Princeton, N.J., Princeton University Press, 1970. pp. 198-221. Bibl. pp. 221) reprinted from

Umemura, Mataji
Factor shares, prices, and population; population and labor force. (K. Ohkawa and M. Shinohara, ed. Patterns of Japanese economic development; a quantitative appraisal. New Haven, Yale Univ. Press, 1979. pp. 241-250)

Umemura, Mataji
Gainful workers. (Kazushi Ohkawa and Yujiro Hayami, ed. Economic growth; the Japanese experience since the Meiji era; proceedings of the second conference held by the Japan Economic Research Centre, June 26-July 1, 1972 in Japan. Tokyo, Japan Economic Research Centre, 1973. v. 1. pp. 95-100)

Young, Arthur
Labor and industry; the rice riots of 1918. (Jon Livingston, ed. Imperial Japan, 1800-1935. New York, Pantheon Books, 1973. pp. 322-326)

III.

Chuang, Liu-Hsiung
The role of human capital in the process of economic development; a case study of Japan. Ph.D. 1975. Stanford University. 166p.

Holden, Karen Cleo Anderson
A comparative study of labor force change; Japan 1920-69 and United States 1890-1955. Ph.D. 1973. University of Pennsylvania. 315p.

Large, Stephen Stocker
The labor movement in Japan, 1912-1919, Suzuki Bunji and the Yūaikai. Ph.D. 1970. The University of Michigan. 405p.

Nagai, Willie Tsunetaka
A christian labor leader; Kagawa Toyohiko (1888-1960). Ph.D. 1976 University of Colorado at Boulder. 388p.

IV.

Ariizumi, Tōru
The strike and the contract of employment in Japan. Annals of the Institute of Social Science, no. 8. 1967. pp. 12-23.

Cole, Robert E.
The late-developer hypothesis; an evaluation of its relevance for Japanese employment patterns. Journal of Japanese studies, v. 4, no.2. Summer 1978. pp. 247-268.

Cole, Robert E.
The theory of institutionalization; permanent employment and tradition in Japan. Economic development and cultural change, v. 20, no.1. Oct. 1971. pp. 47-70.

Crawcour, E. Sydney
The Japanese employment system. Journal of Japanese studies, v. 4, no.2. Summer 1978. pp. 225-247.

Emi, Koichi
Employment structure in the service industires. Developing economies, v. 7, no.2. June 1969. pp. 133-157.

Evans, Robert, Jr.
Evolution of the Japanese system of employer-employee relations, 1868-1945. Business history review, v. 44, no.1. Spring 1970. pp. 110-125.

Hayami, Hiroshi and Jacqueline Kaminski
Japanese labor - management relations and Uno Riemon. Journal of Japanese studies, v. 5, no.1. Winter 1979. pp. 71-106.

Iida, Kanae
The iron worker's union in the earliest stages of the Japanese labour movement; the rise and fall of a craft union. Keio economic studies, v. 10, no.1. 1973. pp. 39-60.

Iida, Kanae
Trends in research on the history of labor movement in Japan. Keio economic studies, v. 2. 1964. pp. 98-107.

Jones, H. J.
Japanese women and the dual-track employment system. Pacific Affairs, v. 49, no.4. Winter 1976/77. pp. 589-608.

Katakami, Akira
Types of joint-consultation and their relations to collective bargaining in the industrial relations in Japan. Bullen of University of Osaka Prefecture, series D. v. 10. 1966. pp. 52-64.

Kawada, Hisashi
Comparative industrial relations; East and South Asian countries and Japan. Keio economic studies, v. 6, no.1. 1969. pp. 41-54.

Kawada, Hisashi
Continuity and discontinuity; an approach to industrial relations systems. Management and labor studies, no. 16. Feb. 1966. pp. 69-84.

Kawada, Hisashi
The government, industrial relations and economic development in Japan. Management and labor studies, no. 9. Nov. 1964. pp. 1-61.

Kishimoto, Eitaro
The characteristics of labour-management relations in Japan and their historical formation (1) (2). Keio University economic review, v. 35, no.2. Oct. 1965. pp. 33-55.
v. 36, no.1. Apr. 1966. pp. 17-38.

Kishimoto, Eitaro
A short history of the labor movements in Japan. Kyoto University economic review, v. 21. no.1. Apr. 1951. pp. 39-56.

Kudo, Kyokichi
Clothiers and wage weavers in the Ashikaga district in the Meiji era, 1868-1912. Waseda business and economic studies, no. 2. 1966. pp. 1-18.

Large, Stephen S.
The Japanese labor movement, 1912-1919; Suzuki Bunji and the Yūaikai. Journal of Asian studies, v. 29. no.3. May 1970. pp. 559-580.

Minemura, Teruo
The role of the government in industrial relations; an outline. Management and labor studies, no. 17. Feb. 1966. pp. 261-267.

Mohri, Shigetaka
Two kinds of labor management. Annals of the Hitotsubashi academy, v. 2, no.2. Apr. 1952. pp. 172-182)

Nishikawa, Shunsaku
Domestic labor migration in Japan. Keio Business Review. no. 1. 1962. pp. 79-99. Reprinted in Management and labor studies. no. 6. Mar. 1963.

Odaka, Konosuke
Indices of the excess demand for labor in prewar Japan, 1929-39; a preliminary study. Hitotsubashi journal of economics, v. 10, no.1. June 1969. pp. 33-55.

Ohkawa, Kazushi
The differential employment structure of Japan. Annals of the Hitotsubashi academy, v. 9, no.2. Apr. 1959. pp. 205-217.

Ohkawa, Kazushi
The phase of unlimited supplies of labor. Hitotsubashi journal of economics, v. 5, no.1. June 1964. pp. 1-15.

Saito, Osamu
Migration and the labor market in Japan, 1872-1920; a regional study. Keio economic studies, v. 10, no.2. 1973. pp. 47-60.

Saxonhouse, Gary R.
The supply of quality workers and the demand for quality in jobs in Japan's early industrialization. Explorations in entrepreneurial history, v. 15, no.1. 1978. pp. 40-68.

Shibata, Ginjiro
Port labor conditions in Japan, particularly in Kobe port. Kobe Economic and Business Review, v. 6. 1959. pp. 75-90.

Sumiya, Mikio
The development of Japanese labor-relations. Developing economies, v. 4, no.4. Dec. 1966. pp. 499-515.

Taira, Koji
Factory legislation and management modernization during Japan's industrialization, 1868-1916. Business history review, v. 44, no.1. Spring 1970. pp. 84-109.

Takamiya, Susumu
Characteristics of management in Japanese enterprise. Annals of the Hitotsubashi academy, v. 10, no.2. Dec. 1959. pp. 181-193.

Totten, George O.
Labor and agrarian disputes in Japan following World War I. Economic development and cultural change, v. 9. no.1, pt. 2. Oct. 1960. pp. 187-212.

Tsuda, Masumi
Study of Japanese management development practices. Hitotsubashi journal of arts and science, v. 18, no.1. Sept. 1977. pp. 1-19.

Tussing, Arlon
The labor force in Meiji economic growth; a quantitative study of Yamanashi prefecture. Journal of economic history, v. 26, no.1. Mar. 1966. pp. 59-92.
also cf. Ohkawa Kazushi, ed. Agriculture and economic growth; Japan's experience, pp. 198-221.

Umemura, Mataji
An analysis of employment structure in Japan. Hitotsubashi journal of economics, v. 2, no.2. Mar. 1962. pp. 16-29.

Umemura, Mataji
Regional differences in the distribution of industrial employment in Japan. Developing economies, v. 7, no.2. June 1969. pp. 117-132.

Yamasaki, Takeo
The forestry labour of Japan. Kyoto University economic review, v. 31, no.2. Oct. 1961. pp. 17-41.

WAGES

II.

Hotani, Rokuro and Takashi Hayashi
Evolution of wage structure in Japan. (Committee for Translation of Japanese Economic Studies. Translations of Japanese economic studies. no.14. Tokyo International House of Japan, 1959-64. 31p.)

Masui, Yukio
The supply price of labor; farm family workers. (Kazushi Ohkawa, ed. Agriculture and economic growth; Japan's experience. Princeton, Princeton University Press, 1970. pp. 222-249. Bibl. pp. 248-249)

Minami, Ryoshin and Akira Ono
Factor shares, prices, and population; wages. (K. Ohkawa and M. Shinohara, ed. Patterns of Japanese economic development; a quantitative appraisal. New Haven, Yale Univ. Press, 1979. pp. 229-240)

Minami, Ryoshin and Akira Ono
Relative income share of labor; long-run trend and fluctuations in prewar Japan and their implications. (International Development Center of Japan. Papers and proceedings of the conference on Japan's historical development experience and contemporary developing countries; issues for comparative analysis. Feb.11-16, 1978. Tokyo, 1978. pp. 303-330)

Noda, Tsutomu
Commodity prices and wages. (Kazushi Ohkawa and Yujiro Hayami, ed. Economic growth; the Japanese experience since the Meiji era; proceedings of the second conference held by the Japan Economic Research Centre, June 26-July 1, 1972 in Japan. Tokyo, Japan Economic Research Centre, 1973. v. 1. pp. 113-132)

Yasuba, Yasukichi
The evolution of dualistic wage structure. (Hugh Patrick, ed. Japanese industrialization and social consequences. Berkeley, University of California Press, 1976. pp. 249-298)

IV.

Kobayashi, Yoshimoto
On some pecurialities of the Japanese wages system. Annals of the School of Business Administration, Kobe Univ. no. 5. 1961. pp. 1-7.

Odaka, Konosuke
A history of money wages in the northern Kyushu industrial area, 1898-1939. Hitotsubashi journal of economics. v. 8, no.2. Feb. 1968. pp. 71-100.

Odaka, Konosuke
On employment and wage-differential structure in Japan; a survey. Hitotsubashi journal of economics. v. 8, no.1. June 1967. pp. 41-64.

Ono, Yoshiteru
Labor's shares in the national income of Japan. Bulletin of University of Osaka Prefecture, series D. v. 10. 1966. pp. 30-33.

Sano, Yoko
The changes in real wages of construction workers in Tokyo, 1830-1894. Management and labor studies. no. 4. Jan. 1963. pp. 1-60.

Sano, Yoko
A quantitative analysis of wage determination in Japan. Keio business review, no. 7. 1968. pp. 65-89. Bibl. 87-89.

Taira, Koji
The inter-sectoral wage differential in Japan 1881-1959. Journal of farm economics, v. 44, no.2. May 1962. pp. 322-334.

Taira, Koji
Market forces and public power in wage determination; early Japanese experience. Social research, v. 30. no.4. Winter 1963. pp. 434-457.

Umemura, Mataji
Labor's relative share in the Japanese manufacturing industry since 1900. Annals of the Hitotsubashi academy, v. 8, no.2. Apr. 1958. pp. 176-187.

TRANSPORTATION AND COMMUNICATION

I.

Hirota, Naotaka
The lure of Japan's railways. Tokyo, Japan Times, 1969. 1 v. (unpaged, chiefly illus.)

Hirota, Naotaka
Steam locomotives of Japan. Tokyo, Kodansha International, 1972. 104p.

Japan. Ministry of Transportation
Seventy five years progress of Japanese Government Railways. Tokyo, Foreign Affairs Unit, Freight Traffic Section, Traffic Bureau. 76p.

II.

Crouzet, F.
When the railways were built; a French engineering firm during the "great depression" and after. (Keiichiro Nakagawa, ed. Marketing and finance in the course of industrialization; proceedings of the 3rd Fuji Conference. Tokyo, University of Tokyo Press, 1978. pp. 169-194)

Minami, Ryoshin
Railroads and electric utilities. (Kazushi Ohkawa and Yujiro Hayami ed. ed. Economic growth; the Japanese experience since the Meiji era; proceedings of the second conference held by the Japan Economic Research Centre, June 26-July 1, 1972 in Japan. Tokyo, Japan Economic Research Centre, 1973. v. 1, pp. 39-50)

Nehmer, Stanley
Transportation and communications. (Hugh Borton, ed. Japan. Ithaca, N.Y., Cornell University Press, 1950. pp. 110-126)

Noda, M.
Corporate finance of railroad companies in Meiji Japan. (Keiichiro Nakagawa, ed. Marketing and finance in the course of industrialization; proceedings of the 3rd Fuji Conference. Tokyo, University of Tokyo Press, 1978. pp. 87-101)

III.

Noguchi, Paul Hideyo
The "One railroad family" of the Japanese national railways; a cultural analysis of Japanese industrial familialism. Ph.D. 1977. University of Pittsburgh. 219p.

IV.

Aoki, Kaizo
The national railways. Japan quarterly, v. 8. no.1. Jan./Mar. 1961. Changing Japan 14. pp. 106-113.

Hatta, Yoshiaki
History of the Japanese railways. Contemporary Japan, v. 22. no.1/3. 1953. pp. 38-52.

Ike, Nobutaka
The pattern of railway development Japan. Far Eastern quarterly, v. 14, no.2. Feb. 1955. pp. 217-229.

Tanaka, Tokihiko
Meiji government and the introductior of railways. pt. 1-2. Contemporary Japan, v. 28, no.3-4. May 1966-May 1967. pp. 567-588, 750-788.

Uda, Tadashi
On the return-sales to the private ownership of the railways nationalized during the wartime 1943-1944 in Japan. Otemon economic studies, no. 1. 1968. pp. 71-80.

Uda, Tadashi
Yukichi Fukuzawa's opinions on the railway to early Meiji era. Otemon economic studies, no. 2. 1969. pp. 37-42.

SHIPPING

IV.

Sasaki, Seiji
The distinction between "Shasen" and "Shagaisen" as historical concepts in Japanese shipping. Kobe economic and business review, v. 3. 1956. pp. 45-54.

Sasaki, Seiji
The early development of Kobe port. Kobe economic and business review, v. 15. 1968. pp. 17-28.

Sasaki, Seiji
The introduction of European-style vessels in Japan; a historical survey. Kobe economic and business review, v. 10. 1963. pp. 41-52.

Sasaki, Seiji
A little study on the transition from sailing vessel to steamer in Japan. Kobe economic and business review, v. 4. Oct. 1957. pp. 165-176.

Sasaki, Seiji
The maritime competitions in the early Meiji era - in relation to the development of "common carrier" type. Kobe economic and business review, v. 2. 1955. pp. 37-52.

Sasaki, Seiji
The modernization of Japanese shipping based on the transportation of Hokkaido marine products. Kobe economic and business review, v. 5. 1958. pp. 67-76.

Sasaki, Seiji
Types of early modern Japanese shipowners. Kobe economic and business review, v. 9, 1962. pp. 15-30.

Shibata, Ginjiro
Curves of diminishing values of Japanese merchant ships in proportion to their age. Kobe economic and business review, v. 5. 1958. pp. 53-66.

Shibata, Ginjiro
Movements for the establishment of free ports in Japan - a historical survey. Kobe economic and business review, v. 2. 1955. pp. 3-20.

Shibata, Ginjiro
Present status of Japan's shipping. Kobe economic and business review, v. 3. 1956. pp. 27-44.

Shibata, Ginjiro
Problems in port administration and finance in Japan. Kobe economic and business review, v. 9. 1962. pp. 1-14.

Taga, Yutaka
Development of shipbuilding industry. Contemporary Japan, v. 24, no.1/3. 1956. pp. 68-87.

Yamamoto, Hiromasa
Development of the marine insurance industry in Japan in the Meiji period. Kobe economic and business review, v. 5. 1958. pp. 77-88.

Yamamoto, Hiromasa
On the employment system of seamen in Japan. Kobe economic and business review, v. 9. 1962. pp. 31-42.

Yamamoto, Hiromasa
Singularity in the structure of the seamen's union of Japan, in comparison with enterprise union. Kobe economic and business review, v. 7. 1960. pp. 47-58.

Yasuba, Yasukichi
Freight rates and productivity in ocean transportation for Japan. 1875-1943. Explorations in entrepreneurial history, v. 15, no.1. Jan. 1978. pp. 11-39.

COMMERCE

I.

Kinoshita, Yetaro
The past and present of Japanese commerce. Reprint ed. N.Y., AMS Press, 1968. 164p.

Nakagawa, Keiichiro, ed.
Marketing and finance in the course of industrialization; proceedings of the 3rd Fuji Conference. Tokyo, Univ. of Tokyo Press, 1978. 227p. (International Conference on Business History 3)
Contents:
- Marketing and financing in the course of industrialization; a comparative analysis of the ways that limiting factors were overcome in three nations; the United States, Japan and the United Kingdom, by R. Iwata. pp. 3-29.
- The financial characteristics of the Zaibatsu in Japan; the old Zaibatsu and their closed finance, by H. Masaki. pp. 33-54.
- Trade credit and the development of the cotton spinning industry; its role and background, by K. Sugiyama. pp. 59-82.
- Corporate finance of railroad companies in Meiji Japan, by M. Noda. pp. 87-101.
- Introduction and diffusion of depreciation accounting in Japan, 1875-1903, by S. Takatera. pp. 105-115.

- Marketing and sales financing in the automobile industry; U.S. and Japan, by K. Shimokawa. pp. 121-142.
- The role of financial intermediaries in American economic growth, by D. C. North. pp. 147-165.
- When the railways were built; a French engineering firm during the "great depression" and after, by F. Crouzet. pp. 169-194.
- Capital and entrepreneurship as factor markets in British industry, 1750-1914, by P. Mathias, pp. 199-218.
- Summary of concluding discussion, by K. Nakagawa. pp. 221-227.

II.

Iwata, R.
Marketing and financing in the course of industrialization; a comparative analysis of the ways that limiting factors were overcome in three nations; the United States, Japan and the United Kingdom. (Nakagawa, Keiichiro, ed. Marketing and finance in the course of industrialization; proceedings of the 3rd Fuji Conference. Tokyo, University of Tokyo Press, 1978. pp. 3-29)

Iwata, R.
Marketing strategy and market structure in three nations; the United States, the United Kingdom, and Japan. (Keiichiro Nakagawa, ed. Strategy and structure of big business; proceedings of the 1st Fuji Conference. Tokyo, Univ. of Tokyo Press. pp. 177-195)

Shimokawa, K.
Marketing and sales financing in the automobile industry; U. S. and Japan. (Keiichiro Nakagawa, ed. Marketing and finance in the course of industrialization; proceedings of the 3rd Fuji Conference. Tokyo, University of Tokyo Press, 1978. pp. 121-142)

Yamamura, Kozo
General trading companies in Japan - their origins and growth. (Hugh Patrick, ed. Japanese industrialization and its social consequences. Berkeley, University of California Press, 1976. pp. 161-200)

Yamazawa, Ippei and Hirohisa Kohama
Trading companies and the expansion of Japan's foreign trade. (International development Center of Japan. Papers and proceedings of the conference on Japan's historical development experience and contemporary developing countries; issues for comparative analysis. Feb. 11-16, 1978. Tokyo, 1978. pp. 153-180)

Yui, T.
The traditional system of middlemen and marketing policies of food manufacturers. (Keiichiro Nakagawa, ed. Strategy and structure of big business; proceedings of the 1st Fuji Conference. Tokyo, Univ. of Tokyo Press. pp. 115-120)

IV.

Eyre, John D.
Patterns of Japanese salt production and trade. <u>Univ. of Michigan, Center for Japanese studies occasional papers</u>, no. 3. 1952. pp. 15-46.

Fukami, Giichi
Department store business in Japan. <u>Annals of the Hitotsubashi academy</u>, v. 3, no.1. Oct. 1952. pp. 114-128.

Kamibayashi, Masanori
Historical development of commodity exchanges in Japan. <u>Annals of the School of Business Administration, Kobe Univ</u>, no. 7. 1963. pp. 1-21.

Sheldon, Charles D.
'Pre-modern' merchants and modernization in Japan. <u>Modern Asian studies</u>, v. 5, no.3. July 1971. pp. 193-206.

Suzuki, S.
Analysis of distribution structure in the iron and steel industry. Kyoto University economic review. v. 21, no.2. Oct. 1951. pp. 98-100.

Suzuki, Shigeaki
On the market milk in Japan around 1900. Japanese studies in the history of science, no. 7. 1968. pp. 71-82.

Uchida, Katsutoshi
Structure of commerce in Japan. Bulletin of University of Osaka Prefecture, series D. v. 6. 1962. pp. 54-66.

Uchida, Katsutoshi
Trading firms of Japan. Bulletin of University of Osaka Prefecture, series D. v. 2. 1958. pp. 97-107.

FOREIGN TRADE

I.

Brode, John
Tables of Japanese foreign trade, 1868-1965. Keijo, Chosen Sotokufu, Chosen Boeki Nempyo. 1967. Mimeo.

Fujii, Shigeru
Japan's trade and her level of living. Tokyo, 1955. 76p. (Science Council of Japan economic series. no.6)

Hollerman, Leon
Japan's dependence on the world economy; the approach toward economic liberalization. Princeton, Princeton Univ. Press, 1967. 291p.

Huh, Kyung-mo.
Japan's trade in Asia; developments since 1926, prospects for 1970. N.Y., 1966. 282p. (Praeger special studies in international economics and development)

Hunsberger, Warren S.
Japan and the United States in world trade. N.Y., Harper and Row, 1964. 492p.

Japan. Economic Counsel Board
Japanese foreign trade during 1934 by commodity and country. Tokyo, 1953. 117p.

Ohara, Keishi, ed.
Japanese trade and industry in the Meiji-Taisho era, tr. and adapted by Okata Tamotsu. Tokyo, Obunsha, 1957. 566p. illus. (Centenary Cultural Council series) under the auspices of Kaikoku Hyakunen Kinen Bunka Jigyokai.

Sill, John Baxter
Trading under sail off Japan, 1860-99; the recollections of Captain John Baxter Will, sailing master and pilot, ed. with a historical introduction by George Alexander Lensen. Tokyo, Sophia Univ., 1968. 190p. illus.

II.

Baba, Masao and Masahiro Tatemoto
Foreign trade and economic growth in Japan; 1858-1937. (L. Klein and K. Ohkawa, ed. Economic growth: the Japanese experience since the Meiji era. Homewood, R. D. Irwin, 1968. pp. 162-196)

Ballantine, Joseph W.
Foreign relations (1931-1945) (Hugh Borton, ed. Japan. Ithaca, N,Y., Cornell University Press, 1950. pp. 285-297)

Hemmi, Kenzo
Primary product exports and economic development; the case of silk. (Kazushi Ohkawa, ed. Agriculture and economic growth; Japan's experience. Princeton, N.J., Princeton University Press, 1970. pp. 303-323. bibl. pp. 322-323

Lockwood, William W.
Trade. (Hugh Borton, ed. Japan. Ithaca, N.Y., Cornell University Press, 1950. pp. 81-93)

Nagazumi, Akira
Toward the abolition of the unequal treaties; the cases of Japan and Thailand. (Carl A. Trocki, ed. The emergence of modern states; Thailand and Japan. Bangkok, Institute of Asian Studies, Chulalongkorn University, 1976. pp. 45-58)

Okada, Shumpei
Shigenobu Okuma; his view on Japan's international balance of payments. (Naosaku Uchida, ed. Social and economic aspects of Japan. Seijo Gakuen Jubilee year 1917-1967. Tokyo, Economic Institute of Seijo Univ., 1967. pp. 17-42)

Rapp, William V.
Firm size and Japan's export structure; a microview of Japan's changing export competitiveness since Meiji. (Hugh Patrick, ed. Japanese industrialization and social consequences. Berkeley, University of California Press, 1976. pp. 201-248)

Shinohara, Miyohei
Economic development and foreign trade in pre-war Japan. (Charles Donald Cowan, ed. The economic development of China and Japan; studies in economic history and political economy. London, George Allen and Unwin. 1964. pp. 220-248)

Shionoya, Yuichi and Ippei Yamazawa
Industrial growth and foreign trade in pre-war Japan. (Economic growth; the Japanese experience since the Meiji era; proceedings of the second conference held by Japan Economic Research Centre, June 26-July 1, 1972 in Japan. Tokyo, Japan Economic Research Centre, 1973. v. 2. pp. 515-548)

Yamazawa, Ippei and Yuzo Yamamoto
Production and trade; trade and balance of payments. (K. Ohkawa and M. Shinohara, ed. Patterns of Japanese economic development; a quantitative appraisal. New Haven, Yale Univ. Press, 1979. pp. 134-158)

III.

Ishii, Osamu
Cotton-textile diplomacy; Japan, Great Britain and the United States, 1930-1936. Ph.D. 1977. Rutgers University, the State U. of New Jersey. 520p.

IV.

Adams, Nassau A.
Import structure and economic growth; a comparison of cross-section and time-series data. Economic development and cultural change, v. 15, no.2. pt.1. Jan. 1967. pp. 43-162.

Baba, Keinosuke
Japanese gains from trade, 1878-1932. Annals of the Hitotsubashi academy, v. 8, no.2. Apr. 1958. pp. 127-142.

Dowd, Laurence P.
The impact of exchange policy on the international economy of Japan during the period 1930-1940. Kobe economic and business review, v. 4. 1957. pp. 1-58.

Feraru, Arthur N.
Japanese trade with China. Far eastern survey, v. 18, no.17. Aug. 24, 1949. pp. 200-204.

Garbuny, Siegfried
Prewar Soviet-Japanese trade. Far estern survey, v. 17, no.1. Jan. 14. 1948. pp. 8-11.

Goodman, Grant K.
The Philippine legislature trade mission to Japan, 1933; a reassessment. Monumenta Nipponica, v. 25, nos.3/4. 1970. pp. 239-248.

Hollerman, Leon
Japan and Far Eastern development. Pacific affairs, v. 24, no.4. Dec. 1951. pp. 372-397.

Hollerman, Leon
The logistic view versus the national income view of foreign trade dependence, with special reference to Japan. Hitotsubashi journal of economics, v. 1, no.1. Oct. 1960. pp. 52-58.

Horie, Yasuzo
Foreign trade policy in the early Meiji era. Kyoto University economic review, v. 22, no.2. Oct. 1952. pp. 1-21.

Horie, Yasuzo
Japan's balance of international payments in the early Meiji period. Kyoto University economic review, v. 24, no.1. Apr. 1954. pp. 16-34.

Huber, Richard J.
Effect on prices of Japan's entry into world commerce after 1858. Journal of political economy, v. 79, no.3. May/June 1971. pp. 614-628.

Ikemoto, Kiyoshi
Japan's export of sundry goods. Kobe University economic review, no. 11. 1965. pp. 59-76.

Inlow, Burke
Japan's "special trade" in north China, 1935-37. Far Eastern quarterly, v. 6, no.2. Feb. 1947. pp. 139-168.

Katano, Hikoji
Econometric determination of foreign exchange rate of Japan for 1926-1953. Kobe economic and business review, v. 3. 1956. pp. 9-26.

Kawata, Fukuo
Japan's trade with South and South-East Asian countries - a statistical analysis. Kobe economic and business review, v. 1. 1954. pp. 37-64.

Kawata, Fukuo
A study on Japan's invisible trade. Kobe economic and business review, v. 9. 1962. pp. 43-60.

Kojima, Kiyoshi
Economic development and import dependence in Japan. Hitotsubashi journal of economics. v. 1, no.1. Oct. 1960. pp. 29-52.

Kojima, Kiyoshi
Japanese foreign trade and economic growth; with special reference to the terms of trade. Annals of the Hitotsubashi academy. v. 8, no.2. Apr. 1958. pp. 143-168.

Koo, Anthony Y. C. and C. C. Liang
The role of Japan in the inter-regional trade of the Far East. Review of economic and statistics. v. 35, no.1. Feb. 1953. pp. 31-40.

Matsui, Kiyoshi
Some notes on Japan's foreign trade. Kyoto University economic review. v. 27, no.2. Oct. 1957. pp. 19-55.

Mehta, Fredic A.
Price-competition between India, Japan, and the U. K. in the Indian cotton textile market during the nineteen-thirties. Review of economic and statistics. v. 39, no.1. Feb. 1957. pp. 75-78.

Mendel, Douglas H., Jr.
Perspective on Japanese foreign policy. Monumenta Nipponica. v. 21. nos.3/4. 1966. pp. 346-353.

Oshima, Kiyoshi
The world economic crisis and Japan's foreign economic policy. Developing economies. v. 5, no.4. Dec. 1967. pp. 628-647.

Rapp, William V.
A theory of changing trade patterns under economic growth; tested for Japan. Yale economic essays, v. 7, no.2. Fall 1967. pp. 69-135.

Saito, Takashi
Japan's foreign policy in the international environment of the nineteen-twenties. Developing economies. v. 5, no.4. Dec. 1967. pp. 685-701.

Stewart, John R.
The position of silk in Japanese exports. Pacific affairs. v. 21, no.1. Mar. 1948. pp. 46-50.

Trotter, Ann
Tentative steps for an Anglo-Japanese rapprochement in 1934. Modern Asian studies. v. 8, pt. 1. Jan. 1974. pp. 59-84.

Unno, Fukuju
The export trade in silk and the Japanese silk reeling industry in the first half of the Meiji period. Rural economic problems. v. 2, no.1. May 1965. pp. 70-82.

Wado, Atsunori
On the trade accommodations of the Yokohama and Kobe harbours in the late years of Meiji. Doshisha Shogaku v. 1, no.4. Apr. 1950. pp. 1-11.

Yamazawa, Ippei
Industrial growth and trade policy in prewar Japan. Developing economies. v. 13, no.1. Mar. 1975. pp. 38-65.

Yamazawa, Ippei and Akira Hirata
Industrialization and external relations; comparative analysis of Japan's historical experience and contemporary developing countries performance. Hitotsubashi journal of economics. v. 18, no.2. Feb. 1978. pp. 33-61.

Yanaihara, Katsu
Problems of the rice trade between Burman and Japan; a case study on exports of primary products in underdeveloped countries. Developing economies. v. 2, no.1. Mar. 1964. pp. 29-57.

Yukizawa, Kenzo
Changes in Japanese-United States productivity differentials and yen-dollar problem. pt. 1: International levels of labor productivity in prewar Japanese manufacturing industry-comparison of Japan, Britain, and the United States. pt. 2: The narrowing Japanese-United States productivity gap - as related to the yen revaluation. Japanese economic studies. v. 1. no.4. Summer 1973. pt. 1: pp. 33-47. pt. 2: pp. 48-62.

FOREIGN INVESTMENT

I.

Allen, George Cyril and Audrey G. Donnithorne
Western enterprise in Far Eastern economic development; China and Japan. London, Allen and Unwin, 1954.
291p.

Islam, Nurul
Foreign capital and economic development; Japan, India and Canada; studies in some aspects of absorption of foreign capital. Tokyo, Tuttle, 1960.
251p.

Jardine, Matheson & Co.
Jardines' centenary in Japan, 1859-1959. Tokyo, 1959.
47p.

II.

Reubens, Edwin P.
Foreign capital and domestic development in Japan. (Simon Kuznets, W. E. Moore and J. J. Spengler, ed. Economic growth; Brazil, India, Japan. Durham, N.C., Duke University Press, 1955. pp. 179-230)

III.

Key, Bernard Merril
The role of foreign contributions in Japanese capital formation, 1868-1936, with special reference to the period 1904-1914. Ph.D. 1971. University of California at Berkeley.
187p.

Taniguchi, Izumi
The financing of Japanese imports with especial reference to foreign investments in the process, 1868-1914. Ph.D. 1970. The University of Texas at Austin.
299p.

IV.

Horie, Yasuzo
Foreign capital and the Japanese capitalism after the World War I. Kyoto University economic review, v. 20, no.1. Apr. 1950. pp. 38-59.

SOCIETY AND SOCIAL PROBLEMS

MODERNIZATION

GENERAL

I.

Benedict, Ruth
The chrisanthemum and the swod; patterns of Japanese culture. Boston, Houghton Mifflin, 1946. 324p.

Chuo-seishonen Dantai Renraku Kyogikai (National Council of Youth Organizations in Japan)
Traditional culture and development. Tokyo, 1978. 129p.

Fukuoka Unesco Association
Report of the Second Kyushu International Cultural Conference; Japan's modernization and the role of Kyushu. Fukuoka, 1968. 95p.

Fese, Toyomasa, ed.
Modernization and stress in Japan. Leiden, E. J. Brill, 1975. 94p. (International studies in sociology and social anthropology, v. 2)
Contents:
- Introduction, by Toyomasa Fuse. pp. 1-11.
- Roots of the modernization experience in Japan, by Peter Mitchell. pp. 12-23.
- Japan's economic devevelopment; success, stress and prospects for the future, by Toyomasa Fuse. pp. 24-40.
- Paradox of Japan's nationalism; relations with Asia, by Savitri Vishwanathan. pp. 41-50.
- Protest and the Japanese political system, by Akira Kubota. pp. 51-61.
- Tradition and modernity in Japanese suicide; the case of Yasunari Kawabata, by Mamoru Iga. pp. 62-73.
- Modernization, social stress and emigration, by K. Victor Ujimoto. pp. 74-83.
- The Koshinjo and Tanteisha; institutionalized ascription as a response to modernization and stress in Japan, by Cullen T. Hayashida. pp. 84-94.
- Contributors, p. 95.

Howes, John F.
Tradition in transition; the modernization of Japan. N.Y., Macmillan, 1975. 102p.

International Conference on the Problems of Modernization in Asia, Seoul, 1965.
Report. Seoul, Korea Univ. Asiatic Research Center, 1966. 821p. illus.
Contents:
- Tradition and modernization in Japan, by Kentaro Hayashi. pp. 261-268.

- Three slogans of modernization in Japan, by Marius B. Jansen. pp. 271-299.
- Dilemmas of growth; the experience of Japan, 1905-1945, by James W. Morley, pp. 300-308.
- The extent to which the Japanese colonial policy toward Korea contributed to her modernization, by Sun-keun Lee. pp. 323-336.
- Modernization of Japan and China in relation to international law, by Toshio Ueda. pp. 454-459.
- The role of government for economic development in transition to modern industrialism with special reference to Japan, by Byong Kuk Kim. pp. 573-585.
- The role of intellectuals in Japan's modernization, by Yuzuru Okada. pp. 692-694.

Jansen, Marius B., ed.
Changing Japanese attitudes toward modernization. Princeton, Princeton Univ. Press, 1965.
546p. illus. (Studies in the modernization of Japan)
Contents:
- Changing conceptions of the modernization of Japan, by John Whitney Hall. pp. 7-42.
- Changing Japanese attitudes toward modernization, by Marius B. Jansen. pp. 43-98.
- The legacy of Tokugawa education, by R. P. Dore. pp. 99-132.
- Science and confucianism in Tokugawa Japan, by Albert Craig. pp. 133-166.
- The development of an orthodox attitude toward the imperial institution in the nineteenth century, by Herschel Webb. pp. 167-192.
- Nishimura Shigeki; a confucian view of modernization, by Donald H. Shively, pp. 193-242.
- The Meiji leaders and modernization; the case of Yamagata Aritomo, by Roger F. Hackett, pp. 243-282.
- Chinese confucianism on the eve of the great encounter, by Hellmut Wilhelm, pp. 283-310.
- Western and indigenous elements in modern Indian thought; the case of Rammohun Roy, by Stephen N. Hay. pp. 311-336.
- Japanese Christians and American missionaries, by John F. Howes, pp. 337-368.
- Ienaga Saburo and the search for meaning in modern Japan, by Robert N. Bellah, pp. 369-424.
- Japanese writers and modernization, by Kato Shuichi, pp. 425-446.
- Modernization and the Japanese intellectual; some comparative observations, by Herbert Passin, pp. 447-488.
- Patterns of individuation and the case of Japan; a conceptual scheme, by Masao Maruyama, pp. 489-532.
- List of contributors, p. 533.

Japan. Ministry of Foreign Affairs
Japan in transition; one hundred years of modernization. Tokyo, 1968.
97p. illus.
enl. issue 1973, 116p.

Kokusai Kirisutokyo Daigaku. (International Christian Univ.)
Studies on modernization of Japan by western scholars. Tokyo, 1962.
150p. (Asia bunka kenkyu no.3)
Contents:
- On studying the modernization of Japan, by Marius B. Jansen. pp. 1-12.
- Values and social change in modern Japan, by Robert N. Bellah, pp. 13-56.
- Conciliar thought in late Tokugawa Time, in the case of Sakamoto Ryōma, by Marius B. Jansen. pp. 57-72.
- The thought of men; the thought of society, the educational system and ideologies of the Tokugawa period, by Ronald Dore. pp. 73-86.
- Political thought and the Meiji Oligarchs, by George Beckmann, pp. 87-102.

- Japanese adaptations of Marx-Leninism, modernization and history, by George Beckmann. pp. 103-114.
- Youth and history, individual changes in postwar Japan, by Robert J. Lifton. pp. 115-136.
- Some value consequences of higher education, by Maurice E. Troyer. pp. 137-149.
- Introduction to the contributors. p. 150.

Shively, Donald H., ed.
Tradition and modernization in Japanese culture. Princeton, Princeton University Press, 1971. 689p. (Studies in the modernization of Japan, 5)
Published for the Conference on Modern Japan.
Contents:
- On the nature of western progress; the journal of the Iwakura embassy, by Eugene Soviak. pp. 7-34.
- Westernization and Japanization; the early Meiji transformation of education, by Michio Nagai. pp. 35-76.
- The Japanization of the middle Meiji, by Donald H. Shively. pp. 77-120.
- The Sino-Japanese War of 1894-95 and its cultural effects in Japan, by Donald Keene. pp. 121-175.
- Western style painting in early Meiji period and its critics, by John M. Rosenfield. pp. 181-229.
- The modern music of Meiji Japan, by William P. Malm. pp. 257-300.
- Natsume Soseki and the psychological novel, by Howars S. Hibbett. pp. 305-346.
- Toson and the autobiographical novel, by Edwin McClellan. pp. 347-378.
- Masaoka Shiki and tanka reform, by Robert H. Brower. pp. 379-418.
- Kobayashi Hideo, by Edward Seidensticker. pp. 419-462.
- Fukuda Tsuneari, modernization and Shingeki, by Benito Ortolani. pp. 463-505.
- Nishida Kitaro; the early years, by Valdo Humbert Viglielmo. pp. 507-562.
- Millenarian aspects of the new religions in Japan, by Carmen Blacker. pp. 563-600.
- Levels of speech (Keigo) and the Japanse linguistic response to modernization, by Roy Andrew Miller. pp. 601-667.

Silberman, Bernard S. and H. D. Harootunian with ten collaborating authors, ed.
Modern Japanese leadership; transition and change. Tucson, Univ. of Arizona Press, 1966.
433p.
Contents:
- Duty, reward, sanction, and power; four-cornered office of the Tokugawa village headman, by Harumi Befu, pp. 25-50.
- From caste patron to entrepreneur and political ideologue; transformation in 19th and 20th century outcaste leadership elites, by John B. Cornell. pp. 51-82.
- Jinsei, jinzai, and jitsugaku; social values and leadership in late Tokugawa thought, by Harry D. Harootunian, pp. 83-119.
- An early Meiji intellectual in politics; Baba Tatsui and the Jiyuto, by Eugene Soviak. pp. 121-170.
- Christian samurai and samurai values, by Irwin Scheiner. pp. 171-194.
- Okubo Toshimich and the first Home Ministry bureaucracy; 1873-1878, by Sidney De Vere Brown. pp. 195-232.
- Elite transformation in the Meiji restoration; the upper civil service 1868-1873, by Bernard S. Silberman, pp. 233-259.
- From closed door to empire; the formation of the Meiji military establishment, by James B. Crowley. pp. 261-287.
- A "Subleader" in the emergence of the diplomatic function; Ikeda Chohatsu (Chikugo no Kami) 1837-1879, by Ardath W. Burks. pp. 289-322.
- Rationality in the Meiji restoration; the Iwakura embassy, by Marlene Mayo. pp. 323-369.
- The Kaishinto as a political elite, by Joyce Lebra. pp. 371-383.

- Political party membership and sub-leadership in rural Japan; a case study of Okayama prefecture, by Alfred B. Clubok. pp. 385-409.

Tobata, Seiichi, ed.
The modernization of Japan, 1. Tokyo, Institute of Asian Economic Affairs, 1966.
298p. map.
Contents:
- A short history of modern Japan, by Yanaihara Tadao. pp. 3-48.
- Modernization reconsidered; with special reference to industrialization, by Otsuka Hisao. pp. 49-66.
- The transformation of national economy; a chapter in Japan's economic history, by Horie Yasuzo. pp. 67-90.
- The financial policy of the Meiji government, by Takeda Takao. pp. 91-114.
- The formation of heavy industry; one of the processes of industrialization in the Meiji period, by Ando Yoshio. pp. 115-135.
- Agriculture and turning-points in the economic growth, by Ohkawa Kazushi. pp. 136-154.
- Land reform and Japan's economic development, by Ronald P. Dore. pp. 155-164.
- Economic development and population growth; with special reference to South-East Asia, by Tachi Minoru and Okazaki Yoichi. pp. 165-184.
- The building of a national army, by Fukushima Shingo. pp. 185-208.
- The course and problems of national education - from the Meiji period to the present day, by Munakata Seiya. pp. 209-228.
- The confucian ideology and modernization of Japan - as illustrated in the Meiji edition of the Denshun Nenju Gyoji, by John R. McEwan. pp. 229-242.
- Modern trend in religious thoughts, by Nakamura Hajime. pp. 243-298.

Ward, Robert E., ed.
Political development in modern Japan. Princeton, Princeton Univ. Press, 1968. 637p. (Studies in the modernization of Japan)
Contents:
- A monarch for modern Japan, by John W. Hall. pp. 11-64.
- Political modernization and Meiji Genro, by Roger F. Hackett. pp. 65-98.
- Fukuzawa Yukichi; the philosophical foundations of Meiji nationalism, by Albert M. Craig. pp. 99-148.
- Modernization and foreign policy in Meiji Japan, by Marius B. Jansen. pp. 149-188.
- War and modernization, by Nobutaka Ike. pp. 189-212.
- Popular political participation and political development in Japan; the rural level, by Kurt Steiner. pp. 213-248.
- Elections and political modernization in prewar Japan, by Robert A. Scalapino. pp. 249-292.
- The development of interest groups and the pattern of political modernization in Japan, by Takeshi Ishida. pp. 293-336.
- Structural and functional differentiation in the political modernization of Japan, by Bernard S. Silberman. pp. 337-386.
- Law and political modernization in Japan, by Dan Fenno Henderson. pp. 387-456.
- Decision-making in the Japanese government; a study of ringisei, by Kiyoaki Tsuji. pp. 457-476.
- Reflections on the allied occupation and planned political change in Japan, by Robert E. Ward. pp. 477-536.
- The politics of Japan's modernization; the autonomy of choice, by Ardath B. Burks. pp. 537-637.

II.

Bellah, Robert N.
Values and social change in modern Japan. (Kokusai Kirisutokyo Daigaku Studies on modernization of Japan by Western scholars. Tokyo, 1962. pp. 13-56)

Borton, Hugh.
Development of the modern state (1850-1945). (Hugh Borton, ed. Japan. Ithaca, N.Y. Cornell University Press, 1950. pp. 271-284)

Hall, John Whitney
Changing conceptions of the modernization of Japan. (Marius B. Jansen, ed. Changing Japanese attitudes toward modernization. Princeton, Princeton University Press, 1965. pp. 7-42)

Hayashi, Kentaro
Tradition and modernization in Japan. (International Conference on the Problems of Modernization in Asia, Seoul, 1965. Report. Seoul, Korea University Asiatic Research Centre, 1966. pp. 261-268)

Ishida, Takeshi
The development of interest groups and the pattern of modernization in Japan. (Australian National University. Papers on modern Japan, v. 1. Canberra, 1965. pp. 1-17)

Jansen, Marius B.
Changing Japanese attitudes toward modernization. (Marius B. Jansen, ed. Changing Japanese attitudes toward modernization. Princeton, Princeton University Press, 1965. pp. 43-98)

Jansen, Marius B.
Modernization and foreign policy in Meiji Japan. (Robert E. Ward, ed. Political development in modern Japan. Princeton, Princeton University Press, 1968. pp. 149-188)

Jansen, Marius B.
On studying the modernization of Japan. (Kokusai Kirisutokyo Daigaku. Studies on modernization of Japan by Western scholars. Tokyo, 1962. pp. 1-12)

Jansen, Marius B.
Three slogans of modernization in Japan. (International Conference on the Problems of Modernization in Asia, Seoul, 1965. Report. Seoul, Korea University Asiatic Research Center, 1966. pp. 271-299)

Lockwood, William W.
Economic and political modernization; Japan. (Robert E. Ward and D. A. Rustow, ed. Political modernization in Japan and Turkey. Princeton, Princeton University Press, 1964. pp. 117-145)

Mitchell, Peter
Roots of the modernization experience in Japan. (Toyomasa Fusé, ed. Modernization and stress in Japan. Leiden, E. J. Bill. 1975. pp. 12-23)

Okada, Yuzuru
The role of intellectuals in Japan's modernization. (International Conference on the Problems of Modernization in Asia, Seoul, 1965. Report. Seoul, Korea University Asiatic Research Centre, 1966. pp. 692-694)

Otsuka, Hisao
Modernization reconsidered; with special reference to industrialization. (Seiichi Tobata, ed. The modernization of Japan, I. Tokyo, Institute of Asian Economic Affairs, 1966. pp. 49-66)

Sumiya, Mikio
The emergence of modern Japan. (Kazuo Okochi, Bernard Karsh, and Solomon B. Levine, ed. Workers and employers in Japan; the Japanese employment relations system. Princeton, N.J., Princeton Univ. Press, 1973. pp. 15-48)

IV.

Epp, Robert
The challenge from tradition; attempts to compile a civil code in Japan, 1866-1878. Monumenta Nipponica, v. 22, nos.1/2. 1967. pp. 15-48.

Horie, Yasuzo
The problems of the modernization of Japan. Kyoto University economic review, v. 26, no.1. Apr. 1956. pp. 1-12.

Nagasu, Kazushi
Introduction to "the modernization of Japan III" Developing economies, v. 5, no.4. Dec. 1967. pp. 551-567.

Nakamura, Katsumi
The modernization of Japan. Keio economic studies, v. 5. 1968. pp. 35-49.

Otsuka, Hisao
Modernization reconsidered, with special reference to industrialization. Developing economies, v. 3, no.4. Dec. 1965. pp. 387-403.

Quo, F. Q.
Democratic theories and Japanese modernization. Modern Asian studies, v. 6, pt.1. Jan. 1972. pp. 17-32.

Smith, Thomas C.
Old values and new techniques in the modernization of Japan. Far Eastern quarterly, v. 14, no.3. May 1955. pp. 355-364.

COMPARISON OF MODERNIZATION PROCESSES

I.

Beckmann, George M.
The modernization of China and Japan. N.Y., Harper and Row, 1962. 724p. illus. maps.

Black, Cyril Edwin and others
The modernization of Japan and Russia; a comparative study. N.Y., Free Press, 1975. 386p.

Chakravarti, Nalini Ranjan
Hundred years of Japan and India, 1878-1968; a comparative study of development. Calcutta, Progressive Publishers, 1978. 382p.

Craig, Albert M., ed.
Japan, a comparative view. Princeton, N.J., Princeton Univ. Press, 1979. 437p.
Contents:
- On foreign borrowing, by Marius B. Jansen. pp. 18-48.
- Tokyo and London; comparative conceptions of the city, by Henry D. Smith II. pp. 49-104.
- Response to the West; the Korean and Japanese patterns, by Seizaburo Sato. pp. 105-129.
- Nation-building in modern East Asia; early Meiji (1868-1890) and Mao's China (1949-1971), by Ezra F. Vogel. pp. 130-159.
- Love and death in the early modern novel; America and Japan by Takehiko Noguchi. pp. 160-181.

- Uchimura Kanzo; Japanese christianity in comparative perspective, by Takeo Doi. pp. 182-213.
- Cultural differences in family socialization; a psychocultural comparison of Chinese and Japanese, by George Devos, Lizabeth Hauswald and Orin Borders. pp. 214-275.
- Pre-industrial landholding patterns in Japan and England, by Kozo Yamamura. pp. 276-323.
- Industrial relations in Japan and elsewhere, by R. P. Dore. pp. 324-370.
- Factory life in Japan and China today, by John C. Pelzel. pp. 371-432.
- List of contributors. pp. 433-434.
- Index. p. 435.

Datta, Amlankusum
A century of economic development of Russia and Japan. Calcutta, World Press, 1963.
187p.

Trocki, Carl A., ed.
The emergence of modern states; Thailand and Japan. Bangkok, Institute of Asian Studies, Chulalongkorn Univ., 1976.
151p.
Contents:
- Forward, p. 2.
- Note on measure, pp. 3-4.
- Introduction, pp. 5-6.
- The modernization base in Japan and Thailand; education and science, by Prasert Chittiwatanapong. pp. 7-25.
- Contrasting modernization in Chulalongkorn's Siam and Meiji's Japan, by Likhit Dhiravegen. pp. 26-44.
- Toward the abolition of the unequal treaties; the cases of Japan and Thailand, by Akira Nagazumi. pp. 45-58.
- Response to the West; the Korean and Japanese patterns, by Seizaburo Sato. pp. 59-84.
- The front palace; the office of the heir apparent? by Charnvit Kaset-Siri. pp. 85-101.
- Forced labor in Thailand, by Deja Chayabongse. pp. 102-116.
- The tin industry as a non-peasant export production of Thailand, by Suthy Prasartset. pp. 117-130.
- The economic thought of Phraya Suriyanuwat, by Chatthip Nartsupha, pp. 131-147.
- Program. pp. 148-149.
- List of participants. p. 150.

Ward, Robert E. and Denkwart A. Rustow
Political modernization in Japan and Turkey. Princeton, N.J., Princeton Univ. Press, 1964.
502p. (Studies in political development).
Contents:
- Introduction, by Dankwart A. Rustow and Robert E. Ward. pp. 3-13.
- The nature of traditional society: A. Japan, by John Whitney Hall. pp. 14-41. B. Turkey, by Halil Inalcik. pp. 42-63.
- Environmental and foreign contributions, A. Japan, by Robert A. Scalapino, pp.64-90. B. Turkey, by Roderic H. Davison. pp. 91-116.
- Economic and political modernization, A. Japan, by William W. Lockwood. pp. 117-145. B. Turkey, by Peter F. Sugar. pp. 146-175.
- Education, A. Japan, by R. P. Dore. pp. 176-204. B. Turkey, by Frederick W. Frey. pp. 205-235.
- The mass media, by Shuichi Kato., pp. 236-254. B. Turkey, by Kemal H. Karpat, pp. 255-282.
- The civil bureaucracy, A. Japan, by Masamichi Inoki. pp. 283-300. B. Turkey, by Richard L. Chambers. pp. 301-327.
- The military, A. Japan, by Roger F. Hackett. pp. 328-351. B. Turkey, by Dankwart A. Rustow. pp. 352-388.
- Political leadership and political parties, A. Japan by Nobutaka Ike pp. 389-410. B. Turkey, by Arif T. Payaslioglu. pp. 411-433.
- Conclusion, by Dankwart A. Rustow, pp. 434-468.
- Bibliography. pp. 469-486.
- Contributors. pp. 487-490.
- Index. p. 491.

II.

Devos, George, Lizabeth Hauswald and Orin Broders
Cultural differences in family socialization; a psychocultural comparison of Chinese and Japanese. (Albert M. Craig, ed. Japan; a comparative view. Princeton, N.J., Princeton Univ. Press, 1979. (pp. 214-275)

Dhiravegen, Likhit
Contrasting modernization in Chulalongkorn's Siam and Meiji's Japan. (Carl A. Trocki, ed. The emergence of modern states; Thailand and Japan. Bangkok, Institute of Asian Studies, Chulalongkorn University, 1976. pp. 26-44)

Dore, Ronald P.
Latin America and Japan compared. (J. J. Johnson, ed. Continuity and change in Latin America. Stanford, Stanford Univ. Press, 1964. pp. 227-249)

Goodman, Mary Ellen
Values, attitudes, and social concepts of Japanese and American children. (Bernard S. Silberman, ed. Japanese character and culture; a book of selected readings. Tucson, University of Arizona Press, 1962. pp. 237-259)

Landes, David S.
Japan and Europe; contrasts in industrialization. (W. W. Lockwood, ed. The state of economic enterprise in Japan. Princeton, N.J., Princeton Univ. Press, 1965. pp. 93-182)

Levy, Marion J., Jr.
Contrasting factors in the modernizations of China and Japan. (Simon Kuznets, W. E. Moore and J. J. Spengler, ed. Economic growth; Brazil, India, Japan. Durham, N.C., Duke University Press, 1955. pp. 496-536)

Mendel, Douglas H.
Japan as a model for developing nations. (Edmund Skrzypczak, ed. Japan's modern century. A special issue of Monumenta Nipponica prepared in celebration of the centennial of the Meiji restoration. Tokyo, Sophia University, 1968. pp. 191-207)

Sato, Seizaburo
Response to the west: the Korean and Japanese patterns. (Carl A. Trocki, ed. The emergence of modern states; Thailand and Japan. Bangkok, Institute of Asian Studies, Chulalongkorn University, 1976. pp. 59-84) also published in (A. M. Craig, ed. Japan; a comparative view. Princeton, N.J., Princeton Univ. Press, 1979. pp. 105-129)

Scalapino, Robert A.
Environmental and foreign contributions; Japan. (Robert E. Ward and D. A. Rustow, ed. Political Modernization in Japan and Turkey. Princeton, N.J., Princeton University Press, 1964. pp. 64-90)

Ueda, Toshio
Modernization of Japan and China in relation to international law. (International Conference on the problems of Modernization in Asia, Seoul, 1965. Report. Seoul, Korea University Asiatic Research Center, 1966. pp. 454-459)

Vogel, Ezra F.
Nation-building in modern East Asia; Early Meiji (1868-1890) and Mao's China (1949-1971) (Albert M. Craig, ed. Japan; a comparative view. Princeton, N.J., Princeton Univ. Press, 1979. pp. 130-159)

III.

Lee, Hwasoo
A comparative study of economic, social and political conditions for political violence from the perspectives of revolution, China, Japan and Korea. Ph.D. 1975, University of Oregon. 289p.

Sinanian, Natalie Joan Robinson
A comparative study of women and the modernization process in Taiwan and Japan. Sp. A. 1975. Western Michigan University. 104p.

IV.

Cole, Allan B.
Factors explaining the desparate pace of modernization in China and Japan. Asian studies, v. 4, no.1. Apr. 1966. pp. 1-15.

Kobayashi, Yoshiaki
Comparative study of the French revolution and the Meiji restoration in Japan. Doshisha shogaku, v. 31, no.3. Sep. 1979. pp. 21-78.

Levy, Marion J., Jr.
Contrasting factors in the modernization of China and Japan. Economic development and cultural change, v. 2. 1953/54. pp. 161-197.

Levy, Marion J., Jr.
Some aspects of "individualism" and the problem of modernization in China and Japan. Economic development and cultural change, v. 10, no.3. Apr. 1962. pp. 225-240.

Scalapino, Robert A.
Democracy in Asia; past and future. Far eastern survey, v. 22, no.6. Mar. 21, 1951. pp. 53-57.

Sheldon, Charles David
Some economic reasons for the marked contrast in Japanese and Chinese modernization. Kyoto University economic review, v. 23, no.2. Oct. 1953. pp. 30-60.

SOCIAL CHANGE

I.

Bennett, John W. and Iwao Ishino
Paternalizm in the Japanese economy; anthropological studies of Oyabun-Kobun patterns. Minneapolis, Univ. of Minnesota Press, 1963.
307p.

Borton, Hugh
Japan since 1931; its political and social developments. Reprinted ed. Westport, Conn., Greenwood Press, 1973.
149p.

Dore, Ronald Philip.
Aspects of social change in modern Japan. Princeton, N.J., Princeton Univ. Press, 1967.
474p. (Studies in the modernization of Japan)
Contents:
- Preconditions of development: a comparison of Japan and Germany, by Reinhard Bendix. pp. 27-68.
- Merit as ideology in the Tokugawa period, by Thomas C. Smith. pp. 71-90.
- Kinship structure, migration to the city, and modernization, by Ezra F. Vogel. pp. 91-111.
- Mobility, equality, and individuation in modern Japan, by R. P. Dore. pp. 113-150.
- Status changes in hamlet structure accompanying modernization, by Erwin H. Johnson. pp. 153-183.
- Associations and democracy in Japan, by Edward Norbeck. pp. 185-200.
- Collective bargaining and works councils as innovations in industrial relations in Japan during the 1920's, by George O. Totten. pp. 203-243.
- Postwar trade unionism, collective bargaining, and Japanese social structure, by Solomon B. Levine. pp. 245-285.
- Organization and social function of Japanese gangs; historical development and modern parallels, by George A. de Vos and Keiichi Mizushima. pp. 289-325.
- Giri-Ninjo; an interpretation by L. Takeo Doi. pp. 327-334.
- Individual mobility and group membership; the case of the Burakumin, by John B. Cornell. pp. 337-372.
- The outcast tradition in modern Japan; a problem in social self-identity, by Hiroshi Wagatsuma and George A. de Vos. pp. 373-407.
- Japanese economic growth; background for social change, by John W. Bennett. pp. 411-453.

Embree, John F.
The Japanese nation; a social survey, N.Y., Rinehart, 1945.
306p. maps.

Fukutake, Tadashi
Man and society in Japan. Tokyo, Univ. of Tokyo Press, 1962.
241p.

Ishida, Takeshi
Japanese society. N.Y., Random House, 1971.
145p.

Koschmann, J. Victor, ed.
Authority and the individual in Japan; citizen protest in historical perspective. Tokyo, Univ. of Tokyo Press, 1978.
328p.
Contents:
Special introductory essay;
The roots of political disillusionment; "public" and "private" in Japan, by Sannosuke Matsumoto. pp. 31-53.
Part I: Prewar Japan
The Meiji state, Minponshugi, and ultranationalism, by Kuno Osamu. pp. 60-81.
- Japanese Christianity; between orthodoxy and heterodoxy, by Takeda Kiyoko. pp. 82-107.

- "Theory" and "organization" in the Japan Communist Party, by Matsuzawa Hiroaki. pp. 108-127.
- The "civil society" ideal and war-time resistance, by Hashikawa Bunzo. pp. 128-143.
Part II. Postwar Japan
The ethics of peace, by Oda Makoto, pp. 154-170.
- Citizen participation in historical perspective, by Matsushita Keiichi, pp. 171-188.
- Citizen's movements; organizing the spontaneous, by Michitoshi Takabatake pp. 189-199,
- Militarism in the management theory, by Kitazawa Masakuni. pp. 200-206.
- The glory and misery of "my home", by Tada Michitaro. pp. 207-219.
- The controversy over community and autonomy, by Sakuta Keiichi. pp. 220-249.
- The survival struggle of the Japanese community, by Irokawa Daikichi. pp. 250-282.

Nakane, Chie
Japanese society. London, Weidenfeld and Nicholson, 1970.
157p. (The nature of human society series)

Silberman, Bernard S. and H. D. Harootunian, ed.
Japan in crisis; essays on Taisho democracy. Princeton, N.J., Princeton Univ. Press, 1974.
469p.

Contents:
- A sense of en ending and the problems of Taisho, by Harry D. Harootunian. pp. 3-28.
- Some reflections on idealism in the political thought of Yoshino Sakuzo, by Tetsuo Najita. pp. 29-66.
- A note on the political thought of Natsume Sōseki in his later years, by Takayoshi Matsuo. pp. 68-85.
- Kawakami Hajime; a Japanese Marxist in search of the way, by Gail Bernstein. pp. 86-109.
- Between politics and culture; authority and ambiguities of intellectual choice in imperial Japan, by H. D. Harootunian. pp. 110-155.
- Aspects of the proletarian literary movement in Japan, by Yoshio Iwamoto. pp. 156-182.
- The bureaucratic role in Japan 1900-1945; the bureaucrat as politician, by Bernard S. Silberman. pp. 183-216.
- Taishō democracy as the pre-stage for Japanese militarism, by Shuichi Katō. pp. 217-236.
- The failure of economic expansion, 1918-1931, by Akira Iriya. pp. 237-269.
- A new Asian order; some notes on prewar Japanese nationalism, by James B. Crowley. pp. 270-298.
- The Japanese economy, 1911-1930; concentration, conflicts, and crises, by Kozo Yamamura. pp. 299-328.
- Incentives, productivity gaps, and agricultural growth rates in prewar Japan, Taiwan and Korea, by James I. Nakamura. pp. 329-373.
- The origins of tenant unrest, by Ann Waswo. pp. 374-397.
- Japanese industrial relations at the crossroads; the great Noda strike of 1927-1928, by George O. Tutten. pp. 398-436.
- Taisho Japan and the crisis of secularism, by Bernard S. Silberman. pp. 437-454.

Smith, Robert J. and Richard K. Beardsley, ed.
Japanese culture; its development and characteristics. Chicago, Aldine Pub. Co., 1962.
193p. illus. (Viking Fund punlisations in anthropology)
Contents:
- Nature of the problem of Japanese cultural origins, by Eiichiro Ishida. pp. 3-6.
- Prehistoric evidence for Japanese cultural origins, by Ichiro Yawata. pp. 7-10.
- Light on Japanese cultural origins from historical archeology and legend, by Namio Egami. pp. 11-16.

- The Japanese language; its origin and its sources, by Susumu Ono. pp. 17-24.
- Stability in Japanese kinship terminology; the historical evidence, by Robert J. Smith. pp. 25-33.
- Corporate emphasis and patterns of descent in the Japanese family, by Harumi Befu. pp. 34-41.
- "Dozoku" and "Ie", in Japan; the meaning, by Seiichi Kitano. pp. 42-46.
- Changing family structure in Japan, by Takashi Koyama. pp. 47-54.
- Notes on primogeniture in postwar Japan, by Y. Scott Matsumoto. pp. 55-72.
- Common-interest associations in rural Japan, by Edward Norbeck. pp. 73-85.
- Village community ("Buraku") in Japan and its democratization, by Tadashi Fukutake. pp. 86-90.
- The emergence of a self-conscious enterpreneurial class in rural Japan, by Erwin Johnson. pp. 91-99.
- Social and technological change in rural Japan; continuities and discontinuities, by Iwao Ishino. pp. 100-114.
- Patterns of emotion in modern Japan, by William Caudill. pp. 115-131.
- "Amae"; a key concept for understanding Japanese personality structure, by L. Takeo Doi. pp. 132-139.
- Entrance examinations and emotional disturbances in Japan's "new middle class", by Ezra F. Vogel. pp. 140-152.
- Deviancy and social change; a psychocultural evaluation of trends in Japanese delinquency and suicide, by George A. De Vos. pp. 153-171.
- Reflections of dependency phenomena as seen in Nisei in the United States, by Charlotte G. Babcock. pp. 172-188.
Index, p. 189.

Tsurumi, Kazuko
Social change and the individual; Japan before and after defeat in World War II. Princeton, N.J., Princeton Univ. Press, 1970. 441p.
Bibl.: pp. 411-427.

Yamamoto, George K. and Tsuyoshi Ishida, ed.
Selected readings on modern Japanese society. Berkeley, McCutchan, Pub. 1971. 250p.

II.

Barre, Weston La.
Some observations on character structure in the Orient; the Japanese. (Bernard S. Silberman, ed. Japanese character and culture; a book of selected readings. Tucson, University of Arizona Press, 1962. pp. 325-359)

Beardsley, Richard K., John W. Hall, and Robert E. Ward.
Community and kinship organizations. (Bernard S. Silberman, ed. Japanese character and culture; a book of selected readings. Tucson, University of Arizona Press, 1962. pp. 68-100)

Befu, Harumi
Corporate emphasis and patterns of descent in the Japanese family. (Robert J. Smith, ed. Japanese culture; its development and characteristics. Chicago, Aldine Pub. Co., 1962. pp. 34-41)

Bennett, John W.
Japanese economic growth; background for social change. (Ronald P. Dore, ed. Aspects of social change in modern Japan. Princeton, N.J., Princeton University Press, 1967. pp. 411-453)

Craig, Albert M.
Perspectives on personality in Japanese history. (Albert M. Craig, ed. Personality in Japanese history. Berkeley, University of California Press, 1970. pp. 1-28)

DeVos, George A.
Achievement orientation, social self-identity, and Japanese economic growth. (Irwin Scheiner, ed. Modern Japan; an interpretive anthology. New York, MacMillan, 1974. pp. 151-164)

Dore, R. P.
Mobility equality, and individuation in modern Japan. (Ronald P. Dore, ed. Aspects of social change in modern Japan. Princeton, N.J., Princeton University Press, 1967. pp. 113-150)

Gorer, Geoffrey
Themes in Japanese culture (Bernard S. Silberman, ed. Japanese character and culture; a book of selected readings. Tucson, University of Arizona Press, 1962. pp. 308-324)

Haring, Douglas G.
Japanese national character; cultural anthropology, psychoanalysis, and history. (Bernard S. Silberman, ed. Japanese character and culture; a book of selected readings. Tucson, University of Arizona Press, 1962. pp. 387-399)

Hayashi, Kentaro
Tradition and modernization in Japan. (International Conference on the Problems of Modernization in Asia, Seoul, 1965. Report. Seoul, Korea University Asiatic Research Center, 1966. pp. 261-268)

Horie, Y.
The tradition of Ie (house) and the industrialization of Japan. (Keiichiro Nakagawa, ed. Social order and entrepreneurship; proceedings of the 2nd Fuji Conference. Tokyo, University of Tokyo Press, 1977. pp. 231-254)

Hulse, Frederick S.
Convention and reality in Japanese culture. (Bernard S. Silberman, ed. Japanese character and culture; a book of selected readings. Tucson, University of Arizona Press, 1962. pp. 298-307)

Ike, Nobutaka
War and modernization. (Robert E. Ward, ed. Political development in modern Japan. Princeton, N.J., Princeton Univ. Press, 1968. pp. 189-212)

Kawashima, Takeyoshi, Michio Nagai, and John O. W. Bennett
A summary and analysis of the "familial structure of Japanese society". (Bernard S. Silberman, ed. Japanese character and culture; a book of selected readings. Tucson, University of Arizona Press, 1962. pp. 101-111)

Kitano, Seiichi
"Dozoku" and "Ie" in Japan; the meaning of family genealogical relationships. (Robert J. Smith, ed. Japanese culture; its development and characteristics. Chicago, Aldine 1962. pp. 42-46)

Koyama, Takashi
Changing family structure in Japan. (Robert J. Smith, ed. Japanese culture; its development and characteristics. Chicago, Aldine, 1962. pp. 47-54)

Okada, Yuzuru
The role of intellectuals in Japan's modernization. (International conference on the problems of modernization in Asia, Seoul, 1965. Report. Seoul, Korea University Asiatic Research Center, 1966. pp. 692-694)

Sano, Chiye
Changing values of the institutional family. (Bernard S. Silberman, ed. Japanese character and culture; a book of selected readings. Tucson, University of Arizona Press, 1962. pp. 112-140)

Smith, Robert J.
The life cycle. (Bernard S. Silberman, ed. Japanese character and culture; a book of selected readings. Tucson, University of Arizona Press, 1962. pp. 187-213)

Vogel, Ezra F.
Kinship structure, migration to the city, and modernization. (Ronald P. Dore, ed. Aspects of social change in modern Japan. Princeton, Princeton University Press, 1967. pp. 91-111)

Wagatsuma, Hiroshi
The social perception of skin color in Japan. (Irwin Scheiner, ed. Modern Japan; an interpretive anthology. N.Y., MacMillan, 1974. pp. 51-78)

III.

Takane, Masa'aki
Factors influencing the mobility of the Japanese political elites; 1860-1920. Ph.D. 1972. University of California at Berkeley.

IV.

Devos, George A.
Achievement orientation, social self-identity, and Japanese economic growth. Asian survey, v. 5, no.12. Dec. 1965. pp. 575-589.

Flershem, Robert G.
Case studies of social change in the region of Oshimizu Gumi. Monumenta Nipponica, v. 23, no.3/4. 1968. pp. 431-443.

Horio, Yasuzo
The rule of the Ie (House) in the economic modernization of Japan. Kyoto University economic review, v. 36, no.1. Apr. 1966. pp. 1-16.

Obelsky, Alvan J.
Japan's transition; socio-economic interpretation. Kobe University economic review, no.9. 1963. pp. 1-12.

Rabinowitz, Richard W.
Law and the social process in Japan. Transactions of the Asiatic Society of Japan, 3rd ser. v. 10. Aug. 1968. pp. 5-96.

EDUCATION

I.

Anderson, Ronald S.
Japan; three epochs of modern education. Washington, U. S. Dept. of Health, Education and Welfare, 1959. 219p. illus.

Aso, Makoto and Ikuo Amano
Education and Japan's modernization. Tokyo, Ministry of Foreign Affairs, 1972.
112p.

Brameld, Theodore
Japan; culture, educatiin, and change in two communities. N.Y., Holt, Reinehart and Winston, 1968.
316p. illus. maps.
Bibl. pp. 303-308.

Cummings, W. K., I. Amano, and K. Kitamura, ed.
The changing Japanese university in comparative perspective. N.Y., Praeger, 1979.
250p. (Comparative education series)
Bibl. pp. 240-250.
Contents:
- 1. Introduction, by William K. Cummings, Ikuo Amano, and Kazuyuki Kitamura. pp. 1-9.
- 2. Continuity and change in the structure of Japanese higher education, by Ikuo Amano. pp. 10-39.
- 3. Finance of higher education, by Shogo Ichikawa. pp. 40-63.
- 4. Mass higher education, by Kazuyuki Kitamura. pp- 64-82.
- 5. Expansion, examination fever, and euality, by William K. Cummings. pp. 83-106.
- 6. The Japanese student and the labor market, by Morikzau Ushiogi. pp. 107-126.
- 7. The changing role of the Japanese professor, by William K. Cummings and Ikuo Amano. pp. 127-148.
- 8. The productivity of the Japanese scholar, by Michiya Shimbori. pp. 149-165.

- 9. The internationalization of Japanese higher education, by Tetsuya Kobayashi. pp. 166-184.
- 10. The organization and administration of individual universities, by Yasumasa Tomoda and Takekazu Ehara. pp. 185-201.
- 11. Japan's postmodern student movement, by Donald F. Wheeler. pp. 202-216.
- 12. The Japanese system of higher education in comparative perspective, by Burton R. Clark. pp. 217-240.

Hokkaido Daigaku (Hokkaido University)
Hokkaido University; its history and calendar. Sapporo, 1953.
80p.

Japan. Ministry of Education
Demand and supply for graduates from secondary schools and universities; Japan. Tokyo, 1961.
69p.

Kaigo, Tokiomi
Japanese education; its past and present. Tokyo, Kokusai Bunka Shinkokai, 1965.
128p. illus. (Series on Japanese life and culture)

Kato, Hidetoshi
Japanese popular culture; studies in mass communication and cultural change, made at the Institute of Science of Thought, Japan. Tokyo, Tuttle, 1959.
223p. illus.

Kobayashi, Tetsuya
Society, schools and progress in Japan. Oxford, 1976.
185p. (Pergamon international library of science, technology, engineering and social studies)

Kobayashi, Victor Nobuo
John Dewey in Japanese educational thought. Ann Arbor, Univ. of Michigan, 1964.
198p. (Comparative education dissertation series)

Passin, Herbert
Society and education in Japan. N.Y., Columbia Univ. Teachers Village, 1965.
347p. (Comparative education series)

Pempel, T. J.
Patterns of Japanese policymaking; experiences from higher education. Boulder, Colo., Westview Press, 1978.
248p.

Roden, D. T.
Schooldays in imperial Japan; a study in the culture of a student elite. Berkeley, Univ. of California, 1980.
300p.

Sugihara, Yoshie and David W. Plath
Sensei and his pupil; the building of a Japanese commune. Berkeley, Univ. of California Press, 1969.
167p. illus.

Tsurumi, E. Patricia
Japanese colonial education in Taiwan, 1895-1945. Cambridge, Mass., Harvard Univ. Press, 1977.
334p.

UNESCO. Japanese National Commission
Development of local school administration and finance in Japan. Tokyo, 1962.
26p.

UNESCO. Japanese National Commission
Development of modern textbook system in Japan 1868-1961. Tokyo, 1961.
76p.

UNESCO. Japanese National Commission
Development of school building in Japan. Tokyo, 1962.
58p. illus.

UNESCO. Japanese National Commission
Development of school curriculum in Japan. Tokyo, 1961.
73p.

UNESCO. Japanese National Commission
Development of school health in Japan. Tokyo, 1962.
61p.

UNESCO. Japanese National Commission
History of industrial education in Japan, 1868-1900. Tokyo, 1959.
197p.

UNESCO. Japanese National Commission
The role of education in the social and economic development of Japan. Tokyo, 1966.
427p.

UNESCO. Japanese National Commission
The treatment of the West in textbooks of Japan - a historical survey. Tokyo, 1958.
58p. illus.

II.

Abe, Hakaru
Education of the legal profession in Japan. (Arthur Taylor von Mehren, ed. Law in Japan; the legal order in a changing society. Cambridge, Mass., Harvard University Press, 1963. pp. 153-187)

Amano, Ikuo
Continuity and change in the structure of Japanese higher education. (W. K. Cummings, I. Amano and K. Kitamura, ed. The changing Japanese university in comparative perspective. New York, Praeger, 1979. pp. 10-39)

Caiger, John
The aims and content of school courses in Japanese history, 1872-1945. (Edmund Skrzypczak, ed. Japan's modern century. A special issue of Monumenta Nipponica prepared in celebration of the centennial of the Meiji restoration. Tokyo, Sophia University, 1968. pp. 51-82)

Chittiwatanapong, Prasert
The modernization base in Japan and Thailand; education and science. (Carl A. Trocki, ed. The emergence of modern states; Thailand and Japan. Bangkok, Institute of Asian Studies, Chulalongkorn University, 1976. pp. 7-25)

Dore, R. P.
Education; Japan. (Robert E. Ward and D. A. Rustow, ed. Political modernization in Japan and Turkey. Princeton, Princeton Univ. Press, 1964. pp. 176-204)

Dore, R. P.
The legacy of Tokugawa education. (Marius B. Jansen, ed. Changing Japanese attitudes toward modernization. Princeton, Princeton University Press, 1965. pp. 99-132

Ichikawa, Shogo
Finance of higher education. (W. K. Cummings, I. Amano, and K. Kitamura, ed. The changing Japanese university in comparative perspective. New York, Praeger, 1979. pp. 40-63)

Kato, Shuichi
The mass media; Japan. (Robert E. Ward and D. A. Rustow, ed. Political modernization in Japan and Turkey. Princeton, Princeton University Press, 1964. pp. 236-254)

Kitamura, Kazuyuki
Mass higher education. (W. K. Cummings, I. Amano, and K. Kitamura, ed. The changing Japanese university in comparative perspective. New York, Praeger, 1979. pp. 64-87)

Lanham, Betty
Aspects of child care in Japan. (Bernard S. Silberman, ed. Japanese character and culture; a book of selected readings. Tucson, University of Arizona Press, 1962. pp. 220-236)

Makino, Tatsumi
Some notes on literacy and education in Japan. (Paul Halmos, ed. Japanese sociological studies. Keele, Univ. of Keele, 1966. pp. 83-94)

Moloney, James Clark
Child training and Japanese conformity. (Bernard S. Silberman, ed. Japanese character and culture; a book of selected readings. Tucson, University of Arizona Press, 1962. pp. 214-219)

Munakata, Seiya
The course and problems of national education; from the Meiji period to the present day. (Seiichi, Tobata. The modernization of Japan - I. Tokyo, Institute of Asian Economic Affairs. pp. 209-228)

Nagai, Michio
Westernization and Japanization; the early Meiji transformation of education. (Donald H. Shively, ed. Tradition and modernization in Japanese culture. Princeton, Princeton University Press, 1971. pp. 35-76)

Nakayama, Shigeru
A history of universities; an overview - from the viewpoint of science history. (Shigeru Nakayama, ed. Science and society in modern Japan; selected historical sources. Tokyo, University of Tokyo Press, 1974. pp. 72-80)

Passin, Herbert
Education and the position of women; the Japanese educational system. (Jon Livingston, ed. Imperial Japan, 1800-1945. New York, Pantheon Books, 1973. pp. 257-270)

Pittau, Joseph
Inoue Kowashi (1843-1895) and the Meiji educational system. (Irwin Scheiner, ed. Modern Japan; an interpretive anthology. New York, MacMillan, 1974. pp. 176-189)

Silberman, Bernard S.
Elite transformation in the Meiji restoration; the upper civil service 1868-1873. (Bernard S. Silberman, etc. ed. Modern Japanese leadership; transition and change. Tucson, University of Arizona Press, 1966. pp. 233-259)

III.

Bender, Fred Augstus
A historical study of the structure and function of the junior college in Japan. Ph.D. 1978. The University of Texas at Austin. 248p.

Bonnallie, Dorothy A.
Education in early Meiji Japan, 1868-1890; Fukuzawa Yukichi, Niijima Jo, and Mori Arinori. Ph.D. 1976. Claremont Graduate School. 205p.

Cummings, William K.
The changing academic market place and University reform in Japan. Ph.D. 1969. Harvert University.

Haslett, Jacqueline G.
A history of physical education and sports in Japan from 1868 through 1972. Ed.D 1977. Boston University School of Education. 1104p.

Kim, Soon-ja
Historical development of Japanese secondary technical education, 1870-1935. Ph.D. 1978. University of Pittsburgh. 254p.

Meynardie, Mary Elizabeth Wood
The role of education in the modernization of Japan. Ed.D. 1973. The University of Toledo, 279p.

Nishihira, Isao
Western influences on the modernization of Japanese education, 1868-1912. Ph.D. 1972. The Ohio State University. 482.p.

Niwata, Yoichi
Economic growth and education as a form of social overhead capital; an empirical investigation, a case of the Japanese economy. Ph.D. 1977. Claremont graduate school. 172p.

IV.

Abe, Hiroshi
Higher learning in Korea under Japanese rule - Keijo Imperial University and the "People's University" campaign. Developing economies. v. 9, no.2. June 1971. pp. 174-196.

Arase, Yutaka
Mass communication between the two world wars. Developing economies, v. 5, no.4. Dec. 1967. pp. 748-766.

Dore, R. P.
Education in Japan's growth. Pacific affairs, v. 37, no.1. Spring 1964. pp. 66-79.

Fujitake, Akira
The formation and development of mass culture. Developing economies, v. 5, no.4. Dec. 1967. pp. 767-782.

Ishizaka, Iwao
Problems in the industrial training in Japan. Keio business review, no. 3. 1964. pp. 29-55.

Ito, Ryoji
Education as a basic factor in Japan's economic growth. Developing economies, v. 1, no.1. Jan/June 1963. pp. 38-54.

Iwauchi, Ryoichi
Institutionalizing the technical manpower formation in Meiji Japan. Developing economies, v. 15, no.4. Dec. 1977. pp. 420-439.

Katagiri, Akinori
Broadcasting. Japan quarterly, v. 8, no.3. July/Sept. 1961. Changing Japan 16. pp. 356-361.

Kawada, Hisashi
Industrialization and educational investment in the Meiji era, 1868-1912. Management and labor studies, no. 8. Feb. 1964. pp. 1-28.

Koga, Hiroshi
The development of industrial training systems in "heavy industry" in Japan, 1860's-1930's. Waseda economic papers, no. 16. 1977. pp. 1-26.

Munakata, Seiya
The course and problems of national education; from the Meiji period to the present day. Developing economies, v. 3, no.4. Dec. 1965. pp. 540-559.

Shimbori, Michiya
The academic marketplace in Japan. Developing economies, v. 7, no.4. Dec. 1969. pp. 617-639.

Taira, Koji
Education and literacy in Meiji Japan; an interpretation. Explorations in entrepreneurial history, v. 8, no.4. Summer 1971. pp. 371-394.

Terasaki, Masao
Development of the study on the history of universities in Japan. Japanese studies in the history of science, no.15. 1976. pp. 15-20.

Tsurumi, E. Patricia
Meiji primary school language and ethics textbooks; old values for a new society. Modern Asian studies, v. 8, pt. 2. Apr. 1974. pp. 247-288.

MEDICAL SYSTEM

I.

Bowers, John Z.
Medical education in Japan; from Chinese medicine to Western medicine. N.Y., Harper and Row, 1965. 174p. (Commonwealth Fund book).

Bowers, John Z.
Western medical pioneers in feudal Japan. Baltimore, J. Hopkins Press, 1970. 245p. illus.

Lock, M. M.
East Asian medicine in urban Japan; varieties of medical experience. Berkeley, Univ. of California, 1979. 300p.

III.

Lock, Margaret Marion
Oriental medicine in urban Japan; a harmony of tradition and science. Ph.D. 1976. University of California, Berkeley. 318p.

IV.

Nakagawa, Yonezo
A survey of the interest for the history of medicine in Japan. Japanese studies in the history of science, no. 1. 1962. pp. 38-44.

Ōtori, Ranzaburo
The acceptance of western medicine in Japan. Monumenta Nipponica, v. 19, nos.3/4. 1964. pp. 21-40.

POLLUTION

I.

Strong, Kenneth
Ox against the storm; a biography of Tanaka Shozo, Japan's conservationist pioneer. Tenterdent, Kent., Kenneth Norbury Pub., 1977. xviii, 231p.

III.

Stone, Alan Atwood
The vanishing village; the Ashio Copper Mine pollution case, 1890-1907. Ph.D. 1974. University of Washington. 254p.

IV.

Notehelfer, F. G.
Japan's first pollution incident, symposium; the Ashio copper pollution case. Journal of Japanese studies, v. 1, no.2. Spring 1975. pp. 351-383.

Pyle, Kenneth B.
Introduction; Japan faces her future, symposium; the Ashio copper mines pollution case. Journal of Japanese studies, v. 1, no.2. Spring 1975. pp. 347-350.

Stone, Alan
The Japanese muckrakers, symposium: the Ashio copper pollution case. Journal of Japanese studies, v. 1, no.2. Spring 1975. pp. 385-407.

URBAN PROBLEMS

I.

Allinson, Gary D.
Japanese urbanizm; industry and politics in Kariya, 1872-1972. Berkeley, Univ. of California Press, 1975.
276p.

Azumi, Atsushi and Hiroshi Kaneko
Tokyo: tradition and the megapolis. Tokyo, Kodansha International, 1972.
126p.

Black, John R.
Young Japan; Yokohama and Yedo 1868-79, with an introduction by Grace Fox. Tokyo, Oxford Univ. Press, 1968.
2 v. illus. (Oxford in Asia historical reprintes)

Busch, Noel F.
Two minutes to noon; the story of the great Tokyo earthquake and fire. N.Y., Simon and Schuster, 1962.
191p. illus. maps.

Dore, Ronald Philip
City life in Japan; a study of a Tokyo ward. Berkeley, Univ. of California Press, 1958.
472p. illus.

Glickman, Norman J.
Financing the Japanese urban system; local public finance and intergovernmental relations. Luxenburg, International Institute for Applied Systems Analysis, 1977.
71p.

Kokusai Kirisutokyo Daigaku, Shakaikagaku Kenkyusho. (Social Science Research Institute, International Christian Univ.)
Local community and urbanization. Tokyo, 1963.
39p.

Kornhauser, David Henry
Urban Japan; its foundations and growth. London, Longman, 1976.
180p.

Poole, Otis Manchester
The death of old Yokohama in the great Japanese earthquake of September 1, 1923. London, George Allen and Unwin, 1968.
135p. illus. maps.

Smith, Thomas C., ed.
City and village in Japan. Chicago, Univ. of Chicago Press, 1960.
257p. (Economic development and cultural change, v. 9, no.1. pt. 2. Oct. 1960)
Contents:
- Urbanization and population change in the development of modern Japan, by Irene B. Taeuber. pp. 1-28.
- The farm population in the national economy before and after World War II, by Masayoshi Namiki. pp. 29-42.
- The role of agriculture in modern Japanese economic development, by Kazushi, Ohkawa and Henry Rosovsky. pp. 43-68.
- Agricultural improvement in Japan; 1870-1900, by R. P. Dore. pp. 69-92.

- Landlords' sons in the business elite, by Thomas C. Smith, pp. 93-108.
- Leaders of modern Japan; social origins and mobility, by James C. Abegglen and Mannari Hiroshi. pp. 109-134.
- Urban-rural differences and the process of political modernization in Japan; a case study, by Robert E. Ward. pp. 135-166.
- Urban-rural differences in voting behavior in postwar Japan, by Jun'ichi Kyogoku and Nobutaka Ike. pp. 167-186.
- Labor and agrarian disputes in Japan following World War I, by George O. Totten. pp. 187-212.
- Modernization and divorce rate trends in Japan, by Takeyoshi Kawashima and Kurt Steiner. pp. 213-240.
- Pre-industrial urbanism in Japan; a consideration of multiple traditions in a feudal society, by Robert J. Smith. pp. 241-257.

Steiner, Jesse F.
Mitaka; from village to suburban city; a study of Tokyo's urban fringe. Tokyo, International Christian Univ., 1957.
39p.

Tokyo-to
Regional and city planning for Tokyo. Tokyo, Tokyo Metropolitan Government, 1964.
32p. maps.

Tokyo-to. Somukyoku
Tokyo's financial history; a century of growth amid change. Tokyo, 1972.
152p. (TMG municipal library. no.7)

UNESCO. Japanese National Commission
Regionalism or regional planning in Japan. Tokyo, 1958.
59p.

White, James W.
Political implications of city-ward migration; Japan as an exploratory test case. Beverly Hills, Calif., Sage Publications, 1973.
61p.

Wilkinson, Thomas O.
The urbanization of Japanese labor 1868-1955. Amherst, Univ. of Massachusetts Press, 1965.
243p. maps.

Yazaki, Takeo
The Japanese city; a sociological analysis. Tokyo, Japan Pub. Trading Co., 1963.
105p. illus. map.

Yazaki, Takeo
Social change and the city in Japan, from earliest times through the industrial revolution. Tokyo, Japan Pub. Trading Co., 1968.
549p. maps.

Yazaki, Takeo
The socioeconomic structure of the Tokyo metropolitan complex, tr. by Mitsugu Matsuda.
Honolulu, Social Science Research Institute, Univ. of Hawaii, 1970.
401p.

II.

Chūbashi, Masayoshi and Koji Taira
Poverty in modern Japan; perceptions and realities. (Hugh Patrick, ed. Japanese industrialization and social consequences. Berkeley, University of California Press, 1976. pp. 391-438)

Kikuchi, Shinzo
Centrifugal and centripetal urbanization in Japan. (International Geographical Union. Regional conference in Japan, 1957. Proceedings of IGU regional conference in Japan. Tokyo, 1959. pp. 367-370)

Numata, Jiro
Shigeno Yasutsugu and the modern Tokyo tradition of historical writing. (W. G. Beasley and E. G. Pulleyblank, ed. Historians of China and Japan. London, Oxford University Press, 1961. pp. 264-287)

Smith, Henry D., II.
Tokyo and London; comparative conceptions of the city. (Albert M. Craig. ed. Japan, a comparative view. Princeton, N.J., Princeton University Press, 1979. pp. 49-104)

Yazaki, Takeo
The countryside and the cities; social change and the city. (Jon Livingston, ed. Imperial Japan, 1800-1945. New York, Pantheon Books, 1973. pp. 135-137)

III.

August, Robert Leslie
Urbanization and local government in Japan; a study of Shibuya, 1889-1932. Ph.D. 1975. University of Pittsburgh.
231p.

Downard, Jack Douglas
Tokyo; the depression years, 1927-1933. Ph.D. 1976. Indiana University.
281p.

IV.

Beika, Minoru
Characteristic approach for regional development in Western Europe and U. S. A. relations to the case in Japan. Kobe economic and business review, v. 15. 1968. pp. 1-8.

Ishida, Takeshi
Urbanization and its impact on Japanese politics; a case of a late and rapidly developed country. Annals of the Institute of Social Science, no. 8. 1967. pp. 1-11.

Kimura Ki and Kotaro Ishii
History of Yokohama. Contemporary Japan, v. 22, nos.10/12. 1954. pp. 633-649.

Kornhauser, David H.
Urbanization and population pressure in Japan. Pacific affairs, v. 31, no.3. Sept. 1958. pp. 275-285.

Kurasawa, Susumu
Japanese city; a study on its structural changes. Developing economies, v. 7, no.4. Dec. 1969. pp. 527-553.

Nee, Brett
Sanya; Japan's internal colony. Bulletin of concerned Asian scholars, v. 6, no.3. Sept./Oct. 1974. pp. 12-18.

Shiota, Shobei
The rice riots and the social problems. Developing economies, v. 4, no.4. Dec. 1966. pp. 516-534.

Smith, Henry D., II.
Tokyo as an idea; an exploration of Japanese urban thought until 1945. Journal of Japanese studies, v. 4, no.1. Winter 1978. pp. 45-80.

Taira, Koji
Urban poverty, rag pickers, and the "Ants villa" in Tokyo. Economic development and cultural change. v. 17, no.2. Jan. 1969. pp. 155-177.

LAW AND LOCAL GOVERNMENT

I.

Aqua, Ronald
Local institutions and rural development in Japan. Ithaca, N.Y., Rural Development Committee, Center for International Studies, Cornell Univ. 1974.
102p. (Special series on rural local government, no.8)

Burks, Ardath W.
The government of Japan, 2d ed. N.Y., Crowell, 1964.
283p. (Crowell comparative government series)

Hall, John Whitney
Government and local power in Japan, 500-1700; a study based on Bizen Province. Princeton, Princeton University Press, 1966.
446p.

Hoven W. and A. van den Elshout
Local government in selected countries; Ceylon, Israel, Japan. N.Y., United Nations, 1963.
113p.

Minear, Richard H.
Japanese tradition and Western law; emperor, estate, and law in the thought of Hozumi Yatsuka. Cambridge, Mass., Harvard Univ. Press, 1970.
244p. (Harvard East Asian series)

Steiner, Kurt
Local government in Japan. Stanford, Stanford Univ. Press, 1965.
564p.

Von Mehren, Arthur Taylor, ed.
Law in Japan; the legal order in a changing society. Cambridge, Mass., Harvard Univ. Press. 1963.
706p.
Contents:
- A century of innovation: the development of Japanese law, 1868-1961, by Kenzo Takayanagi. pp. 5-40.
- Dispute resolution in contemporary Japan, by Takeyoshi Kawashima. pp. 41-72.
- The process of litigation; an experiment with the adversary system, by Kohji Tanabe. pp. 73-110.
- The legal profession in Japan; its historical development and present state, by Takaaki Hattori. pp. 111-152.
- Education of the legal profession in Japan, by Hakaru Abe. pp. 153-187.
- Commentary: part I, by Arthur T. von Mehren. pp. 188-204.
- The rule of law; constitutional development, by Masami Ito. pp. 205-238.
- The rule of law; some aspects of judicial review of administrative action, by Kiminobu Hashimoto. pp. 239-273.

- The accused and society; some aspects of Japanese criminal law, by Ryuichi Hirano. pp. 274-296.
- The accused and society; the administration of criminal justice in Japan, by Atsushi Nagashima. pp. 297-323.
- The accused and society; therapeutic and preventive aspects of criminal justice in Japan, by Haruo Abe. pp. 324-363.
- The family and the law; the individualistic premise and modern Japanese family law, by Yozo Watanabe. pp. 364-398.
- The treatment of motor-vehicle accidents; a study of the impact of technological change on legal relations, by Ichiro Kato, pp. 399-421.
- Commentary; part II, by Arthur T. von Mehren. pp. 422-438.
- The regulation of the employer-employee relationship; Japanese labor-relations law, by Kichiemon Ishikawa. pp. 439-479.
- The regulation of corporate enterprise; the law of unfair competition and the control of monopoly power, by Yoshio Kanazawa. pp. 480-506.
- The letal structure for economic enterprise; some aspects of Japanese commercial law, by Shinichiro Michida. pp. 507-546.
- The legal structure for corporate enterprise; shareholder-management relations under Japanese law, by Makoto Yazawa. pp. 547-566.
- Computation of income in Japanese income taxation; a study in the adjustment of theory to reality, by Morio Uematsu. pp. 567-621.
- Commentary; part III, by Arthur T. von Mehren. pp. 622-630.
- Laws, orders, and related materials cited. pp. 631-648.
- Table of cases. pp. 649-686.
- Index. p. 687.

Zenkoku Chiho Jichi Kyogikai (Japan Local Self-Government Institute)
Guide to local government in Japan. Tokyo, 1959.
27p. map.

II.

Hattori, Takaaki
The legal profession in Japan; its historical development and present state. (Arthur Taylor von Mehren, ed. Law in Japan; the legal order in a changing society. Cambridge, Mass. Harvard University Press, 1963. pp. 111-152)

Henderson, Dan F.
Japanese law: a profile (Arthur E. Tiedemann, ed. An introduction to Japanese civilization, New York, Colombia Univ. Press, 1974. pp. 569-591)

Inoki, Masamichi
The civil bureaucracy; Japan. (Robert E. Ward and D. A. Rustow. Political modernization in Japan and Turkey. Princeton, Princeton University Press, 1964. pp. 283-300)

Takayanagi, Kenzo
A century of innovation; the development of Japanese law, 1868-1961. (Arthur Taylor von Mehren, ed. Law in Japan; the legal order in a changing society. Cambridge, Mass., Harvard University Press, 1963. pp. 5-40)

Tanabe, Kohji
The process of litigation; an experiment with the adversary system. (Arthur Taylor von Mehren, ed. Law in Japan; the legal order in a changing society. Cambridge, Mass., Harvard University Press, 1963. pp. 73-110)

III.

Kramer, Robert Johnston
The politics of legal modernization; the roman and Japanese experiences. Ph.D. 1975. New York University. 290p.

Staubitz, Richard Lousis
The establishment of the system of of local self-government (1888-1890) in Meiji Japan; Yamagata Aritomo and the meaning of "Jichi" (self government). Ph.D. 1973. Yale University.
268p.

IV.

McClain, James L.
Local politics and national integration; the Fukui prefectural assembly in the 1880's. Monumenta Nipponica. v. 31, no.1. Spring 1976. pp. 51-75.

Miyamoto, Ken'ichi
Local self-government and local finance. Developing economies. v. 6, no.4. Dec. 1968. pp. 587-615.

Pyle, Kenneth B.
The technology of Japanese nationalism; the local improvement movement, 1900-1918. Journal of Asian studies. v. 33, no.1. Nov. 1973. pp. 51-65.

Totten, George Oakley
Adoption of the Prussian model for municipal government in Meiji Japan; principles and compromises. Developing economies. v. 15, no.4. Dec. 1977. pp. 487-510. Bibl. pp. 508-510.

GEOGRAPHY AND REGIONAL PROBLEMS

GEOGRAPHY

I.

Ackerman, Edward A.
Japan's natural resources and their relation to Japan's economic future. Chicago, Univ. of Chicago Press, 1953.
655p. illus. maps.

Allen, George Cyril
Japan as a market and source of supply. Oxford, Pergamon Press, 1967. 140p. (The Commonwealth and international library)

Andrews, Ron L.
Japan; a social and economic geography. Melbourne, George Philip and O'Neil, 1971.
150p.

Dempster, Prue
Japan advances; a geographical study. London, Methuen, 1967.
329p.

International Geographical Union. Regional Conference in Japan, 1957.
Proceedings of IGU Regional Conference in Japan. Tokyo, 1959.
606p. illus. maps.
Contents:
- Geography of the industrialization of Japan, by Ryuziro Isida. pp. 349-354.
- Geographical function of the reclamation settlements during the period of the Shogunate, 1603-1867. pp. 362-366.
- Centrifugal and centripetal urbanization in Japan, by Shinzo Kiuchi. pp. 367-370.
- The formation of citrus growing areas in Japan, by Setsutaro Murakami. pp. 420-428.
- Traditional manufacturing industry in Japan, by Mutsuo Nishimura. p. 439.
- Japanese and American world-views and their landscapes, by Forrest Ralph Pitts. pp. 447-452.
- Maki-Hata; the four-field system in Japan, by Toyoji Tanaka. pp. 497-502.

Trewartha, Glenn T.
Japan; a physical, cultural and regional geography. Madison, Univ. of Wisconsin Press, 1945.
607p. illus. maps.

II.

Ginsbury, Norton
Economic and cultural geography. (Arthur E. Tiedemann, ed. An introduction to Japanese civilization. New York, Columbia Univ. Press, 1974. pp. 423-460)

Ishida, Ryuziro
Geography of the industrialization of Japan. (International Geographical Union. Regional conference in Japan, 1957. Proceedings of IGU regional conference in Japan. Tokyo, 1959. pp. 349-354)

Pitts, Forrest Ralph
Japanese and American world-views and their landscapes. (International Geographical Union. Regional conference in Japan, 1957. Proceedings of IGU regional conference in Japan. Tokyo, 1959. pp. 447-452)

IV.

Ishida, Ryuziro
The industrialization of Japan; a geographical analysis. Annals of the Hitotsubashi academy. v. 7. no.1. Oct. 1956. pp. 61-80.

Kuroha, Hyojiro
A historio-geographical sketch of Osaka Prefecture. Bulletin of University of Osaka Prefecture, series D. v. 2. 1958. pp. 1-8.

Oya, Eiichi
A few aspects about the economic geography of Japan. Hokudai economic papers, v. 1. 1968/1969. pp. 94-101.

Takeuchi, Keiichi
The origins of human geography in Japan. Hitotsubashi journal of arts and sciences, v. 15, no.1. Sept. 1974. pp. 1-13.

Takeuchi, Keiichi
Some remarks on the history of regional description and the tradition of regionalism in modern Japan. Hitotsubashi journal of social studies, v. 10, no.1. Apr. 1978. pp. 36-49.

HOKKAIDO

I.

Harrison, John A.
Japan's northern frontier; a preliminary study in colonization and expansion with special reference to the relations of Japan and Russia. Gainesville, Univ. of Florida Press, 1953. 202p.

Jones, Francis Clifford
Hokkaido; its present state of development and future prospects. London, Oxford Univ. Press, 1958. 146p.

Salwey, Charlotte M.
The island dependencies of Japan; an account of the islands that have passed under Japanese control since the restoration, 1867-1912. London, Eugene L. Morice, 1913. 148p.

MINORITIES

I.

De Vos, George A.
Socialization for achievement; essays on the cultural psychology of the Japanese. Berkeley, Univ. of Clifornia Press, 1973. 597p.

De Vos, George and Hiroshi Wagatsuma
Japan's invisible race; caste in culture and personality. Berkeley, Univ. of Clifornia Press, 1966.
415p. illus.
Bibl. pp. 387-406.

De Vos, George and William O. Wetherall
Japan's monorities; Burakumin, Koreans and Ainu. Rev. ed. London, Minority Rights Group, 1974.
20p.

Mitchell, Richard Hanks
The Korean minority in Japan. Berkeley, Univ. of California Press, 1967.
186p.

Munro, Neil Gordon
Ainu creed and cult. N.Y., Columbia Univ. Press, 1963.
182p. illus.

Takakura, Shinichiro
The Ainu of northern Japan. Philadelphia, American Philosophical Society, 1960.
88p. map. (Transactions of the American Philosophical Society)

Tull, Chu
Political attitudes of the overseas Chinese in Japan. Hong Kong, Union Research Institute, 1967.
203p.

Wagner, Edward W.
The Korean minotiry in Japan 1906-1950. N.Y., Institute of Pacific Relations, 1951.
108p.

II.

Cornell, John B.
Buraku social organization and community life. (Bernard S. Silberman, ed. Japanese character and culture; a book of selected readings. Tucson, University of Arizona Press, 1962. pp. 36-67)

Cornell, John B.
From caste patron to entrepreneur and political ideologue; transformation in 19th and 20th century outcaste leadership elites. (Bernard S. Silberman, etc. ed. Modern Japanese leadership; transition and change. Tucson, University of Arizona Press, 1966. pp. 51-82)

Cornell, John B.
Individual mobility and group membership; the case of the Burakumin. (Ronald P. Dore, ed. Aspects of social change in modern Japan. Princeton, Princeton University Press, 1967. pp. 337-372)

Wagatsuma, Hiroshi and George A. de Vos.
The outcast tradition in modern Japan; a problem in social self-identity. (Ronald P. Dore, ed. Aspects of social change in modern Japan. Princeton, Princeton University Press, 1967. pp. 373-407)

IV.

Passin, Herbert
Untouchability in the Far East. <u>Monumenta Nipponica</u>. v. 11, no.3. Oct. 1955. pp. 27-47.

Totsuka, Hideo
Korean immigration in prewar Japan. <u>Annals of the Institute of Social Science</u>. no. 17. 1976. pp. 89-110.

RYUKYU ISLANDS

I.

Glacken, Clarence J.
The great Loochoo; a study of Okinawan village life. Berkeley, Univ. of California Press, 1955.
324p. illus. maps.

Haring, Douglas G.
Okinawan customs; yesterday and today. Tokyo, Tuttle, 1969.
192p. illus. map.

Kerr, George H.
Okinawa; the history of an island people. Tokyo, Tuttle, 1958.
542p. illus. maps.

Lebra, William P.
Okinawa religion; belief, ritual, and social structure. Honolulu, Univ. of Hawaii Press, 1966.
241p.

Maretzki, Thomas W. and Hatsumi Maretzki
Taira; an Okinawan village. N.Y., John Wiley, 1966.
176p. (Six cultures series)

Morris, M. D.
Okinawa; a tiger by the tail. N.Y., Hawthorn Books, 1968.
238p. illus.

Robinson, James C.
Okinawa; a people and their gods. Tokyo, Tuttle, 1969.
110p.

Smith, Allan H., ed.
Ryukyuan culture and society; a survey. Honolulu, Univ. of Hawaii Press, 1964.
111p. (Tenth Pacific Congress series)

Zabilka, Gladys, ed.
Customs and culture of Okinawa. Rev. ed. Tokyo, Tuttle, 1959.
200p. illus.

IV.

Lebra, William P. and Thomas W. Maretzi
The community cooperative in northern Okinawa. Economic development and cultural change, v. 2, no.3. pt. 1. Apr. 1953. pp. 225-238.

Matsuda, Mitsugu
The Ryukuan government scholarship students to China, 1392-1868 - based on a short essay by Nakahara Zenchu, 1962. Monumenta Nipponica. v. 21, nos.3/4. 1966. pp. 273-304.

EXTERNAL PROBLEMS

JAPANESE IN FOREIGN COUNTRIES

I.

Bennett, John William, Herbert Passin, and Robert K. McKnight
In search of identify; the Japanese overseas scholar in American and Japan, Minneapolis, Univ. of Minnesota Press, 1958.
369p. illus.

California. State Board of Control
California and the oriental; Japanese, Chinese and Hindus. New York, Arno Press, 1978.
231p.
Reprint ed.

Coman, Katharine and Andrew W. Lind
The history of contract labor in the Hawaiian Islands, and Hawaii's Japanese. New York, Arno Press, 1978.
264p.
Reprint ed.

Conroy, Francis Hilary
The Japanese expansion into Hawaii, 1868-1898. San Francisco, R. and E. Research Associates, 1973.
246p.
Reprint ed.

Conroy, Francis Hilary
The Japanese frontier in Hawaii, 1868-1898. Berkeley, Univ. of California Press, 1953.
175p. (Univ. of Calif. publications in history)

Daniels, Roger, ed.
Two monographs on Japanese Candaians. New York, Arno Press, 1978.
43,98p.
Reprint ed.

Gardiner, C. Harvey
The Japanese and Peru, 1873-1973. Albuquerque, Univ. of New Mexico Press, 1975.
202p.

Hata, Donald Teruo, Jr.
"Undesirables"; early immigrants and the anti-Japanese movement in San Francisco, 1892-1893, prelude to exclusion. New York, Arno Press, 1978.
168p.
Reprint ed.

Heller, H. Robert and Emily E. Heller
Japanese investment in the United States; with a case study of the Hawaiian experience.
N.Y., Praeger, 1974.
161p.

Kachi, Teruko Okada
The treaty of 1911 and the immigration and alien land law issue between the United States and Japan, 1911-1913. New York, Arno Press, 1978.
266p.
Reprint ed.

La Violette, Forrest Emanuel
Americans of Japanese ancestry; a study of assimilation in the American community. New York, Arno Press, 1978.
185p.
Reprint ed.

Matsuda, Mitsugu
The Japanese in Hawaii, 1868-1967; a bibliography of the first hundred years. Honolulu, Univ. of Hawaii Social Science Research Institute, 1968.
232p. (Hawaii series)

Mears, Eliot Grinnell
Resident orientals on the American Pacific coast. New York, Arno Press, 1978.
545p.
Reprint ed.

Millis, Harry Alvin
The Japanese problem in the United States. New York, Arno Press, 1978.
334p.
Reprint ed.

Normano, Joao Feederico and Antonello Gerbi
The Japanese in South America; an introductory survey with special reference to Peru. New York, AMS Press, 1978.
135p. (Institute of Pacific Relations)
Bibl. pp. 127-130.
Rep. of the 1943 ed.

Ogawa, Dennis M.
Jan Ken Po; the world of Hawaii's Japanese Americans. 2d ed. Honolulu, Univ. Press of Hawaii, 1978.
183p.

Shapiro, Harry Lewis
Migration and environment; a study of the physical characteristics of the Japanese immigrants to Hawaii and the effects of environment on their descendants. New York, Arno Press, 1978.
594p.
Reprint ed.

Stewart, Norman R.
Japanese colonization in eastern Paraguay. Washington, National Academy of Sciences, 1967.
202p. illus. maps. (Foreign field research program report)

U. S. Congress. House. Committee on Immigration and Naturalization
Japanese immigration; hearings before the Committee on Immigration and Naturalization. New York, Arno Press, 1978.
1490p.
Reprint ed.

U. S. Dept. of State
Report of the Honorable Roland S. Morris on Japanese immigration and alleged discriminatory legislation against Japanese residents in the United States. New York, Arno Press, 1978.
282p.
Reprint ed.

Young, Charles Hurlburt
The Japanese Canadians. New York, Arno Press, 1978.
295p.
Reprint ed.

III.

Kikumura, Akemi
The life history of an Issei woman; conflicts and strain in the process of acculturation. Ph.D. 1979, University of California, Los Angeles.
256p.

Shimada, Koji
Education, assimilation and acculturation; a case study of a Japanese-American community in New Jersey. Ed.D. 1975. Temple University.
244p.

Tsuchida, Nobuya
The Japanese in Brazil, 1908-1941. Ph.D. 1978. University of California, Los Angeles.
415p.

IV.

Ono, Kazuichiro
The problem of Japanese emigration. _Kyoto University economic review_, v. 28, no.1. Apr. 1958. pp. 40-54.

Tanaka, Kaoru
Japanese immigrants in Amazonia and their future. _Kobe University economic review_, no.3. 1957. pp. 1-24.

Titiev, Mischa
The Japanese colony in Peru. _Far Eastern quarterly_, v. 10, no.3. May 1951. pp. 227-237.

Williams, Emilio
The Japanese in Brazil. _Far eastern survey_, v. 18, no.1. Jan. 12, 1949. pp. 6-8.

INTERNATIONAL RELATIONS

I.

Battistini, Lawrence H.
Japan and America, from earliest times to the present. N.Y., John Day, 1953.
189p. maps. (Asia book.)

Battistini, Lawrence H.
The United States and Asia. Tokyo, Maruzen, 1955.
370p. maps.

Beers, Burton F.
Vain endeavor; Robert Lansing's attempts to end the American-Japanese rivalry. Durham, N.C., Duke Univ. Press, 1962.
207p.

Borg, Dorothy
The United States and the Far Eastern crisis of 1933-1938, from the Manchurian incident through the initial stage of the undeclared Sino-Japanese War. Cambridge, Mass., Harvard Univ. Press, 1964.
674p. (Harvard East Asian series)

Burdick, Charles B.
The Japanese siege of Tsingtau; World War I in Asia. Hamden, Conn., Archon Books, 1976.
274p.

Burnell, Elaine H.
Asian dilemma; United States, Japan and China; a special report from the Center for the Study of Democratic Institutions.
Santa Barbara, Center for the Study of Democratic Institutions, 1969.
238p. illus. (Center occasional paper)

Carnegie Endowment for International Peace.
The Imperial Japanese Mission to the United States, 1917.
Washington, 1918.
125p.

Coox, Alvin D. and Hilary Conroy, ed.
China and Japan; search for balance since World War I. Santa Barbara, Calif., Clio Press, 1978.
468p.
Contents:
- I. Overview - 1. How China and Japan see each other, by Chalmers Johnson. pp. 3-18.
- II. Administration, government, diplomacy to 1931.
- 2. The Japanese intervention in Shantung during World War I, by Tsing Yuan. pp. 19-34.
- 3. From the twenty-one demands to the Sino-Japanese military agreements, 1915-1918; ambivalent relations, by Hsi-Ping Shao. pp. 35-58.
- 4. From the Paris Peace Conference to the Manchurian Incident; the beginnings of China's diplomacy of resistance against Japan, by Pao-chin Chu. pp. 59-84.
- III. Japanese attitudes and Chinese resistance.
- 5. Comparing Japan and China; some theoretical and methodological issues, by Frances V. Moulder. pp. 85-112.
- 6. China in Japanese textbooks, by Harry Wray. pp. 113-132.
- Notes on the cultural relationship between Japan and China, by Ryozo Kurai. pp. 133-140.
- 7. The Chinese communist party and the Anti-Japanese movement in Manchuria; the initial stage, by Chong-Sik Lee. pp. 141-176.
- IV. "Experts and meddlers"
- 8. Doihara Kenji and the North China autonomy movement, 1935-1936, by B. Winston Kahn. pp. 177-210.
- 9. A new look at Chinese nationalist "appeasers", by Han-Sheng Lin. pp. 211-242.
- 10. Peace advocacy during the Sino-Japanese incident, by John Hunter Boyle. pp. 243-264.
- 11. A botched peace effort; the Miao Pin Kasaku, 1944-1945, by Yoji Akashi. pp. 265-288.
- Commentary on the Yoji Akashi essay, by Han-Sheng Lin. pp. 289-292.

- V. The faces of force
- 12. Recourse to arms; the Sino-Japanese conflict, 1937-1945, by Alvin D. Cock. pp. 293-322.
- 13. Japanese agression against China; the question of responsibility, by Martin Bagish and Hilary Conroy. pp. 323-334.
- VI. Chill and thaw
- 14. Ending the State of War between Japan and China; Taipei (1952), by Yu San Wang. pp. 335-354.
- 15. The roots of détente, by Yung H. Park. pp. 355-384.
- 16. The Tanaka government and the mechanics of the China decision, by Yung H. Park. pp. 385-398.
- VII. Concluding overview - 17. Sino-Japanese relations in the 1970s, by Tang Tsou, Tetsuo Najita, and Hideo Otake. pp. 399-438.
- Photographs. pp. 439-446.
- Index. pp. 447.

Crowley, James B.
Japan's quest for autonomy; national security and foreign policy 1930-1938. Princeton, Princeton Univ. Press, 1966.
428p.

Emmerson, John K.
The Japanese thread; a life in the U. S. foreign service. New York, Holt, Rindart and Winstor, 1978.
465p.

Esthus, Raymond A.
Theodore Roosevelt and Japan. Seattle, Univ. of Washington Press, 1969.
329p.

Farley, Miriam S., ed.
American Far Eastern policy and the Sino-Japanese war; a report of seven discussion conference held under the auspices of the American Council, Institute of Pacific Relations, March to May 1938. New York, AMS Press, 1978.
68p.
Reprint ed.

Friedman, Donald J.
The road from isolation; the campaign of the American Committee for Non-Participation in Japanese Aggression, 1938-1941. Cambridge, Mass., Harvard Univ. Press, 1968.
122p. (Harvard East Asian monographs

Griswold, Alfred Shitney
The Far Eastern policy of the United States. New Haven, Yale Univ. Press, 1962.
530p.

Heinrichs, Waldo H., Jr.
American ambassador; Joseph C. Grew and the development of the United States diplomatic tradition. Boston, Little Brown, 1966.
460p. illus.

Ienaga, Saburo
Japan's last war; World War II and Japanese, 1931-1945. Oxford, B. Blackwell, 1979.
332p.

Ikle, Frank William
German-Japanese relations, 1936-1940. N.Y., Bookman Associates, 1956.
243p.

Iriye, Akira
Across the Pacific; an inner history of American-East Asian relations. N.Y., Harcourt, Brace and World, 1967.
361p.

Iriye, Akira
After imperialism; the search for a new order in the Far East, 1921-1931. Cambridge, Mass., Harvard Univ. Press, 1965.
375p. (Harvard East Asian series)

Issraeljan, V. and L. Kutakov
Diplomacy of aggression; Berlin-Rome-Tokyo axis, its rise and fall. Moscow, Progress Publishers, 1970.
438p.

Jansen, Marius B.
Japan and China; from war to peace, 1894-1972. Chicago, Rand McNally College Pub., 1975.
547p.

Jones, Francis Clifford
Extraterritoriality in Japan, and the diplomatic relations resulting in its abolition, 1853-1899. N.Y., AMS Press, 1970.
237p.

Jones, Francis Clifford
Japan's new order in East Asia; its rise and fall, 1937-45. London, Oxford Univ. Press, 1954.
498p.
Bibl. pp. 480-484.

Kajima, Morinosuke
A brief diplomatic history of modern Japan. Tokyo, Tuttle, 1965.
216p. maps.

Kamikawa, Hikomatsu
Japan-American diplomatic relations in the Meiji-Taisho era, compiled and ed. by Kamikawa Hikomatsu, tr. and adapted by Kimura Michiko. Tokyo, Pan-Pacific Press, 1958.
458p. illus. (Centenary Cultural Council series)

Kennedy, Malcolm D.
The estrangement of Great Britain and Japan 1917-34. Manchester, Univ. Press, 1969.
363p. illus. maps.

King, Wunsz
China and the league of nations; the Sino-Japanese controversy. N.Y., St. John's Univ. Press, 1965.
104p. (Asia in the modern world)

Koginos, Manny T.
The Panay incident; prelude to war. Lafayette, Ind., Purdue Univ. Studies, 1967.
154p. illus.

Kuno, Yoshisaburo
Japanese expansion on the Asiatic continent; a study in the history of Japan with special reference to her international relations with China, Korea, and Russia. Port Washington, N.Y., Kennikat Press, 1967.
2 v. illus. maps.

Kuo, Ting-yee, comp.
Sino-Japanese relations 1862-1927; a checklist of the Chinese Foreign Ministry Archives, ed. by James W. Morley. N. Y., East Asian Institute, Columbia Univ. 1965.
228p.

Leng, Shao-chuan
Japan and Communist China. Kyoto, Doshisha Univ. Press, 1958.
169p.

Lensen, George Alexander
Japanese diplomatic and consular officials in Russia; a handbook of Japanese representatives in Russia from 1874 to 1968, compiled on the basis of Japanese and Russian sources with a historical introduction. Tokyo, Sophia Univ., 1968.
230p. (Monumenta Nipponica monographs)

Lensen, George Alexander
Japanese recognition of the U.S.S.R.; Soviet-Japanese relations 1921-1930. Tokyo, Sophia Univ., 1970.
419p. illus. maps.

Lensen, George Alexander, ed.
Korea and Manchuria between Russia and Japan 1895-1904; the observations of Sir Ernest Satow, selected and ed. with a historical introduction by George Alexander Lensen. Tullahassee, Fla., Dipolomatic Press, 1966.
296p. illus.

Lensen, George Alexander
Russian diplomatic and consular officials in East Asia; a handbook of the representatives of Tsarist Russia and the provisional government in China, Japan and Korea from 1858 to 1924, and of Soviet representatives in Japan from 1925 to 1968, compiled on the basis of Russian, Japanese and Chinese sources with a historical introduction. Tokyo, Sophia Univ., 1968.
294p. (Monumenta Nipponica monographs)

Lensen, George Alexander
The Russian push toward Japan; Russo-Japanese push toward Japan; Russo-Japanese relations, 1697-1875. Princeton, Princeton Univ. Press, 1959.
553p. illus. maps.

Lensen, George Alexander
Russia's Japan expedition of 1852 to 1855. Gainesville, Univ. of Florida Press, 1955.
208p. illus.

Lintulahti, Martti
A treatise of the Finno-Japanese relations from the early contacts to the present. Tokyo, 1963.
130p.

Lowe, Peter
Great Britain and Japan 1911-15; a study of British Far Eastern policy. London, Macmillan, 1969.
343p. illus. maps. (The making of the twentieth century series)

Maki, John M.
Selected documents; Far Eastern international relations 1689-1951. Seattle, Univ. of Washington, 1951.
333p.

Malozemoff, Andrew
Russian Far Eastern policy, 1881-1904, with special emphasis of the Russo-Japanese War. Berkeley, Univ. of California Press, 1958.
358p. (Russian and East European studies)

Maxon, Yale Candee
Control of Japanese foreign policy; a study of civil-military rivalry, 1930-1945. Berkeley, Univ. of California Press, 1957.
286p.

Meskill, Johanna Menzel
Hitler and Japan; the hollow alliance. N.Y., Atherton Press, 1966.
245p.

Morley, James William, ed.
The fateful choice; Japan's advance into Southeast Asia, 1939-1941, tr. by Peter A. Burton and Robert A. Scalapino. N.Y., Columbia Univ. Press, 1980.
368p.

Morley, James William
The Japanese thrust into Siberia, 1918. N.Y., Columbia Univ. Press, 1957.
395p. map. (Studies of Columbia Univ.)

Morris, Ivan, ed.
Japan 1931-1945, militarism, fascism, Japanism? Boston, Heath, 1963.
77p. (Problems of Asian civilizations)

Moulton, Harold G. and Louis Malio
The control of Germany and Japan. Washington, Brookings Institution, 1944.
116p. maps.

Neu, Charles E.
An uncertain friendship; Theodore Roosevelt and Japan, 1906-1909. Cambridge, Mass., Harvard Univ. Press, 1967.
347p.

Neumann, William L.
America encounters Japan, from Perry to MacArthur. Baltimore, Johns Hopkins Press, 1963.
353p. (Goucher College series)

Nichi-Bei Shuko Tsusho Hyakunen Kinen Gyoji Uneikai
Colleted documents of the Japanese mission to America 1860. Tokyo, Kazama Shobo, 1961.
7 v. illus.

Nish, Ian H.
The Anglo-Japanese alliance; the diplomacy of two island empires 1894-1907. London, Univ. of London, 1966.
420p. (Univ. of London historical studies)
also published by Westport, Conn., Greenwood Press, 1976.

Ogata, Sadako
Defiance in Manchuria; the making of Japanese foreign policy, 1931-1932. Berkeley, Univ. of California Press, 1964.
259p. map.

Okumiya, Masatake, Jiro Horikoshi, and Martin Caidin
Zero; the story of the Japanese Navy Air Force 1937-1945. London, Cassell, 1957.
364p. illus. maps.

Oliphant, Laurence
Elgin's mission to China and Japan, with an introduction by J. J. Gerson. Tokyo, Oxford Univ. Press, 1970.
2 v. illus. maps. (Oxford in Asia historical reprints)

Osgood, Robert E, George R. Packard III, and John H. Badgley
Japan and the United States in Asia. Baltimore, J. Hopkins Press, 1968.
65p. (Studies in international affairs)

Presseisen, Ernst L.
Germany and Japan; a study in totalitarian diplomacy 1933-1941. The Hague, Martinus Nijhoff, 1958.
368p. (International scholars forum)

Rappaport, Armin
Henry L. Stimson and Japan 1931-33. Chicago, Univ. of Chicago Press, 1963.
238p.

Reischauer, Edwin O.
The United States and Japan. 3d ed. Cambridge, Mass., Harvard Univ. Press, 1965.
396p. maps. (American foreign policy library)

Schroeder, Paul W.
The Axis alliance and Japanese American relations, 1941. Ithaca, N.Y. Cornell Univ. Press, 1958.
245p.

Schwantes, Robert S.
Japanese and Americans; a century of cultural relations. N.Y., Harper, 1955.
380p.

Storry, Richard
Japan and the decline of the West in Asia, 1894-1943. London, Macmillan Press, 1979.
186p.

Takagi, Yasaka
Toward international understanding, Tokyo, Kenkyusha, 1954.
180p.

U. S. Dept. of State
Foreign relations of the United States, diplomatic papers, 1940; the Far East. Washington, U. S. Govt. Print. Off. 1955.
1022p.
2 v.

White, John Albert
The diplomacy of the Russo-Japanese War. Princeton, Princeton Univ. Press, 1964.
410p. illus.

II.

Bagish, Martin and Hilary Conroy
Japanese aggression against China; the question of responsibility. (A. D. Coox and H. Conroy, ed. China and Japan; search for balance since World War I. Santa, Barbara, Calif., Clio Press, 1978. pp. 323-334)

Coox, Alvin D.
Recourse to arms; the Sino-Japanese conflict, 1937-1945. (A. D. Coox and H. Conroy, ed. China and Japan; search for balance since World War I. Snata Barbara, Calif., Clio Press, 1978. pp. 293-622)

Kahn, B. Winston
Doihara Kenji and the North China autonomy movement, 1935-1936. (A. D. Coox and H. Conroy, ed. China and Japan' search for balance since World War I. Santa Barbara, Calif., Clio Press, 1978. pp. 177-210)

Vishwanathan, Savitri
Paradox of Japan's nationalism; relations with Asia. (Toyomasa Fusé, ed. Modernization and stress in Japan. Leiden, E. J. Bill. 1975. pp. 41-50)

III.

Herzberg, James Richard
American economic policies towards Japan, 1931-1941. Ph.D. 1977. The University of Texas at Austin.
368p.

Kunimoto, Iyo Iimura
Japan and Mexico, 1888-1917. Ph.D. 1975. The University of Texas at Austin.
288p.

Lyman, Donald Roy
The United States and Japan, 1913-1921. Ph.D. 1976. The University of North Carolina at Chapel Hill.
577p.

Lyon, Jessie C.
Diplomatic relations between the United States, Mexico and Japan; 1913-1917. Ph.D. 1975. Claremont Graduate School.
214p.

Morita, Hideyuki
Preliminary planning in the state department relative to American-Japanese relations once World War II ended, 1939-1943. M. A. 1976. Northeast Missouri State University.
130p.

Roebuck, James Randolph, Jr.
The United States and East Asia 1909-1913; a study of the Far Eastern diplomacy of William Howard Taft. Ph.D. 1977. University of Virginia.
349p.

IV.

Altman, Albert A. and Harold Z. Schiffrin
Sun Yat-sen and the Japanese, 1914-1916. Modern Asian studies, v. 6, pt. 4. Oct. 1972. pp. 385-400.

Sutton, Joseph L.
Territorial claims of Russia and Japan in the Kurile Islands. Univ. of Michigigan, Center for Japanese studies occasional papers. no. 1. 1951. pp. 35-61.

COLONIES

I.

Banvai, Richard A.
Money and banking in China and South-east Asia during the Japanese military occupation, 1937-1945. Taipei, Taiwan Enterprises, 1974. 150p.

II.

Ho, Samuel P. S.
The development policy of the Japanese colonial government in Taiwan, 1895-1945; comments, by Hugh T. Patrick. (Gustav Ranis, ed., Government and economic development. New Haven, Yale Univ. Press, 1971. pp. 287-331)

Lee, Chong-Sik
The Chinese communist party and the anti-Japanese movement in Manchuria; the initial stage. (A. D. Coox and H. Conroy, ed. China and Japan; search for balance since World War I. Santa Barbara, Calif., Clio Press, 1978. pp. 141-176)

Lee, Sun-keun
The extent to which the Japanese colonial policy toward Korea contributed to her modernization. (International Conference on the Problems of Modernization in Asia, Seoul, 1965. Report. Seoul, Korea University Asiatic Research Center, 1966. pp. 323-336)

Shao, Hsi-Ping
From the twenty-one demands to the Sino-Japanese military agreements, 1915-1918; ambivalent relations. (A. D. Coox and H. Conroy, ed. China and Japan; search for balance since World War I. Santa Barbara, Calif., Clio Press, 1978. pp. 35-58)

III.

Ch'en, Ch'ing-ch'ih
Japanese socio-political control in Taiwan, 1895-1945. Ph.D. 1973. Harvard University. vi, 596p.

Chen, Shih-ta
Enclave growth in an open agrarian economy; Manchuria under Japanese colonialism. Ph.D. 1973. Cornell University. 345p.

Eng, Robert Yeok-Yin
Imperialism and the Chinese economy; the Canton and Shanghai silk industry, 1861-1932. Ph.D. 1978. University of California, Berkeley. 315p.

Salter, Christopher Lord
The geography of marginality; a study of migration, settlement, and agricultural development in the Rift Valley of eastern Taiwan. Ph.D. 1970. University of California at Berkeley. 256p.

Selya, Roger Mark
The industrialization of Taiwan; a geographic analysis. Ph.D. 1971. University of Minnesota. 332p.

Tsurumi, Elisabeth Patricia
Japanese colonial education in Taiwan, 1895-1945. Ph.D. 1971. Harvard University. v. 307p.

Wang, I-shou
Chinese migration and population change in Manchuria, 1900-1940. Ph.D. 1971. University of Minnesota. 243p.

IV.

Brudnoy, David
Japan's experiment in Korea. Monumenta Nipponica, v. 25, nos. 1/2. 1970. pp. 155-195.

Chen, Edward I-te
Formosan political movements under Japanese colonial rule, 1914-1937. Journal of Asian studies. v. 31, no.3. May 1972. pp. 477-498.

Chen, Edward I-te
Japanese colonializm in Korea and Formosa. Harvard journal of Asiatic studies, v. 30. 1970. pp. 126-158.

Culver, Margaret S.
Manchuria; Japan's supply base. Far eastern survey, v. 14, no.12. June 20, 1945. pp. 160-163.

Cutlack, F. M.
The Manchurian arena; an Australian view of the Far Eastern conflict. Sydney, Angus and Robertson, 1934. 76p. map.

Hunter, Janet
Japanese government policy, business opinion and the Seoul-Pusan railway, 1894-1906. Modern Asian studies. v. 11, pt. 4. Oct. 1977. pp. 573-599.

King, Betty L.
Japanese colonialism and Korean economic development. Asian studies. v. 13, no.3. Dec. 1975. pp. 1-22.

Koo, T. K.
Some economic documents relating to the genesis of the Japanese-sponsored regime in north China. Far Eastern quarterly. v. 6, no.1. Nov. 1946. pp. 65-77.

Kublin, Hyman
The evolution of Japanese colonialism. Comparative studies in society and history. v. 2, no.1. Oct. 1959. pp. 67-84.

Kublin, Hyman
The Ogasawara venture, 1861-1863. Harvard journal of Asiatic studies. v. 14, no.1/2. June 1951. pp. 261-284.

Mizoguchi, Toshiyuki
Consumer prices and real wages in Taiwan and Korea under Japanese rule. Hitotsubashi journal of economics. v. 13, no.1. June 1972. pp. 40-56.

Mizoguchi, Toshiyuki
Foreign trade in Taiwan and Korea under Japanese rule. Hitotsubashi journal of economics. v. 14, no.2. Feb. 1974. pp. 37-53.

RELIGION AND THOUGHT

I.

Arima, Tatsuo
The failure of freedom; a portrait of modern Japanese intellectuals. Cambridge, Mass., Harvard Univ. Press, 1969.
296p. (Harvard East Asian series)

Asakawa, Kanichi
The documents of Iriki, tr. and ed. by Kan-ichi Asakawa. Reprinted with the complete Japanese text by the Committee for the Publication of Dr. K. Asakawa's works. Tokyo, Japan Society for the Promition of Science, 1955.
1 v. illus.

Beard, Mary R.
The force of women in Japanese history. Washington, Public Affairs Press, 1953.
196p.

Blacker, Carmen
The Japanese enlightnment; a study of the writings of Fukuzawa Yukichi. Cambridge, Mass., Cambridge Univ. Press, 1964.
186p.

Bowen, R. W.
Rebellion and democracy; a study of commoners in the popular rights movement of the early Meiji period. Berkeley, Univ. of California, 1979.
350p.

Brown, Delmer M.
Nationalism in Japan; an introductory historical analysis. Berkeley, Univ. of California Press, 1955.
336p.

Chang, Richard T.
Historians and Meiji statesmen. Gainesville, Univ. of Florida Press, 1970.
105p. (Social science monographs series, no. 41)

Cressey, Earl Herbert
Daughters of changing Japan. N.Y., Farrar, Straus and Cudahy, 1955.
305p.

Fukuzawa, Yukichi
The autobiography of Fukuzawa Yukichi. New translation by Eiichi Kiyooka. Tokyo, Hokuseido, 1960.
401p. illus.

Fukuzawa, Yukichi
An encouragement of learning, tr. with an introduction by David A. Dilworth and Umeyo Hirano. Tokyo, Sophia Univ., 1969.
128p. (Monumental Nipponica monographs.)

Fukuzawa, Yukichi
The speeches of Fukuzawa; a translation and critical study by Wayne H. Oxford. Tokyo, Hokuseido Press, 1973.
300p.

Hay, Stephen N.
Asian ideas of East and West; Tagore and his critics in Japan, China and India. Cambridge, Mass., Harvard Univ. Press, 1970.
478p. illus. maps. (Harvard East Asian series)

Hinton, Harold C. and Marius B. Jansen, ed.
Major topics on China and Japan; a handbook for teachers.
N.Y., Institute of Pacific Relations, 1957.
326p. maps.

Ijichi, Sumimasa
The life of Marquis Shigenobu Okuma; a biographical study in the rise of democratic Japan, by Junesay Iddittie. Tokyo, Hokuseido, 1956.
423p. illus.

Ishii, Ryosuke, ed.
Japanese legislation in the Meiji era, tr. and adapted by William J. Chambliss. Tokyo, Pan-Pacific Press, 1959.
741p. illus. (Centenary Cultural Council series)

Iwata, Masakazu
Okubo Toshimich; the Bismarck of Japan. Berkeley, Univ. of California Press, 1964.
376p.

Jansen, Marius B.
The Japanese and Sun Yat-sen. Cambridge, Mass., Harvard Univ. Press, 1954.
274p.
also published in Stanford Univ. Press, 1979.

Kanda Memorial Committee
Memorials of Naibu Kanda. Tokyo, Toko Shoin, 1927.
516p. illus.

Kitasawa, Sukeo
The life of Dr. Nitobe. Tokyo, Hokuseido, 1953.
93p. illus.

Koblin, Hyman
Asian revolutionary; the life of Sen Katayama. Princeton, Princeton Univ. Press, 1964.
370p. illus.

Kosaka, Masaaki, ed.
Japanese thought in the Meiji era. tr. and adapted by David Abosch. Tokyo, Pan-Pacific Press, 1958.
512p. illus. (Centenary Cultural Council series)

Mitchell, Richard Hanks
Thought control in prewar Japan. Ithaca, Cornell Univ. Press, 1976.
226p.

Mushanokoji, Saneatsu
Great Saigo; the life of Takamori Saigo, adapted by Moriaki Sakamoto. Tokyo, Kaitakusha, 1942.
507p. illus. maps.

Nitobe, Izano
Japan, some phases of her problems and development; Japanese traits and foreign influences. Tokyo, Kyobunkan, 1970.
647p. (Nitobe Inazo zenshu)

Nitobe, Inazo
Western influences in modern Japan; a series of papers on cultural relations, by Inazo Nitobe and others. Chicago, Univ. of Chicago Press, 1931.
532p. illus.

Notehelfer, F. G.
Kotoku Shusui; portrait of a Japanese radical. Cambridge, Mass., Cambridge Univ. Press, 1971.
227p.

Okakura, Kazuo
The ideals of the East, with special reference to the art of Japan. Tokyo, Tuttle, 1970.
244p. illus.

Peattie, Mark R.
Ishiwara Kanji, and Japan's confrontation with the West. Princeton, N.J., Princeton Univ. Press. 1975.
430p.

Pittau, Joseph
Political thought in early Meiji Japan, 1868-1889, Cambridge, Mass., Harvard Univ. Press, 1967.
250p. (Harvard East Asian series.)

Pyle, Kenneth
The new generation in Meiji Japan; problems of cultural identity, 1885-1895. Stanford, Stanford Univ. Press, 1969.
240p.

Saito, Hiroshi
Japan's policies and purposes; selections from recent addresses and writings. Boston, Marshall Jones, 1935.
231p.

Scheiner, Irwin
Christian converts and social protest in Meiji Japan. Berkeley, Univ. of California Press, 1970.
268p.

Smith, Warren W., Jr.
Confucianism in modern Japan; a study of conservatism in Japanese intellectual history. Tokyo, Hokuseido, 1959.
285p. illus.

Storry, Richard
The double patriots; a study of Japanese nationalism. London, Chatto and Windus, 1957.
335p.

Tanin, O. and E. Yohan
Militarism and fascism in Japan, Reprint ed. Westport, Conn. Greenwood Press, 1975.
320p.

Totten, George O, ed.
Democracy in prewar Japan; groundwork of facade? Boston, D. C. Heath, 1965.
107p. (Problems in Asian civilizations)

Tsuda, Sōkichi
What is the Oriental culture?, tr. by Yasotaro Morri. Tokyo, Hokuseido, 1955.
103p.

Wilson, George M., ed.
Crisis politics in prewar Japan; institutional and ideological problems of the 1930's. Tokyo, Sophia Univ., 1970.
87p. (Monumental Nipponica monographs)

Wilson, George M.
Radical nationalist in Japan; Kita Ikki, 1883-1937. Cambridge, Mass., Harvard Univ. Press, 1969.
230p.

II.

Altman, Albert A.
Shinbunshi; the early Meiji adaptation of the Western-style newspaper. (W. G. Beasley, ed. Modern Japan; aspects of history, literature and society. London, G. Allen & Unwin, 1975. pp. 52-66)

Hashikawa, Bunsō
The "civil society" ideal and wartime resistance. (J. Victor Koschmann, ed. Authority and the individual in Japan. Tokyo, Univ. of Tokyo Press, 1978. pp. 128-143)

Ike, Nobutaka
Ideology for the new society; evolution of the family. (Jon Livingston, ed. Imperical Japan, 1800-1945, New York, Pantheon Books, 1973. pp. 159-161)

Kuno, Osamu
The Meiji state, minponshugi, and ultranationalism. (J. Victor Koschmann, ed. Authority and the individual in Japan; citizen protest in historical perspective. Tokyo, Univ. of Tokyo Press, 1978.
pp. 60-89)

Maruyama, Masao
Japanese thought. (Irwin Scheiner, ed. Modern Japan; an interpretive anthology. New York, MacMillan, 1974. pp. 208-215)

Matsumoto, Sannosuke
The roots of political disillusionment; "Public"and "Private" in Japan. (J. Victor Koschmann, ed. Authority and the individual in Japan. Tokyo, Univ. of Tokyo Press, 1978. pp. 31-53)

Matsuzawa, Hiroshi
"The "civil society" ideal and wartime resistance. (J. Victor Koschmann, ed. Authority and the individual in Japan; citizen protest in historical prespective. Tokyo, University of Tokyo Press, 1978. pp. 128-143)

Miwa, Kimitada
Fukuzawa Yukici's 'departure from Asia'; a prelude to the Sino-Japanese war. (Edmund Skrzypczak, ed. Japan's modern century. A special issue of Monumenta Nipponica prepared in celebration of the centennial of the Meiji restoration. Tokyo, Sophia University, 1968. pp. 1-26)

Moloney, James Clark
Selections from understanding the Japanese mind. (Bernard S. Silberman, ed. Japanese character and culture; a book of selected readings. Tucson, University of Arizona Press, 1962. pp. 360-386)

Passin, Herbert
Ideology for the new society; Mori Arinori. (Jon Livingston, ed. Imperial Japan, 1800-1945. New York, Pantheon Books, 1973. pp. 148-150)

Yazaki, Takeo
Ideology for the new society; civil law and the family. (Jon Livingston, ed. Imperial Japan, 1800-1945. New York, Pantheon Books, 1973. pp. 162-164)

Yuan, Tsing
The Japanese intervention in Shantung during World War I. (A. D. Coox and H. Conroy, ed. China and Japan; search for balance since World War I. Santa Barbara, Calif., Clio Press, 1978. pp. 19-34)

III.

Hopper, Helen Marlys
The conflict between Japanese tradition and western learning in the Meiji intellectual Mori Ogai, 1862-1922. Ph.D. 1976. Washington University. 301p.

Oxford, Wayne Hemphill
A critical edition of selected speeches of Fukuzawa Yukichi dealing with the modernization of Japan, translated from the Japanese with an introductions and notes. Ph.D. 1969. University of California at Los Angeles, 1969. 449p.

IV.

Cho (Takeda) Kiyoko
An essay on Kagawa Toyohiko; the place of man in his social theory. <u>Asia bunka kenkyu</u>, no.2. Sept. 1960. pp. 33-40.